# SCARLET EXPERIMENT

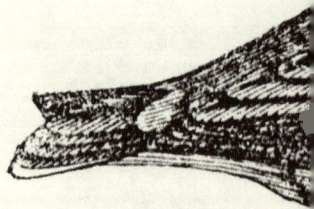

# Scarlet Experiment

## Birds and Humans in America

JEFF KARNICKY

University of Nebraska Press  LINCOLN AND LONDON

Acknowledgments for the use of copyrighted
material appear on pages xi–xii, which
constitute an extension of the copyright page.

∞

Publication of this volume was assisted by
the Virginia Faulkner Fund, established
in memory of Virginia Faulkner, editor in
chief of the University of Nebraska Press.

Library of Congress Cataloging-in-Publication Data
Names: Karnicky, Jeffrey, author.
Title: Scarlet experiment: birds and humans
in America / Jeff Karnicky.
Description: Lincoln: University of Nebraska Press,
[2016] | Includes bibliographical references and index.
Identifiers: LCCN 2016022223
ISBN 9780803294981 (hardback: alk. paper)
ISBN 9780803295735 (epub)
ISBN 9780803295742 (mobi)
ISBN 9780803295759 (pdf)
Subjects: LCSH: Animals and civilization—United
States. | Human-animal relationships—United States.
| Birds—Social aspects—United States. | Animals—
Social aspects—United States. | BISAC: NATURE
/ Animals / Birds. | NATURE / Environmental
Conservation & Protection. | LITERARY CRITICISM /
American / General.
Classification: LCC QL85 .K37 2016 | DDC 598.0973—dc23
LC record available at https://lccn.loc.gov/2016022223

Set in Fanwood Text by John Klopping.
Designed by N. Putens.

*For the birds*

# CONTENTS

# ILLUSTRATIONS

# ACKNOWLEDGMENTS

I would like to thank Linda Birke for asking me to submit my first piece of writing for what eventually became this book, my essay on the red knot, to Society and Animals. I also thank the members of the Society for Literature, Science, and the Arts who heard me present my work, and gave me important feedback, at the slsa conference over the past ten years. Tom Gannon and Spencer Schaffner wrote scholarly books on birds that inspired my work. I thank my colleagues at Drake University with whom I talked about this manuscript. I thank the Drake Center for the Humanities for supporting this book. Without Jeff Nealon's and Rich Doyle's instruction at Penn State, this book would not have been possible. Suki and Pippa were by my side during the writing of much of this book. I cannot thank Megan and Max enough for their love and support.

A portion of chapter 2 originally appeared as "Ornithological Biography, Animal Studies, and Starling Subjectivity," in *Humanimalia: A Journal of Human/Animal Interface Studies* 2, no. 3 (2011): 31–59. A portion of chapter 4 originally appeared as "What Is Red Knot Worth?: Valuing Human/Avian Interaction," in *Society and Animals* 12, no. 3 (2004): 253–66. All appear with permission.

# INTRODUCTION
## Split the Lark

This is not a birding memoir. I am not writing about how birds have impacted my life. I am not writing about a wild bird I took in and befriended. I am not writing about what I have learned from studying extinct birds. I am not writing about what I have learned from a life of bird-watching. There are already a lot of these books out there. I like them and I am haunted by them: their narratives; their personal revelations; their memoir-like qualities; their calls for conservation. But I have never named or lived with a bird and my experiences watching birds have been rather pedestrian. I do not believe that hope is the thing with feathers. I do, however, believe that humans have been conducting a "scarlet experiment" on birds in America for at least the past two centuries.

### HOPE IS NOT THE THING WITH FEATHERS

Christopher Cokinos used Emily Dickinson's famous line as the title for his 2000 book *Hope Is the Thing with Feathers: A Personal Chronicle of Vanished Birds*. Cokinos writes with poetic detail of the decline and extinction of six American birds: the Carolina parakeet, the ivory-billed woodpecker, the heath hen (technically a subspecies of the greater prairie chicken), the passenger pigeon, the Labrador duck, and the great auk. These birds, along with the Eskimo curlew and the Bachman's warbler, have all become extinct since the mid-nineteenth century, mostly as the result of human action, and mostly because of overhunting and habitat destruction. Cokinos is a poet, not an ornithologist; he calls his book "a personal chronicle, in which I weave together these accounts with my attempts to understand them—which led me to visit the places where these birds once lived and died."[1] As a result, he "resolved to grapple with hope in this environmentally complicated time."[2] While he never explicitly discusses Dickinson's poem, the notions of hope and birds interconnect throughout his text. Cokinos writes about extinct birds with a mix of hope, guilt, and despair, for the futures of both humans and birds. In this way, Dickinson's poem seems a fair representation of what he writes, as the "hope" of the poem "perches in the [assumedly human] soul."[3] For many birding memoirists, then, the human soul of Dickinson's poem learns from birds, and what has been learned often becomes the writer's focus. For instance, Cokinos and his wife "perform the rote chores of the perpetually guilt-ridden" and decide not to have children because he "cannot imagine explaining to a child of mine what the Loggerhead Shrike *used* to be . . . or what the song of the Hermit Thrush *once* sounded like."[4] Birds become a means of learning about the self, and what it desires and what it despairs about. Nonetheless, hope remains, as Cokinos writes, "on good days, I believe in our capacity to heal, to form communities of concern and action, to recognize loveliness and protect it. On good days, I smile to hear the caroling of a Carolina Wren and know that we are capable of adoration."[5]

This sense of hope, and a companion feeling of self-understanding that Cokinos locates within his self-described "middle-class American life," resounds through other memoirs focused on birds.[6] In *To See Every Bird on Earth: A Father, a Son, and a Lifelong Obsession*, Dan Koeppel describes his father's quest to see every bird species on earth. As he accompanies his father on some of his journeys, Koeppel learns about birds, but his focus shifts to his relationship with his father. "On our trip, Dad and I connected in ways that were both lovely and difficult. I saw his self-destructive side, a part of him that for years has shut out family and love. And I saw his best qualities, a man with a gentle heart, hidden by pain, but not hard to detect upon careful inspection. The triumph of the list is the triumph of that hidden heart because it is proof not just of obsession, but also grace, and glory."[7] I take "grace" and "glory" here to be kin to hope; the father's bird list of over seven thousand species speaks both to his hard work and to the beauty and diversity of bird life. Listing birds reveals the human heart and strengthens a familial relationship.

To cite just one more example, Kenn Kaufman's 1997 *Kingbird Highway: The Story of a Natural Obsession That Got a Little Out of Hand* is about his formative years birding across the United States in the 1970s. In a book-jacket blurb, Pete Dunne, a well-known birder and author, aptly compares the book to Kerouac's *On the Road*. Kaufman (who is now a renowned writer of essays and books about birding, and an author of numerous field guides) writes of his time hitchhiking across the country, hanging out with friends, and looking for birds, which he spontaneously follows from state to state. He ends the book in the present time, looking back on his younger self. "Now, when I look back many years later, as though from a great distance, I can still see the young man standing out on that jetty. And at least on my better days, I can see myself standing there with him: shaken by experience, perhaps, but still confident that the light will be better, that the birds will come in closer, that we will see everything more clearly at last, before the day is over."[8] Kaufman, as an experienced ornithologist, can surely speak to the "experience" that has shaken his faith in conservation, but he is also clearly referring to his personal life. Nonetheless, he remains "confident"; in short, he has hope that things will turn out well, for him and for the birds.

All of these books, and many more like them, share in the hope that can be found in Dickinson's poem. These books, as personal narratives, make for great reading. Readers can learn a lot about the human character from them. Many of these books carry at least an implicit conservation message, but because this aspect is often downplayed, it remains rather vague. Cokinos writes, "The birds taught me that we can learn from these losses, take comfort in what remains, and redefine hope from 'wish' to 'work.' We can work to protect the still-astonishing nonhuman lives that have come to depend on us for patience and care."[9]

As I have watched birds and researched how humans in America have interacted with them, I am somewhat skeptical of any large sense of "patience and care." In turn, I am not convinced that hope is the thing with feathers, or that the things with feathers have much hope if they need to depend on human benevolence. Rather, I take my inspiration for this book about birds and humans from another Dickinson poem, not about hope and souls, but about doubt and blood.

> Split the lark– and you'll find the music–
> Bulb after Bulb, in Silver rolled–
> Scantily dealt to the Summer Morning
> Saved for your Ear when Lutes be old–
>
> Loose the Flood–you shall find it patent–
> Gush after Gush, reserved for you–
> Scarlet Experiment! Sceptic Thomas!
> Now, do you doubt that your Bird was true?[10]

I want to cite this "scarlet experiment" as a marker of all the birds killed in America since the nineteenth century as a direct result of human actions. It is impossible to determine the exact number, and many studies of bird mortality are based on small samples. Loss et al. write, "Quantification of direct anthropogenic mortality, although critical for conservation efforts, remains imprecise."[11] To increase precision, they suggest that "a standardized database of avian mortality" be created. This database would be modeled on the eBird database, which has become, over the last ten years, an immense collection of information on bird populations and movements.[12] (I discuss eBird in detail in chapter 5.) Essentially, then, they are calling for a "dead eBird" interface. Even without this precise data, Loss et al. assert that "hundreds of millions to more than one billion North American birds are directly killed each year by human stressors."[13] Considering the role that habitat destruction and climate change play in bird mortality, the number is most likely in the high end of their estimation.

Twenty-first-century humans kill birds in multiple ways. The American Bird Conservancy (ABC) has identified "major, human-induced bird mortality threats," of which habitat destruction is primary. Other causes listed by ABC are:

Climate change
Energy development
Pesticide poisoning
Tower and building collisions
Free-roaming cat predation
Invasive species
Fishery bycatch
Poorly planned development[14]

One study estimates that between 1.4 and 3.7 billion birds are killed annually by domestic cats.[15] As for the number killed by these other threats, the U.S. Fish and Wildlife Service (USFWS) "does not have an official estimate of the number of birds killed from wind turbines or other sources," even as they note that these deaths "may for some species be causing impacts at the population level."[16] As I will discuss in chapters 2 and 4, U.S. Wildlife Services (USDA WS) kills millions of nuisance birds per year, including 1,500,459 European starlings, 657,134 red-winged blackbirds, 846,633 brown-headed cowbirds, and 23,700 Canada geese in 2011.[17]

Global climate change also takes a toll on bird life. The "State of the Birds: 2010 Report on Climate Change," part of a series of yearly reports published by the U.S. Department of the Interior, asks: "How will the impacts of climate change influence our bird populations and their habitats?"[18] While the report does not cite specific population numbers, it does note that oceangoing and Hawaiian birds face a high level of vulnerability, along with species that are already of conservation concern. Other birds, such as those in "coastal, arctic/alpine, and grassland habitats," face an intermediate level of vulnerability.[19]

In 2007 the National Audubon Society noted that even common birds were in steep decline. Audubon defines "common" birds as those with a population of at least 500,000 and a range of at least 385,000 square miles.[20] According to Audubon, "Since 1967 the average population of the common birds in steepest decline have fallen

70 percent, from 17.6 million to 5.35 million individuals." To cite just a few examples from the "top ten" common birds in decline, the northern bobwhite has declined from "31 million to 5.5 million (82 percent)," the evening grosbeak from "17 million to 3.8 million (78 percent)," and the northern pintail from "16 million to 3.6 million (77 percent)." In addition to common birds being in decline, ninety-three species of North American (including Hawaiian) birds are on the federal endangered species list (USFWS Species Reports), which means that such birds are "in danger of extinction throughout all or a significant portion of its range."[21] Lesser number of birds have been killed by scientific experimentation, collection for classification purposes, and hunting (which also serves to protect habitat and may yield a net positive result; nonetheless, millions of birds are killed by hunters each year).

The conservation movement that started in the late nineteenth and early twentieth century successfully protected many species from overhunting and changed public attitudes toward birds. Legislation like the Lacey Act of 1900, which outlawed the interstate market in birds and banned the importation of bird feathers for ornamental use, and the Migratory Bird Treaty Act of 1918, which banned the killing of most species of migratory birds, saved the lives of countless birds.[22] In his history of American ornithology in the nineteenth and twentieth centuries, Mark V. Barrow Jr. writes of the success of these conservation campaigns that began to gain force late in the nineteenth century. "In a highly successful educational, legislative, and enforcement campaign, the AOU's [American Ornithologists' Union] bird protection committee joined forces with a second, more enduring Audubon movement that continues to this day. This fruitful collaboration resulted in not only an American public alerted to the problem of bird destruction, but also an impressive series of state and federal legislative victories."[23]

Barrow is of course right that the "Audubon movement" is still a strong voice for conservation today, but much has changed since the early days of bird protection. The risks to birds in the twenty-first century are far less visible than they were in the nineteenth century, when the focus was on ending plume hunting and changing minds about using feathers as fashion. For many people, the sometimes slow pace of habitat alteration and climate change makes these threats seem invisible, while the threats posed by cat predation, pesticide poisoning, building collisions, and so on might be viewed as "accidental." Nineteenth- and early twentieth-century conservation movements acted against those whose intention was to kill birds. For twenty-first-century conservationists, such is not the case. Most bird kills are unintentional and even unknown.

Intention, though, hardly matters. Birds are being killed in incredibly large numbers, and these numbers have increased despite conservation laws. Since roughly the time Dickinson wrote "Split the Lark," human understanding of and interaction with birds has changed profoundly. As birds came to be seen as beautiful creatures worthy of protection and study, they became subject to all kinds of experiments that altered their relationship with humans. Taking a wide view, the primary result of the human-bird interactions that I call a "scarlet experiment" has been the death of countless birds, whether intentionally, inadvertently, or indifferently. Since Dickinson's time, and since the early days of the conservation movement, humans have "discovered" birds' cognitive abilities and existence as both individuals and populations. More recently, new means of measuring and understanding bird populations with great accuracy has led to a new form of experimentation, which in turn has led to the intensified, unending management of bird life.

In short, my argument is this: In the twenty-first century, birds have become cognitive individuals and populations, subject to human governmental policy. In the interests of 'population management,' governmental and nongovernmental agencies regulate bird life through legislation, public policy, and scientific study. Birds are managed, then, through multiple aspects of what Michel Foucault calls biopolitical power, for better and for worse, depending on the species and the situation. Some birds, such as the European starling and the house sparrow, thrive under this intensive management; others, such as the red knot and birds on the federal endangered species list, may not.

Regardless of the result of human experiments on birds, the ways humans interact with birds have changed radically. My claim here roughly coincides with Jacques Derrida's claim that "for about two centuries, intensely and by means of an alarming rate of acceleration, for we no longer have a clock or a chronological measure of it, we, we who call ourselves men or humans, we who recognize ourselves in that name, have been involved in an unprecedented transformation. This mutation affects the experience of what we continue to call, imperturbably, as if there were nothing wrong with it, the animal and/ or animals."[24] Derrida is writing here specifically about contemporary farming practices that have led to changes in how humans consider animals as food. He writes that this "unprecedented change" has happened "by means of farming and regimentation at a demographic level unknown in the past, by means of genetic experimentation, the industrialization of what can be called the production for consumption of animal meat."[25] Certainly birds—specifically chickens—are subject to these intensified farming procedures. My interest, though, is in "wild" birds, which (in ways similar to and different from farm animals) have been subject to regimentation as their populations have become objects of knowledge. Derrida writes, "No one can deny this event—that is the *unprecedented* proportions of this subjection of the animal."[26] The deaths of birds that I describe above differ immensely from how animals are killed within the world of industrialized farming; at the same time, the immensity of human-caused bird deaths is surely an aspect of the subjection of the animal.

Dickinson's "scarlet experiment," taken very literally, can be read as a dissection of the bird to map out its sound organs—to scientifically understand bird song at the expense of the living bird. The "gush after gush" that Dickinson writes of can stand in for Derrida's subjection of the animal and for my claim about the subjection of birds in America. As humans have watched and studied birds with greater and greater intensity through the twentieth century and into the twenty-first century, birds have become subject to multiple human experiments, some scientific, some literary, some governmental. "Experiment" here should be taken in multiple senses, not just the narrow scientific meaning of testing a hypothesis. More broadly, experiment can mean "the action of trying anything, or putting it to proof; a test, trial."[27] This meaning resonates with Dickinson's poem, and her challenge at the end: "Now, do you doubt that your bird was true?" Of course, the implication here is that the knowledge that becomes "patent," or obvious, as a result of the experiment, comes at the expense of the bird's life. My use of "experiment" is inflected too by this idea that birds' lives are continually at stake in their interactions with humans. "Experiment" can also mean "a tentative procedure; a method, system of things, or course of action, adopted in uncertainty whether it will answer the purpose." This definition, in a sense, goes against the strict scientific definition of testing a hypothesis, but it seems more apt perhaps for many of the human/avian interactions I will discuss. Finally, I want to highlight a more archaic use of "experiment," to mean "practical acquaintance with a person or thing; experience," as a large part of my argument relies on the fact that humans have become more acquainted with birds over the past two hundred years or so (to a lesser degree, I would argue that birds have also become more acquainted with humans).[28] How these experiments, in all senses of the word, have affected both humans and birds is the subject of this book.

Each chapter of *Scarlet Experiment* focuses on a specific bird species; my hope is not to be comprehensive, but to use these species—the blue jay, the European starling, the red knot, the Canada goose, and the tufted titmouse and black-crested titmouse—as a means of exploring a few specific aspects of human-avian interactions. I limit my discussion to North American birds, as defined by the American Birding Association, for bird-listing purposes, as "the ABA Area": "The 49 continental United States, Canada, the French islands of St. Pierre and Miquelon and adjacent waters to a distance of 200 miles from land or half the distance to a neighboring country, whichever is less."[29] Birds, of course, do not follow these boundaries; the red knot, for instance, migrates from the Tierra del Fuego to the Arctic, with only a brief but important stop along the East Coast of the United States. The European starling has spread worldwide and thrives on every continent except Antarctica. Nonetheless, all of the birds I write about have large populations in North America.

In chapter 1, "Emotion and Intelligence: The Blue Jay," I focus on how human interactions with blue jays in the nineteenth and twentieth centuries developed into an understanding of the cognitive ability of birds. Broadly speaking, nineteenth-century writers such as John James Audubon, Emily Dickinson, and Henry David Thoreau fit blue jays into (or in Dickinson's case, outside of) a Christian moral and emotional framework. Twentieth- and twenty-first-century accounts reconfigure the question of emotions, as the bird's mind is taken seriously as a site of cognition. Contemporary accounts of blue jays—scientific works, Don DeLillo's novel *The Body Artist*, and biographical writings on specific birds—strive to understand how the blue jay mind works. Cognitive ethology supports many of the artistic and literary claims made about blue jays, as scientific experimentation has proven the blue jay's ability to use tools and to make complex decisions.

Blue jays, like the focus of chapter 2, "Interpellation and Interiority: The European Starling," have adapted to human alterations of the environment and thrived as a result. Starlings were introduced to the United States in the nineteenth century as part of an experiment to bring every bird written about by William Shakespeare to America. I focus on starling subjectivity in this chapter to argue that starlings have their own way of being in the world. They are also the ultimate companion species to humans, as their population growth parallels human alteration of the world. Starlings can be seen as an important site for thinking about the kinds of ethical relations that exist between human and nonhuman animals. In this ethical relationship starlings have benefited as their affinity for humans has helped them to increase their range and population immensely—starlings have survived and thrived in a human-created world. From a human perspective, starlings can provide a new way of thinking about, and living in, this world. Thinking with starlings leads toward ways of thinking about animal subjectivity and animal studies. In this chapter I engage the work of Jacques Derrida and Donna Haraway, along with other animal studies scholarship, to look for ways of understanding both individual and group subjectivity as not just human conditions. I also write about how bird biographies—human-written stories of interactions with wild birds—might lead to new ways of thinking about avian subjectivity.

Taken together, these first two chapters argue that the cognitive abilities of birds can be understood as a form of avian subjectivity that bears similarities to, but is also quite different than, human subjectivity.

If chapters 1 and 2 argue for an avian subjectivity that brings birds into the existential and ethical world of the human, chapters 3 and 4 focus on how two species—the red knot and the Canada goose—live within a world of intensely administered human governmentality. Both of these chapters rely on Michel Foucault's conception of bio-political power, or biopower, as a productive force that acts on human population from within "the ensemble formed by the institutions, procedures, analyses and reflections, the calculations and tactics that allow the exercise of this very specific albeit complex form of power."[30] Biopower uses what Foucault calls a "formation of a whole series of specific governmental apparatuses" to produce knowledge of human subjects in both the public realms of work and education, and the private realms of home and personal life.[31] Statistics, measurements, norms, and censuses are some of the tools of biopower-driven govern-mentality, and while Foucault and those who follow him write about how these things affect humans, I argue that birds, in the twenty-first century, have become subject to very similar forms of management.

Chapter 3, "Capital and Conservation: The Red Knot," focuses on the imminent extinction of the *rufa* subspecies, whose population has decreased by more than 90 percent in the past twenty years. In looking at how capitalism and conservation have become entwined for better and for worse, I follow Michael Hardt's and Antonio Negri's claim in *Empire* that "all nature has become capital" to argue that "all birds have become capital."[32] From this perspective, I write about how conservation measures to save the red knot have embraced both science and marketing, as I question whether endangered species can continue to exist within what Felix Guattari calls "integrated world capitalism," a dominant form of subjectivity that places an exchange value on all forms of life.

Chapter 4, "Nuisance and Neighbor: Canada Goose," asks a similar question of a bird whose population has increased immensely. The resident Canada goose has thrived so successfully in human-created habitats that it now poses health risks to human populations. As Wildlife Services, a branch of the U.S. Department of Agriculture, exterminates tens of thousands of resident geese per year, the birds have become subject to intensive population management through a series of regulations and behavior modifications of both geese and humans. Multiple community-formed groups have argued against "lethal control" of resident Canada geese, citing the complex social lives of geese as a ground for protection and ethical treatment.

Chapter 5, "Confusion and Classification: Black-Crested Titmouse or Tufted Titmouse," focuses on the human drive to classify and organize all bird life. This chapter looks at how bird species have been "split" and "lumped," that is, either divided into new species or grouped together in a single species as part of this drive toward the classification of all life. This chapter also looks at the emergence of eBird and other databases of bird information that have led to increasingly accurate measurement of bird populations. As birds become data points, they also become much more easily subject to governmentality. With the incredibly detailed population maps produced by eBird and other forms of data management, ornithologists, government administrators, corporations, and citizens know more about bird demographics and movements than has ever been known. What humans will do with this information is the final "scarlet experiment." As more and more complex knowledge of bird life gets produced, the costs that human decisions will have on both birds and humans will become apparent, as I discuss in my conclusion, "The Future of Birds."

A final introductory note: I mention above that I am "haunted" by birding memoirs. This haunting manifests itself in a brief personal narrative introduction to each chapter. These personal narratives are all quickly abandoned, though, as they cannot come close to offering a wide enough perspective for understanding anything beyond my own personal experience with birds. While I cannot deny that my personal experience with birds informs the writing of this book (and is perhaps my motivation for writing it), such experience only works as a narrow starting point for a wider experiment.

# 1

## *Emotion and Intelligence*

### The Blue Jay

*I am walking on the lawn of Emily Dickinson's house and experiencing a strong feeling of historical continuity thanks to two birds in my field of vision. I see an eastern phoebe flitting around the garden. A couple of minutes later, I hear, and then see, a blue jay screaming in the pines a few yards away from the garden. Dickinson wrote the poem that starts "I was a Phebe–nothing more" in 1865. My sense of historical continuity comes from the fact that today's phoebe behaves much like Dickinson's. It is barely noticeable as it flies quietly among low branches and disappears from view, or, as Dickinson wrote, "I dwelt too low that any seek– / Too shy, that any blame–."[1] I watch the phoebe for only a moment before it is gone, and probably unnoticed by the few other people walking near the garden. Again, Dickinson perfectly describes the phoebe's place in the human world: "A phebe makes a little print / Opon the Floors of Fame–."[2] The blue jay, though, gets, and holds, my attention. Like the phoebe, today's blue jay behaves much like the ones Dickinson describes in detail in three poems, and to a lesser extent in four others. It shouts, "bold as a Bailiff's hymn . . . confident and straight" as it chases another jay through the pines that Dickinson called "Just a Sea—with a Stem" in a poem that describes blue jays moving through trees very similar to these, as it announces its arrival at each new branch.[3]*

It is, of course, not at all surprising that one should see a blue jay in Amherst, Massachusetts, in either 2005 or 1865. Blue jays have inhabited the eastern woods of the North American continent for centuries. They are noisy, bold, and brightly colored, which helps to explain why blue jays were "one of the first North American birds to become well known to Europeans."[4] Illustrations of the bird date to John White's watercolor in the sixteenth century; Mark Catesby painted and wrote about the blue jay in 1754.[5] Blue jays thrived as forest was converted to farmland in the nineteenth century and as suburbs sprang up in the twentieth century; they continue to thrive today as forest habitat shrinks and fragments. In fact, blue jays are one of the few species of indigenous birds of North America that has thrived, in part, *because of* human alteration of habitat. In his *The Sibley Guide to Birds*, David Allen Sibley writes that the blue jay "has become increasingly common west of its traditional range east of the Great Plains" as humans have altered the landscape of America.[6] Forest fragmentation, due to logging and development, creates edge habitat that is unsuitable for many forest-nesting birds such as wood thrushes. Blue jays and other species, such as crows, thrive in this habitat. In addition, bird feeders give blue jays a fairly reliable source of winter food. Because the blue jay is not shy of bird feeders, because it is often seen in forest edges that humans tend to frequent, and because it has a boisterous voice and bright colors, humans have long taken notice of blue jays and written about what they have seen. In addition to Dickinson's admiration of the jay's "shrill felicity," many nineteenth-century naturalists wrote about and painted blue jays.[7] Alexander Wilson, in 1831, wrote that the blue jay "makes himself still more conspicuous by his loquacity, and the oddness of his tones and gestures."[8] Henry David Thoreau wrote in his journal that "it is the more glorious to live in Concord because the jay is so splendidly painted";[9] John James Audubon painted the jay's portrait and wrote that it was "exceedingly garrulous [and] may be easily followed to any distance."[10] Along with noting the prominent voice and plumage of jays, these nineteenth-century accounts tend to focus on the blue jay's "character," be it "warrior"-like, possessed of "a singular wildness," or full of "selfishness, duplicity, and malice."[11]

Human perception of blue jays and other birds broadly shifts from a nineteenth-century ascription of human-like emotions to blue jays to a twentieth-century investigation of the human-like intelligence of the birds. Twentieth-century scientific, artistic, and literary accounts of blue jays, as I discuss in detail in this chapter, tend rather to focus on the jay's intelligence and adaptability. In both laboratory and field studies, blue jays and other members of its *corvid* family, such as crows and ravens, have been found to be quite intelligent in a number of ways, including food selection, tool use and invention, and memory. Jays and other corvids exhibit a complex intelligence. Candace Savage, in *Bird Brains*, a book that provides an overview of avian intelligence, writes that such birds "show every sign of enjoying a rich awareness" of their worlds.[12]

Contemporary artistic texts explore just what type of awareness a blue jay might exhibit. Roger Tory Peterson's revision of Audubon's blue jay painting strives to portray the blue jay outside of a moral frame. Don DeLillo's 1998 novel *The Body Artist* tries to imagine what a blue jay might see when it looks through a window into a house. Vicki Formato's biography *Jayson: The True Story of a 20 Year Old Blue Jay* builds a case for avian individuality. This shift in artistic portrayal mirrors the development of cognitive ethology, which studies how animal minds work within their environment. One of the founding scientists of cognitive ethology, Donald Griffin, writes that "the challenging scientific question is, how widespread among animals is conscious awareness?"[13] This question undoubtedly has scientific import, but it also has import in a broader sense of how humans live in the world as they interact with other forms of life, and how we read and understand various kinds of texts. A shift in the way that humans see the world can change the way that humans act in the world. This difference can lead to questions of ethics, conservation, and otherness. Griffin writes, "Our ethical judgments about how we should treat members of other species are strongly influenced by what we believe about their consciousness."[14] If we believe that blue jays and other birds have a consciousness that is more similar to our own than previously thought, in what ways might human behavior change? How might human interactions with differently conscioused beings—in this case blue jays but also birds in general—change? I will attempt to answer these questions in what follows, as I map out how human perceptions of blue jays have altered over the past two hundred years in ways that lead to a rethinking of human-animal relations.

## "HIS CHARACTER A TONIC": BLUE JAYS AND HUMANS IN THE NINETEENTH CENTURY

Emily Dickinson's poetry shows an admiration of the jay's appearance, voice, and demeanor. In two poems, Dickinson compares the jay to a "brigadier": in poem 1022 the jay is "Sitting a Bough like a Brigadier"; in 1596 Dickinson writes, "No brigadier throughout the Year / So civic as the Jay."[15] These descriptions are clearly influenced by close observation of the bird—its bold markings resemble military dress, "Warrant in every line," and one can easily see why Dickinson would compare the jay's bright color and defined pattern to a nineteenth-century military uniform.[16] The poems go beyond this aesthetic comparison, though. Dickinson's jays not only have a military look, they also have a military demeanor and character. Blue jays in Dickinson's poems are "bold" in voice, and their orders must be followed by all who hear them call.[17] In poem 1670 Dickinson writes that the jay's call signals the approach of winter, and that "the Tippet that ignores his voice / Is impudent to nature."[18] In their behavior, Dickinson's jays are "civic" "warrior[s]," who are "bold ... confident and straight" and "prompt" and "executive." In short, the blue jay, in these poems, embodies the virtues of civic-minded nineteenth-century American citizens, and Dickinson's poetic speaker enjoys watching them for just this reason. "Good is the look of him in March / As a Benefit."[19] But this admiration of the jay as model citizen is not the only thing worth noting.

Dickinson writes that the jay's "character" is "a tonic." While this line certainly refers to the jay's virtue, it also gestures toward something a bit more obscure. Poem 1596 twice calls the jay a "neighbor" to humans. Even more broadly, the jay is "The Brother of the Universe," deserving of immortality. "Unfair an immortality / That leaves this neighbor out." Dickinson's poem forges a strong human-bird bond; both inhabit the same world, and perhaps the same afterworld. At the same time, though, Dickinson's jay resists total inscription into the nineteenth-century human world of citizenship and spirituality. This contradiction is best expressed by the poem's description of the jay's "larder": on the one hand it is "terse and militant," on the other it is "unknown." The jay can be watched—as the same poem notes, "I've often seen them"[20]—but it cannot be fully understood. Dickinson's jays may be virtuous like humans, but they are also still jays, flying through the pines, as they "split their route to the Sky."[21]

Henry David Thoreau shared Dickinson's admiration of blue jays, although perhaps to a lesser degree. On moving into his cabin in Walden Woods, Thoreau wrote, "I found myself suddenly neighbor to the birds."[22] In both his journals and in *Walden*, Thoreau writes of his close observations of blue jays. He admired the bird's vitality, which he saw reflected in its voice, plumage, and behavior. In his journal of November 3, 1858, he writes, "The jay is the bird of October. It, too, with its bright color, stands for some ripeness in the bird harvest. And its scream! It is as if it blowed on the edge of an October leaf . . . It is wide awake to what is going on, on the *qui vive*."[23] In other journal entries from the 1850s, Thoreau writes admiringly of blue jays. On July 8, 1853, he notes that the bird's call "suggests a singular wildness."[24] On February 2, 1854, he writes, "The scream of the jay is a true winter sound. It is wholly without sentiment, and in harmony with winter."[25] On November 13, 1858, Thoreau admires the jay's beauty, proclaiming that "it is the more glorious to live in Concord because the jay is so splendidly painted."[26] Like the speaker of Dickinson's poem, Thoreau clearly enjoys having the jay as his neighbor.

While Thoreau's journals show a clear appreciation of the jay, a short passage in *Walden* tempers this enthusiasm, as Thoreau now writes about the jay in terms of human morality, which he does not do in his journal. A passage from his journal of November 10, 1858, compared with an excerpt from the "Winter Animals" section of *Walden*, can serve to illustrate this disparity. First, in the journal entry, Thoreau describes the foraging and eating behavior of a group of jays.

Hearing in the oak and near by a sound as if someone had broken a twig, I looked up and saw a jay pecking at an acorn. There were several jays busily gathering acorns on a scarlet oak. I could hear them break them off. They then flew to a suitable limb and, placing the acorn under one foot, hammered away at it busily, looking round from time to time to see if any foe was approaching, and soon reached the meat and nibbled at it, holding up their heads to swallow, while they held it very firmly with their claws. (Their hammering made a sound like the woodpecker's.) Nevertheless it sometimes dropped to the ground before they had done with it.[27]

This almost purely factual account contrasts strongly with Thoreau's discussion in *Walden* of similar blue jay behavior.

At length the jays arrive, whose discordant screams were heard long before, as they were *warily* making their approach an eighth of a mile off, and in *a stealthy and sneaking manner* they flit from tree to tree, nearer and nearer, and pick up the kernels which the squirrels have dropped. Then, sitting on a pitch pine bough, they attempt to swallow *in their haste* a kernel which is too big for their throats and chokes them; and after great labor they disgorge it, and spend an hour in the endeavor to crack it by repeated blows with their bills. They were *manifestly thieves, and I had not much respect for them*; but the squirrels, though at first shy, went to work as if they were taking what was their own.[28] (emphasis added)

Certainly the passage from *Walden* reads as more literary than the dry, natural science observation from the journal. Whereas the journal describes the jays only as working "busily" to secure their meal, in *Walden* Thoreau sees the birds as "sneaky and stealthy" and as "thieves." The birds enter a human moral framework and are judged harshly. To a reader of his journals, which voice only admiration, Thoreau's claim in *Walden* that "I had not much respect for them" comes as something of a surprise.

*Walden* was published in 1854, so one might suppose that Thoreau's view of the jay changed from one of condemnation to admiration over the course of the four years between the publication of *Walden* and the 1858 journal entry. But Thoreau's pre-*Walden* journal entries of 1853–54 make no moral judgments of the jay. Perhaps the blue jays of *Walden* only look bad in contrast to the smaller, friendlier chickadees that Thoreau discusses immediately after his discussion of blue jays. The chickadee seems to appeal to Thoreau as a neighbor who acknowledges Thoreau's presence. He writes, "They were so familiar that at length one alighted on an armful of wood which I was carrying in, and pecked at the sticks without fear."[29] The jay can be observed at close range, but it remains distant from the observer.

Thoreau's interactions with a common loon might say more about what he was getting at when he described the birds of Walden Woods as his neighbors. In an extended passage, he details a "game" that he plays with a loon, Thoreau rowing his boat toward the loon, the loon diving, and Thoreau attempting to row to the spot where he thinks the loon will resurface. "While he was thinking one thing in his brain, I was endeavoring to divine his thought in mine. It was a pretty game, played on the smooth surface of the pond, a man against a loon."[30] Finally, at the end of this "game," Thoreau concludes in admiration "that he laughed in derision of my efforts, confident of his own resources."[31] Like the chickadee, the loon shows an awareness of Thoreau, at least from Thoreau's perspective. Likewise, he describes the thrill he felt when a sparrow alit on his shoulder. "I felt that I was more distinguished by that circumstance than I should have been by any epaulet I could have worn."[32] Thoreau's best bird neighbors might be the ones who acknowledge his presence, the ones that seem to accept him as part of their "wild" world. In a sense, then, the blue jay was a bad neighbor—a thief who does not acknowledge his neighbor's presence in the woods. The jay escapes human contact; it remains wild, and it sets a bad moral example.

Dickinson and Thoreau both obviously closely studied blue jays before rendering them into literature. John James Audubon, though, had much more detailed encounters with blue jays. He describes his interactions with jays in his journals and in his *Ornithological Biography*, where, like Thoreau, he wavers between admiration for the jay's vitality and approbation of what he sees as its immoral behavior.

Audubon's moral vision of the jay is perhaps best illustrated in the painting of blue jays that appears in *Birds of America*. In the painting, the jays are destroying the eggs of another bird's nest. The yolk is falling from the eggs, and the jays seem to be enjoying the carnage. As one female jay pokes at a broken egg, another female, with wings spread and mouth open, gorges on the seeping yolk. The male jay, slightly lower and on the back of the branch, is shown in profile, looking proud with its crest erect and an egg, dripping yolk, impaled on his beak.

In his description of the painting, Audubon highlights what he sees as the dual nature of the jay:

> Reader, look at the plate in which are represented three individuals of this beautiful species,—rogues though they be, and thieves, as I would call them, were it fit for me to pass judgment on their actions. See how each is enjoying the fruits of his knavery, sucking the egg which he has pilfered from the nest of some innocent dove or harmless pigeon! Who could imagine that a form so resplendent, should harbor so much mischief; that selfishness, duplicity, and malice should form the moral accompaniments of so much physical perfection! Yet so it is, and how like beings of a much higher order, are these gay deceivers! Aye, I could write you a whole chapter on this subject, were not my task of a different nature.[33]

Audubon, while claiming to withhold judgment, condemns the jay because its behavior does not match its appearance. Because the jay is a "resplendent" embodiment of "physical perfection," Audubon expects that it will act accordingly. Instead, Audubon views the seeming inherent deception between appearance and behavior as a mark of the human. Jays, "like beings of a much higher order"—that is, humans— are able to act duplicitously. Like humans, jays can hide their interior moral failings under their exterior beauty.

Audubon goes on to amass evidence of the jay's immorality. He writes that "every where it manifests the same mischievous disposition." Among the blue jays' sins are nest robbing, pecking out the eyes of an injured grouse, eating a caged flying squirrel, and destroying "all the birds of one aviary" in Charleston.[34] What makes this aggressive

John James Audubon, *Blue Jay*, from *Birds of America*.

behavior especially reprehensible for Audubon is the jay's otherwise cowardly behavior. Audubon notes that blue jays will freeze in fear at the sight of a hawk, or fly away to avoid confrontation with cardinals, robins, and mockingbirds. This behavior, which from a contemporary perspective seems merely adaptive, illustrates to Audubon the jay's cowardly behavior. He writes that the jay hides from the hawk "as if ever conscious of deserving punishment." Likewise, the jay's strategy of avoiding confrontation with other birds tells Audubon that the jay is "more tyrannical than brave, and, like most boasters, domineers over the feeble, dreads the strong, and flies even from his equals." Not only is the jay a coward, it also displays an awareness of its own immorality and acknowledges its need to repent. In what can only be read as a parable, Audubon writes that the jay will sneakily eat the eggs and young of the birds that it otherwise avoids in order "to be even with them." But in seeking retribution, the jay does not go unpunished. On returning to its nest, the jay finds "its mate in the jaws of a snake, the nest upset, and the eggs all gone." The jay, and Audubon's readers, can learn a lesson, which Audubon proceeds to spell out. "I have thought that more than once on such occasions that, like all great culprits, when brought to a sense of their enormities, it evinced a strong sense of remorse."[35]

What should a twenty-first-century reader make of Audubon's moral reading of the blue jay? Given his nineteenth-century context, Audubon was not alone in seeing a reflection of Christianity in the natural world. (Remember that Darwin put off publication of *The Origin of Species* for years because it refuted the Christian doctrine of special creation.) There is nothing surprising here; one would be more surprised to find a European or American nineteenth-century writer reflecting on the natural world without injecting a Christian worldview. This moral reading of blue jay's appearance and behavior, though, obscures the ornithological, evolutionary, and ethological insight contained in Audubon's writing.

Perhaps it takes a nineteenth-century philosopher who didn't see the natural world as a reflection of Christian morality to help clarify Audubon's insights. Friedrich Nietzsche's critique of morality provides another way of thinking about Audubon's writing, and thus another way of thinking about human-blue jay interactions.

Nietzsche, of course, was not a natural scientist. Nonetheless, in works such as "On Truth and Lying in a Non-moral Sense" and *The Genealogy of Morals*, he does discuss the human—both scientific and religious—propensity to view the natural world from a moral perspective. One could argue that Nietzsche's use of animals is merely rhetorical or metaphoric. But as Ralph Acampora argues in

*A Nietzschean Bestiary,* Nietzsche's discussion of animals can also be seen as a "zoological recontextualization of humanity as an organic life form set in the natural (versus a metaphysical or supersensory) environment."[36] That is, Nietzsche sees humans as one animal among others. As Acampora quotes Nietzsche: "When one speaks of humanity, underlying this idea is the belief that it is humanity that separates and distinguishes human beings from nature. But, there is, in reality, no such distinction: the 'natural qualities' and those properly called 'human' grow inseparably."[37] Much has been written on Nietzsche's arguments with Darwinian theory, but here he is unintentionally describing the idea of evolutionary continuity that humans are one form of life among others, all interrelated. (This insight, as I will discuss later, is quite important to the field of cognitive ethology, the study of animal cognition in its environment.) In writing of resentment and the origins of good and evil in *The Genealogy of Morals*, Nietzsche considers the relationship between the "lamb" and the "bird of prey." He writes:

> There is nothing very odd about lambs disliking birds of prey, but this is no reason for holding it against large birds of prey that they carry off lambs. And when the lambs whisper among themselves, "these birds of prey are evil, and does not this give us a right to say that whatever is the opposite of a bird of prey must be good?" there is nothing intrinsically wrong with such an argument—though the birds of prey will look somewhat quizzically and say, "*We* have nothing against these good lambs; in fact, we love them; nothing tastes better than a tender lamb."[38]

For Nietzsche, the bird of prey cannot be judged "evil" in and of itself, as its devouring of lambs is simply a manifestation of what he calls the bird's "will." The bird of prey does what it does outside of any encompassing moral context. Within the limited context of the prey, it makes sense to view the bird of prey as evil, and within the limited context of the bird of prey it makes sense to love the lamb. But there is no greater context from which one can judge either animal. For Nietzsche, the moralist overreaches when he or she "assume[s] the right of calling the bird of prey to account for being a bird of prey." To assume, even metaphorically, that a blue jay feels "bad" for devouring the eggs of another bird is, as Nietzsche writes, to "divorce strength from its manifestations, as though there were behind the strong a neutral agent, free to manifest its strength or contain it."[39] For Nietzsche, this "neutral agent" does not exist, except as a mistake of human language. For Audubon, this "neutral agent" is precisely what links the blue jay to the human. Both are "gay deceivers" who might do bad things, but both can feel remorse, and both can repent.

If one strips away Audubon's implicit moral anthropomorphism, the blue jay's will is revealed. Rather than holding the jay to account for its humanly immoral behavior, a more Nietzschean question can emerge: what does the blue jay will? Nietzsche writes that "to expect that strength will not manifest itself as strength, as a desire to overcome, to appropriate, to have enemies, obstacles, and triumphs, is every bit as absurd as to expect that weakness will manifest itself as strength. A quantum of strength is equivalent to a quantum of urge, will, activity."[40] In this sense, the blue jay's actions are nothing more or less than an expression of its will to live. A blue jay devours the eggs of another bird because it desires food, just as the snake devours the blue jay's mate and eggs for the same reason. Both animals manifest their strength as nest raiders. To ask what the blue jay wills, then, is to ask how it acts in its environment, how it adapts to and survives in its world.

Obviously, a sense of moral culpability would not be an adaptive trait for blue jays. But many of the jay's other traits described by Audubon are manifestations of a strong adaptive will. The abilities to choose from a wide variety of food options, to enter into complex social relations, and to deceive, among others, point toward an adaptive intelligence that links jays and other birds more strongly to humans than a common morality does. From this viewpoint, Audubon's writings about the blue jay anticipate twentieth-century understandings of birds and other nonhuman animals.

Regarding the blue jay's diet, Audubon writes that "the Blue Jay is truly omnivorous, feeding indiscriminately on all sorts of flesh, seeds, and insects." While Audubon draws the moral conclusion that jays are thus "more tyrannical than brave," contemporary ornithology and ethology have shown that such foraging behavior is a strong sign of intelligence.[41] In both laboratory and field studies, blue jays and other members of its *corvid* genera such as crows and ravens have been found to be quite intelligent in a number of ways, including food selection, tool use and invention, and memory. Jays and other corvids eat a wide variety of foods and are known as "generalists" because of this. Candace Savage notes in *Bird Brains* that "a generalist has to run a regular inventory on dozens of edible items, an occupation that calls for curiosity, perception, memory, and, often, inventiveness. For such an animal, a well-stocked brain may be an essential means to a well-stuffed belly."[42] Marc Bekoff has demonstrated that Steller's jays (a close western relative of the eastern blue jay), in addition to being able to make complex decisions about what to eat, evaluate numerous complex stimuli in making decisions as to where to feed. He writes, "Jays were making complex decisions after evaluating the total situation, not just one variable at a time."[43] In other words, Bekoff's experiment showed that jays simultaneously evaluate many variables as they consider what and where to eat. Feeding behavior and social behavior are linked, as Bekoff, Allen, and Grant note that one variable of feeding decisions was "the presence of conspecifics and other animals."[44]

Audubon conducted an "experiment" on blue jays that a contemporary reader might see as prefiguring Bekoff's conclusions, even as Audubon characterized his findings in terms of the jay's moral failings. In 1830 Audubon bought twenty-five jays in Louisville, Kentucky, "with the view of turning them out in the English woods."[45] Audubon took the birds to England, but his release experiment failed, as most of the jays died from "a disease occasioned by insects adhering to every part of their body."[46] Only one bird remained alive when Audubon reached London; this jay, though, was so covered in "insects" that Audubon "immersed it in an infusion of tobacco, which, however, killed it in a few hours."[47] Clearly, these aspects of Audubon's experiment have no scientific interest today except as a curiosity. But Audubon's experiment does reveal something about jays' complex social relations.

Audubon did not purchase all twenty-five jays at once. He writes that "they were caught in common traps, baited with maize, and were brought to me one after another as soon as secured."[48] As each jay was caught, it was introduced into the "large cage" that Audubon planned to use to take the birds to England. This slow introduction over the course of numerous days produced an inadvertent means of observing the social behavior of jays. Audubon described how each bird behaved when placed in the cage. "The newcomer ... would run into a corner, place his head almost in a perpendicular position and remain silent and sulky, with an appearance of stupidity quite foreign to his nature. He would suffer all the rest to walk over him and trample him down, without ever changing his position."[49] In observing this behavior, Audubon "was surprised to see how *cowardly* each newly caught bird was when introduced to his brethren."[50] After a day or two in the cage, Audubon noted that the cowardly jays "were as gay and frolicksome as if at liberty in the woods."[51] Audubon saw this behavioral change in emotional, even moral terms: the jay is at first a coward; only eventually does it return to its bold behavior.

With its moral trappings removed, Audubon's sequential placement of jays in a cage can be seen as an experiment on jay social behavior. Over one hundred and forty years later, according to Tarvin and Woolfenden, the editors of the *Birds of North America*, human "understanding of the breeding biology, demography, and sociality of Blue Jays remains poor."[52] Nonetheless, the editors are able to draw certain conclusions in their entry on blue jays from, among other sources, "the sketchy accounts in the published literature." One of their postulated conclusions could perhaps be applied to Audubon's experiment: Jays "do not breed cooperatively, but conduct group social displays and mob predators and intruders, perhaps as members of a loosely organized neighborhood flock."[53] In other words, Audubon's "cowardly" jays might have been displaying the kind of complex social behavior that can be considered a mark of intelligence. Where Audubon saw a moral failing, contemporary readers can see avian social dynamics.

In a similar way, removing Audubon's moral framing of the jay's deceptive behavior can reveal more signs of avian intelligence. Earlier in this chapter, I discuss Audubon's conclusion that a jay, silently hiding from a hawk, is exhibiting feelings of guilt. Forgetting this ascription of guilt, a contemporary reader can see something more interesting in Audubon's description of the jay's response to a predator. Seeing a predator, jays will, according to Audubon, "either remain motionless for a while, or sneak off silently into the closest thickets, where they remain concealed as long as their dangerous enemy is near."[54] Audubon concludes that jays are capable of deception, and are thus capable of exhibiting the moral failings of humans. More recent studies, though, have concluded that the ability to deceive might be a marker of intelligence. As Donald Griffin writes in *Animal Minds*, "deceptive communication may be more likely to require conscious thinking than the honest expression of what an animal feels, desires, or believes."[55] In other words, the ability to deceive does indeed link humans and birds. This link, though, may be less of a moral link, as Audubon posits, and more of an intelligence link. If both blue jays and humans can practice deception, one can argue that they share a similar adaptive intelligence. The ability to deceive implies an ability to consciously plan, and to anticipate reactions from others. Birds and humans can lie because both have brains that allow them to do so. Morality does not enter the picture.

Despite both Thoreau's and Audubon's moral condemnation of blue jays, both admired the bird as much as Dickinson did. Audubon writes that the jays' "graceful form and lovely tints, never fail to delight the observer."[56] The blue jay even becomes a happy reminder of the United States for Audubon. He writes, "After an absence of several months from the United States, the voice of the blue jay sounded melodious to me."[57] In short, the nineteenth-century blue jay was both admired and judged. The blue jay was a civic-minded neighbor, but also a thief; it was aesthetically brilliant but morally weak.

## "HIS FUTURE A DISPUTE": BLUE JAYS IN THE TWENTIETH AND TWENTY-FIRST CENTURIES

In the early 1970s two psychologists conducted an experiment with blue jays. The subject of the experiment was a young jay captured from a nest in Amherst, Massachusetts, at the "estimated age of 7 to 10 days." Over the next sixteen months, this possible descendant of the birds that Emily Dickinson wrote about was placed three times on a "food-deprivation schedule" lasting two to five weeks. During these times, the blue jay learned to use the newspaper that lined its cage to reach food pellets that had collected on a ledge just outside its cage. When hungry, "the jay ripped a piece of newspaper from the pages kept beneath its cage, manipulated the piece of paper, and then proceeded to thrust it back and forth between the wires of its cage, raking in food pellets too distant to be picked up directly with its beak."[58] The blue jay had invented and used a tool. Jones and Kamil later presented the jay with a feather, a piece of grass, a paper clip, and a plastic bag tie. On each occasion, the jay used these implements to procure food. Furthermore, six other jays in the lab began to use pieces of newspaper as tools to pull food into their cages. Jones and Kamil argue that these six jays likely learned this behavior "through observational learning or imitation." Not only could jays invent and use tools, they could learn to use tools by watching other tool-using jays. Jones and Kamil conclude that flexible intelligence "may be indicative of a particular potential for behavioral adaptations typical of some species with highly generalized feeding behaviors, such as the Northern Blue Jay."[59]

In 2004 a group of twenty-nine scientists published a paper called "The Avian Brain Nomenclature Forum: Terminology for a New Century in Comparative Neuroanatomy," in which they argue for renaming certain structures in avian brains to reflect their similarity to mammalian brains. They write that "as deeper insight has been gained into the evolution, development, and functions of the brains of birds and mammals," certain terminology flaws "have greatly hindered communication among avian and mammalian brain research specialists and perpetuated an outdated view of avian brain evolution."[60] This proposed change in terminology is meant to reflect a new understanding of avian brains, an understanding that holds out the possibility that the brains of birds and mammals may be more similar than previously thought. A *New York Times* write-up of the nomenclature forum essay notes that the scientists argue that "the avian brain is as complex, flexible and inventive as any mammalian brain."[61] What might it mean to humans if bird brains are understood as more similar to our brains than we had believed before? What might it mean to us if birds can be thought to have some form of consciousness?

Among other things, it might mean that blue jays and other birds are indeed "neighbors" to humans, but not necessarily in a spiritual and moral sense. Rather, birds and humans can be viewed as evolutionarily continuous—both have the ability to learn, to deceive, to invent, to flexibly respond to situations—to the point that, in the words of Marc Bekoff, "it is difficult to justify the belief that we are the only species on this planet in which individuals are self-conscious."[62] If we believe that blue jays and other birds have a consciousness that is more similar to our own than previously thought, our view of interactions with birds and other conscious beings might change. Indeed, our understanding of what it means to be a conscious inhabit of the planet might be radically altered.

Bekoff has noted that "claims that only humans use tools or language, are artists, have culture, or reason are no longer defensible given the enormous growth in our knowledge of our animal kin."[63] Twentieth- and twenty-first-century engagements with blue jays have taken heed of this growth in knowledge to display an altered understanding of both blue jay's and human's places in the world. A close look at three specific examples—a novel by Don DeLillo, a nonfiction account of life with a blue jay by Vicki Formato, and a painting by Roger Tory Peterson—can help to illustrate this changed perspective.

Don DeLillo's short 1998 novel *The Body Artist* shows a strong interest in birds. Lauren Hartke, the "body artist" of the title, live in a circumscribed world; she barely ventures away from the rented house she shares with her husband. After his suicide, Hartke spends most of her time alone, perfecting a performance art piece and closely observing her surroundings. As part of her daily routine, she feeds birds. "She'd been putting up feeders since her return. This was the basic range of her worldly surround, the breadth of nature that bordered the house."[64] Hartke puts up a multitude of feeders—"a different seed for each receptacle, sometimes two seeds layered light and dark in a single feeder, and they come and peck, or don't and the feeders are different as well, cages, ringed cylinders, hanging saucers, mounted trays"—and closely observes the comings and goings of the birds, noting sparrows, crows, hawks, and jays.[65] She notices when "it was one of the birdless mornings" and when "the birds were going crazy on the feeders."[66] In short, Hartke spends a lot of time maintaining her bird feeders and thinking about birds. "She cleaned and filled the bird feeders, shaping the day around a major thing with all its wrinkles and twists, its array of swarming variations."[67] Hartke's close attention to birds leads her to focus on birds' sensory perception and its differences from human sensory experience. *The Body Artist*, in the details of this close attention, invents a way of closing the distance between human and animal consciousness. Through Hartke's eyes, readers are led to question the human-animal border, much as recent critical work in animal studies and cognitive ethology has done.

At one point, Hartke notes, "the sparrows were at the feeder, wing-beating, fighting for space on the curved perches."[68] As she moves around the kitchen, "birds scattered when she moved near the window"; then, "she moved toward the table and the birds went cracking off the feeder again."[69] A few pages, and a few minutes, later, "she heard the crows in large numbers now, clamorous in the trees, probably mobbing a hawk." Hartke only barely notices this action outside her window, as her attention is divided among the routine events of reading, talking, listening, and daydreaming. As she watches the birds fly into the glare of the sun, "it was an action she only partly knew, elusive and mutely beautiful, the birds so sunstruck they were consumed by light, disembodied, turned into something sheer and fleet and scatter-bright."[70] A few minutes later, though, a singular event at the bird feeders gets all of Hartke's attention. Immersed in routine, "she went to pour water for her tea and paused at the stove waiting for him to say yes or no to coffee. When she started back she saw a blue jay perched atop the feeder. She stopped dead and held her breath."[71] Hartke's encounter with this blue jay takes only a few seconds of perception, but it is described over two and a half pages of the novel. Seeing the blue jay leads her thoughts in at least three directions.

First, she is in awe of the bird; she wants to tell her husband to look at it, but she fears that any movement will scare the bird off. As she continues looking at the bird, Hartke pays minute attention to how her perception works. In essence, the encounter with the blue jay teaches Hartke how vision works. Second, and I would argue most importantly, Hartke attempts to imagine what the blue jay sees. The narrative notes the difficulty of entering into the consciousness of another living being even as it tentatively describes what the blue jay might be seeing. This scene offers a way of beginning to understand interactions across species lines (and across genus, family, order, and class lines). Third, Hartke sees the jay looking back at her, and is overwhelmed by the experience of a nonhuman animal perceiving her. Taken together, Hartke's encounter with the blue jay exemplifies a way of perceiving the world that attempts to take nonhuman perception seriously. In short, Hartke looks at the blue jay and the blue jay looks back.

When Hartke first sees the blue jay, time seems to come to a halt and space reduces to the area occupied by the bird. As she notes the bird's appearance, Hartke realizes that her vision is somehow being altered by this experience. Philip Nel convincingly argues that this detailed passage highlights the metaphorical nature of language, even as DeLillo writes with concrete detail. Nel writes that "DeLillo's description of a blue jay acknowledges the inevitable mediations of metaphor."[72] Likewise, the blue jay scene shows how language itself is connected to human perception. Nel writes that "for all the sharpness of [his] imagery, . . . DeLillo's birds highlight the subjectivity of perception—through how Lauren sees the birds themselves."[73] The scene builds a strong connection between DeLillo's descriptions and Lauren's experience. That is, the clarity of detail in the scene is dependent on Hartke's keen visual perception. She realizes that "she'd never seen a thing so clearly and it was not simply because the jay was posted where it was, close enough for her to note the details of cresting and color."[74] In fact, the event itself—the correspondence of Hartke looking out the window just as the jay appears on the feeder—alters Hartke's perception of how her own vision works. As she notes the bird's appearance—"it stood large and polished and looked royally remote from the other birds busy feeding"—Hartke realizes that her vision is somehow being altered by this experience. "She could nearly believe she'd never seen a jay before."[75] As she continues to stare, "she thought she'd somehow only now learned how to look."[76] She realizes that "this must be like what it means to see if you've been near blind all your life."[77] As Nel writes, "the clarity of DeLillo's rendition brings us as close as possible to Lauren's experiences."[78] Through the mediation of language, readers gain access to Hartke's vision of a blue jay even as the visual encounter with the blue jay overwhelms Hartke and reorders her perceptions.

As she watches the blue jay, the birds that have been in the background of her morning move to the center of her consciousness. Her mundane breakfast becomes "a normal morning going crazy."[79] What, exactly, causes her morning to go "crazy"? The blue jay's proximity seems to be a primary cause. Even with a bird as common and gregarious as the blue jay, such close proximity between human and bird is not an everyday occurrence. This closeness allows Hartke to note details of the bird's appearance, but it also seems to give her access to something else. She forges some sort of perceptual connection with the blue jay that, at least for the moment, causes her to see the world differently. Writing of science and technology, Donna Haraway notes that no act of vision is passive. She writes that "all eyes, including our own organic ones, are active perceptual systems, building in translations and specific ways of seeing, that is, ways of life. . . . There are only highly specific visual possibilities, each with a wonderfully detailed, active, partial way of organizing worlds."[80] Hartke's seeing of the blue jay may only be enabled by the basic technologies of window glass and bird feeders—because of proximity she needs no other optics to see the bird up close—but Haraway's claim that our vision leads to new "ways of life" and of "ordering the world" rings true for Hartke's experience. That is, Hartke's momentary, time-stopping encounter with the blue jay creates what Haraway has famously described as "situated knowledge." Haraway writes, "Situated knowledges require that the object of knowledge be pictured as an actor and agent, not a screen or ground or a resource, never finally as slave to the master that closes off the dialectic in his unique agency and authorship of 'objective' knowledge."[81] Hartke realizes that the blue jay is not just an object to be looked at and described. She senses some kind of agency in the bird as she realizes that the blue jay is looking back at her. The bird becomes an active participant in the act of looking. When Hartke first sees the jay, she imagines it "seeing whatever it saw."[82] But as the moment progresses she begins to wonder just what it is that the bird might be seeing. The bird becomes an agent in this slowed-down period of time carved out of a "normal morning."

As Hartke continues to stare at the bird, "she tried to work past the details to the bird itself, nest thief and skilled mimic, to the fixed interest in those eyes, a kind of inquisitive chill that felt a little like a challenge."[83] Her desire to somehow experience "the bird itself" is quickly located in the bird's eyes. In these eyes, Hartke sees an interest that may or may not be human. She doesn't see herself, and she doesn't see human emotions emanating from the bird's eyes. The bird takes in its surroundings, searching for food and looking out for danger. Later in the novel DeLillo notes that the birds at the feeder sometimes fly off for reasons that are outside of human perception, as "they read a message in some event outside the visible spectrum."[84] Bird senses are not the equivalent of human senses; their life depends on their ability to sense a hawk or a cat lurking nearby. David Sibley notes that "the acuity of avian eyesight is unparalleled among vertebrates: On average, birds can see two to three times more sharply than humans, and some raptors can sight small prey more than a mile away."[85] Later in the novel, Hartke cannot find the right words to describe this acute sense of awareness that birds possess. Looking at the feeder she sees that "there were five birds on the feeder and they all faced outward, away from the food and identically still. She watched them. They weren't looking or listening so much as feeling something, intent and sensing." But Hartke finally realizes that "all of these words are wrong."[86] Human language is incapable of describing bird perception. And, as ornithologist George A. Clark Jr. reminds us, "we cannot experience the perceptions of other organisms."[87]

Nevertheless, Hartke tries to understand exactly what the blue jay might be seeing. "When birds look into houses, what impossible worlds they see. Think. What a shedding of every knowable surface and process. She wanted to believe the bird was seeing her, a woman with a teacup in her hand, and never mind the folding back of day and night, the apparition of a space set off from time."[88] The one-word sentence "Think" is key here. Hartke is indeed thinking outside the usual realm of thought that would never consider what the blue jay sees when it looks at her. She is thinking outside of what DeLillo calls elsewhere in the novel "the easy sway of either/or."[89] In a similar vein, Gilles Deleuze and Felix Guattari write in *What Is Philosophy?* that "subject and object give a poor approximation of thought. Thinking is neither a line drawn between subject and object nor a revolving of one around the other."[90] In her fascination with the blue jay, Hartke clearly blurs the boundaries between subject and object. She first sees the bird as an object, as she describes its coloration and markings. She then tries to enter into the bird's consciousness as she wonders what it might be seeing. These two moments are not mutually exclusive; her vision of the blue jay combines an objectification of the bird with an awareness of its agency.

In a similar way, the notion that birds see "impossible worlds" when they look into houses can be taken in two ways. From the bird's perspective these worlds might be impossible in that it is beyond the ability of the bird to comprehend all that the human term "house" encompasses. At the same time, it is impossible for a human to enter fully into a bird's consciousness in order to experience what the bird is seeing. Regardless of this double impossibility, Hartke is able, through perception and thought, to forge some connection with the blue jay. She becomes, to a certain degree, what Deleuze and Guattari call a "partial observer." They write that "the role of a partial observer is *to perceive* and *to experience*, although these perceptions and affections are not those of a man, in the currently accepted sense, but belong to the thing studied."[91] In short, Hartke's perceptions can be fully located in neither herself nor in the bird. She cannot find the language to explain her experience. In fact, she cannot prolong this ecstatic experience beyond a moment's time. "She looked and took a careful breath. She was alert to the clarity of the moment but knew it was ending already. She felt it in the blue jay. Or maybe not. She was making it happen herself because she could not look any longer."[92] Even as the moment ends, Hartke cannot be sure if what is happening is coming from her or from the blue jay. In a way that she cannot express, the experience is coming from both of them as they perceive the other.

As Hartke falls out of the moment, she has a strong emotional reaction to what has just happened. Returning to conversation with her husband, she asks: "Did you see it?" A brief conversation follows.

> "Don't we see them all the time?"
> "Not all the time. And never so close."
> "Never so close. Okay."
> "It was looking at me."
> "It was looking at you."
> . . . . . . . . . . . . . . . . . . . .
> "It was watching me."
> "Did it make your day?"
> "It made my day. My week. What else?"[93]

Her husband is unable to understand how such a mundane event can take on such importance. Hartke's short declarative sentences make no real attempt to explain the significance of her encounter. Her "what else?," though, points to both the importance of this experience and her inability to express this importance. She may have encountered another consciousness, or the whole thing may have taken place inside her head. Regardless, something about this moment overwhelms Hartke. Later in the novel, a man unexpectedly appears in Hartke's driveway. She had thought she was in solitude, and his appearance is described as "the shock of the outside world, the blow, the stun of intrusion."[94] Her reaction to this man also fits her experience with the blue jay. Perception and thought have put her into contact with a life outside herself and outside her usual experience of the world. Her brief awareness of the blue jay's consciousness implies a whole other perceptual consciousness that is both distant and close. The blue jay's experience of the world is foreign to Hartke's experience, but both she and the blue jay are alive to their respective experiences of the world. Hartke's shock is the shock of awareness of other forms of life that understand shared space in wholly different ways. Blue jays live in a world that overlaps and comes into contact with the human world, yet remains apart from it. Thoreau's nineteenth-century blue jay marks out some of this same distance, as unlike the chickadee, sparrow, and loon it never acknowledges Thoreau's presence in its world. Hartke's desire to have the blue jay see her seems quite different from Thoreau's, though. When she looks into a blue jay's eyes, she does not see a morally fallible creature; instead, she sees a perceiving consciousness staring back at her with intelligence.

It is worth noting here that Hartke's notion that the blue jay was watching her is not outside the realm of scientific possibility. Numerous scientific studies have examined how birds respond to the human gaze. One experiment was able to "show that hand-raised ravens not only visually co-orient with the look-ups of a human experimenter but also reposition themselves to follow the experimenter's gaze around a visual barrier."[95] Another experiment has shown that starlings respond to the gaze of predators. Carter et al. "present wild-caught European starlings (*Sturnus vulgaris*) with human 'predators' whose frontal appearance and gaze direction are manipulated independently, and show that starlings are sensitive to the predator's orientation, the presence of eyes and the direction of eye-gaze."[96] These experiments suggest that birds are attuned to the vision of other animals, including humans. Bugnyar, Stöwe, and Heinrich conclude, "The ability for tracking gaze behind obstacles may provide a basis for future studies on higher-level socio-cognitive processes."[97] In its own way, *The Body Artist* offers an approach for thinking about precisely the same thing.

Likewise, Hartke's belief that the blue jay has some kind of intelligence resonates with recent critical work in animal studies and cognitive ethology. Many cognitive ethologists argue that human and other animal consciousnesses share many similarities. Humanities scholars such as Donna Haraway and Cary Wolfe have argued that, in the words of Haraway, "Nothing really convincingly settles the separation of human and animal."[98] Marc Bekoff concludes that consciousness exists outside of the human realm, "if we pay attention to some basic and well-accepted biological ideas, especially evolutionary continuity."[99] DeLillo's novel offers a kind of literary support for this claim, as it imagines just how humans might understand the self-consciousness of a blue jay.

DeLillo's close focus on this momentary encounter between a human and a blue jay resonates with Wendell Berry's call for "a new, or renewed, propriety in the study and the use of the living world."[100] For Berry, the notion of "propriety" can remind us that humans are not alone in the world. "Its value is in its reference to the fact that we are not alone. The idea of propriety makes an issue of the fittingness of our conduct to place or circumstances, even to our hopes."[101] From such a viewpoint, other creatures (such as, in the case I am considering, a blue jay) cannot be fully comprehended by the human mind. He writes, "The mystery surrounding our life probably is not significantly reducible. And so the question of how to act in ignorance is paramount."[102] Hartke's ability to perceive the blue jay, coupled with her ability to perceive the blue jay looking back at her, establishes a relationship between two living creatures. Neither creature can wholly understand the other, but some of the power of DeLillo's novel resides in his ability to portray the incompleteness of understanding between human and bird. To put it another way, *The Body Artist* makes visible an "impossible world" without reducing that world to the clear possibility of the world as usually understood. Readers are left to consider the propriety of life as a part of the blue jay's world.

Don DeLillo presents a compelling fictional account of what a blue jay might think about when it looks into a human house. To look at things from a different angle, I turn now to the story of "Jayson," a blue jay who has lived in a human house for twenty years. In her book *Jayson: The True Story of a 20 Year Old Blue Jay*, Vicki Formato details what it is like to live with a blue jay who "has made an indelible mark" on her.[103] Formato adopted the female blue jay, which she had thought was male, after a wildlife clinic diagnosed the jay with bone deformities. The clinic was going to euthanize the bird, but Formato convinced the veterinarian to let her care for the bird until it could be released. After six weeks, the vet examined the bird; its deformities had not healed, so the vet allowed Formato to keep the bird. Twenty years later, Jayson still lived with Formato.

Formato's narrative account of life with Jayson is by no means scientific. Nevertheless, many of the conclusions Formato draws from her interactions with Jayson fit nicely with twenty-first-century scientific understandings of birds. Formato provides a wealth of anecdotal evidence that suggests Jayson is an intelligent, curious, social being who has adapted to life in a human house. Perhaps most interestingly, Formato claims that "the jay had quite a personality, nothing like what might be expected from a wild bird."[104] One might even conclude, as Formato does, that Jayson exhibits emotional responses to her world. Everything in Formato's account suggests that Jayson does indeed have a "personality," a sense of his place in the larger context of his life.

As I note above, the blue jay's "flexible intelligence" is well documented. Jayson has clearly been "humanized" and "anthropomorphized" in her unnatural environment; nevertheless, within this environment, she exhibits many traits that can only be understood as manifestations of intelligence. As generalists, blue jays must evaluate multiple food sources. Jayson, while obviously having quite different food options from wild blue jays, selects and caches the food she is offered. Formato writes in detail how Jayson "manag[es] her food supply" by exhibiting preferences for certain foods over others and by eating some food items immediately, and caching some food items for later consumption. While Jayson's "core diet" is dog food, she is offered many other food choices. The bird refuses all fruit (a favorite of wild blue jays) and only eats two vegetables (corn and peas).[105]

Jayson has adapted the "generalist" feeding habits that she would have used in the wild to the habitat of Formato's home. The bird loves "junk food"—"popcorn, potato chips, pretzels, corn chips, and crackers, for example, are now among Jayson's favorite foods"—to such an extent that "she actually will spit out other food if she sees someone walk by with a chip or something else she likes."[106] The bird also clamors for pancakes when she sees Formato's family eating breakfast. Jayson displays curiosity toward novel food items such as junk food, to the point that Formato sees Jayson taking pleasure in the exploration of possible new foods. "She likes to try new and different things, and we enjoy giving them to her."[107] Jayson's instinctual generalism would be a survival mechanism in the "wild"; in Formato's home, this generalism becomes a marker of something like preference and pleasure, or, in other words, taste.

While Jayson displays desire for "human" food, Formato notes that the bird also enjoys foods more typically associated with blue jays, such as seeds and bugs. On seeing Jayson eat a bug, Formato exclaims: "Finally there was a 'natural' food that Jayson liked!"[108] Jayson also rejects foods that blue jays typically reject. "In the wild, blue jays don't eat ants. Well, in captivity, they don't eat them either."[109] Jayson also displays behavior that anyone who has watched a blue jay at a bird feeder is probably familiar with. "Jayson has developed what I believe is her own, unique sorting scheme for finding just the seeds she likes and wants. She approaches her seed dish, looks it over in minute detail . . . then uses her beak to scatter seed all over the cage . . . She bounces from seed to seed, one at a time, inspecting each one, eating some on the spot, ignoring others, and burying certain select ones."[110] At this point, a reader might be wondering about the significance of Jayson's unique food preferences. Surely anyone with a pet bird, cat, or dog could tell similar stories. What makes Jayson's feeding choices and behavior particularly interesting lies in the way that Formato's discussion overlaps with scientific experimentation exploring the social behavior (and implicitly, the intelligence) of blue jays.

At the beginning of this chapter, I reference Bekoff, Allen, and Grant's study of the feeding selection of Steller's jays. This study, with a few scientific controls and detailed statistical methods, gathered its data from observing jays at a human-constructed feeding station. Likewise, a 1997 study by Keith Tarvin and Glen E. Woolfenden examined "Patterns of Dominance and Aggressive Behavior in Blue Jays at a Feeder." Taken together, these two studies illustrate the complexity of both feeding behavior and social organization in the genus that includes blue and Steller's jays. Bekoff concludes, "We found that the selection of feeding sites by Steller's jays was simultaneously influenced by food type, food configuration, animal type, and animal configuration."[111] That is, behind every blue jay visit to a feeder lies a set of complex decisions that cannot be reduced to one or even two factors. Blue jays appear to evaluate multiple variables as they decide where to feed.

Likewise, they enter into complex social milieus as they make these feeding choices. Tarvin and Woolfenden explain why jays have overlapping feeding and social interactions. "Because blue jays do not defend or maintain exclusive territories, individuals encounter many other individuals from within and beyond the local neighborhood, and perhaps engage with them in competition for food, nest sites, etc." As they examined birds at a feeding station in Florida, Tarvin and Woolfenden discovered that blue jay social behavior is quite complex. They conclude that "dominance hierarchies, characterized by reversals, circular triads, and unknown relationships, were not linear . . . we suspect the variable constituency and instability of flocks precludes the emergence of strictly linear hierarchies in the genus *Cyanocitta*."[112] This scientific documentation of the complexity of jay behavior makes Formato's anecdotal evidence all the more interesting.

Jayson clearly lives in a space that is neither "wild" nor completely human. But then again, blue jays in general cannot be said to live in a purely "wild" environment. As I note at the beginning of this chapter, jays often visit feeders and their populations have grown in proportion to human alterations of habitat. Jayson's contact with humans goes beyond that of most blue jays, but the species as a whole certainly has benefited from its relatively close contact with humans. Jayson's world, though, is one of particularly strong border crossings. The bird eats what it would select in the wild, but it also loves junk food. Likewise, Jayson's social behavior is as complex, if not more complex, than that of "wild" blue jays. Not only does Jayson sometimes interact with other blue jays, she also complexly interacts with humans.

Formato writes that Jayson would communicate with other birds when a certain door was opened, thus allowing Jayson to hear birds outside. "She developed a dialogue with them, mostly with the jays.

If a jay squawked, J answered. I got a real kick out of watching the outside jay look feverishly for J, but not being able to find her." At the same time, Jayson has vocal social interactions with humans. Jayson tells Formato when she wants food by "muttering," a vocalization that Formato describes as "sort of chirping under her breath." This muttering, though, is directed only at Formato. The bird has never muttered in anyone else's presence—"her communication apparently is intended specifically for me."[113] Jayson does communicate with other humans in different ways, though. When Formato's son was learning to play a Chopin *polonaise* on the piano, Jayson learned to sing the whole piece. "Listening to the bird gave the impression that she had memorized the score, her accompaniment was that faithful."[114] Jayson also can imitate a ringing phone. Formato has not rigorously studied Jayson's vocabulary, but she concludes that Jayson understands at least ten words and probably "recognizes people's names."[115]

Jayson's social interactions are not limited to vocalizations. After being left at the vet's office all day, Jayson saw Formato and her husband arrive "and immediately began chirping very loudly and flitting around the cage . . . Her vet looked at her, looked at us some distance down the hall, and was astonished at the bird's behavior. He turned to his colleagues and explained how amazed he was that Jayson seemed not only to recognize us, but also to be genuinely happy to see us."[116] Jayson is also noticeably happier when people are present near her cage. Formato succinctly sums up her family's social relation with Jayson: "She knows us, and she likes us."[117]

In short, it seems difficult not to ascribe a certain sense of individuality to Jayson. She displays preferences for certain foods over others and for specific social interactions with certain people, and she possibly exhibits emotional responses to her surroundings. When Formato writes that Jayson "likes" a specific food or person, one might be tempted to dismiss such a claim as purely anthropomorphic. But some evidence exists that birds could indeed be thought of as individuals. Indeed, a whole genre of books exists based on such claims. Perhaps more importantly, cognitive ethologists have made compelling arguments about why we should think of animals as individuals.

Marc Bekoff has argued that an understanding of animals as individuals can have great scientific and ethical import. He calls for close attention to individual differences when he writes that "variation is not noise to be dispensed with."[118] Bekoff calls for a new scientific paradigm. "We must seek to understand each and every individual in his or her own world and be extremely cautious of thinking of differences in terms of their being 'good' or conferring more 'value' on an individual's life."[119] Formato's account of Jayson moves this discussion from the abstract to the concrete. She convincingly argues that Jayson is an intelligent, individual member of *Cyanocitta cristata*.

If Audubon's blue jay portrait exemplifies certain nineteenth-century attitudes toward the bird, then perhaps Roger Tory Peterson's 1976 *Blue Jays with Autumn Oak Leaves* exemplifies twentieth-century attitudes. Peterson, of course, is best known for his field guide, with its brief descriptions and schematic illustrations. Lesser known are his bird "portraits" that have much in common with Audubon's and Louis Agassiz Fuertes's bird paintings. Peterson clearly considered Fuertes's to be the more realistic paintings. He said that "Audubon's birds are relatively static because he wired his birds and stood them up to paint them. He also had a flamboyant personality. Audubon always expressed Audubon, whereas Fuertes always expressed the bird—the integrity of the species."[120] Peterson seemed to dislike the romantic, action-oriented aspects of Audubon's paintings. William K. Zinsser writes that "Peterson has always been careful to make respectful comments about Audubon's pioneering work, but he has left no doubt that his stronger respect and allegiance are to Fuertes. He once wrote: 'Those who really know birds insist there is more latent life in a Fuertes bird, composed and at rest, than in an Audubon bird wildly animated.'"[121] What is described here as Audubon's wild animation and flamboyance connects, I think, to the moralism present in many of Audubon's paintings.

Peterson's rejection of Audubon's dramatic aesthetic can best be seen in Peterson's field guide paintings. The field guide removes all extraneous detail; the birds are usually painted with no background

Roger Tory Peterson, *Blue Jays with Autumn Oak Leaves*, © Estate of Roger Tory Peterson, used by permission.

or context. Field guide readers want to see field marks presented simply; Peterson's field guide illustrations serve the needs of those who want to be able to quickly identify birds. In contrast, Peterson's bird portraits contain much more detail and context. He paints active and interactive birds perching on various fauna that they are associated with. His pair of bobolinks perch on black-eyed Susans and clover; his Baltimore orioles sing in the branches of flowering dogwood. His northern mockingbird does a wing display; his Atlantic puffins seem to be reacting to the winds and waves around them. And even as he rejects Audubon's influence, one cannot look at Peterson's blue jay portrait without thinking of both Fuertes and Audubon.

At first glance, Peterson's blue jays most closely resemble Fuertes's 1903 lithograph, "Blue Jay." Peterson has noted that his first bird painting was a copy of Fuertes, made at the urging of his seventh-grade teacher, who had brought in a collection of Fuertes's prints for her class to emulate. "Each of us was given a small box of watercolors and a color plate from Fuertes's book to copy. I was given the blue jay, and that was my first bird painting."[122] The influence of Fuertes is clear in Peterson's 1976 painting, from the position of the birds to the oak tree that they pose in. Peterson's birds seem more lively, though, almost as if he is combining Fuertes's "integrity" and Audubon's "flamboyance." (Peterson has written that Audubon and Fuertes are the two bird painters who "will be remembered far into the future."[123])

Both Audubon and Peterson portray three birds on the top of a tree limb that is mostly out of the frame. The respective limb tops both start in the lower-left corner of their paintings and move toward the upper-right corner of the frame. Both paintings even portray a similar white glint in the black eye of the jay. And of course, the markings and coloration of the jays are similar. Nonetheless, in looking at both paintings, it is clear that Peterson rejected many of Audubon's painting ideals. Peterson's blue jays can be seen as a corrective to, if not a rebuke of, Audubon's morally culpable jays.

The biggest difference in the paintings lies in the action of each. As I discuss above, Audubon's jays greedily gorge on the eggs of another bird, as if Audubon has caught them in the act of committing a great crime. Peterson's jays are no less vibrant—two of them have their beaks open in apparent screams; the close-billed bird seems poised to fly off out of the frame. It is not clear exactly what Peterson's jays are doing. Clearly, they are not devouring the eggs of another bird. Since they are in an oak in the fall, perhaps they are searching for food. If so, their quarry seems to be the much more morally benign and less dramatic, and more typical food, the acorn.

In essence, then, I look at Peterson's portrait and I see Audubon minus morality. Peterson's jays do not evoke any specific moral stand in this viewer; they are simply jays, caught together, not in a moment of criminality, but in a moment of existence. It might be a stretch to say that Peterson directly critiques Audubon's morality with his portrait. Nevertheless, Peterson did take special interest in the blue jay, as it was the first bird he painted, and one of his favorites. "People often ask me what my favorite bird is, and I have to say it's the blue jay, though many people dislike its aggressive ways."[124] Maybe it is not such a stretch to see Peterson's painting as an attempt at de-emphasizing the blue jay's "aggressive ways" that Audubon was so keen on amplifying.

Even more important than this possible rehabilitation of the blue jay, though, might be the ethic contained in Peterson's painting, an ethic that one might view as a twentieth-century replacement of Audubon's nineteenth-century moralism. Peterson sums up this ethic when he talks about how human-bird relations have changed in the twentieth century. "This is a time of enormous change in people's thinking. The attitude of people towards birds has changed the attitude of birds toward people. Even crows are becoming tamer. Gulls have increased—they're the cleanup crew at garbage dumps. People have begun to see that life itself is important—not just ourselves, but all life."[125] Note that Peterson sees changes in both people's attitude toward birds *and* birds' attitudes toward people. The ethical import of this statement is strong. The way that humans think about birds affects the actual lives of what Peterson calls "all life." Birds are affected by humans; they respond to human actions, and they can be understood as thinking creatures in a continuum of consciousness and intelligence. Peterson's jays do not say to humans: we reflect your Christian guilt. Instead, they seem to say: we inhabit the world, too. We have an avian intelligence that you cannot fully comprehend. Peterson's painting gestures toward making this intelligence visible.

So how might this survey of human interactions with blue jays help to answer the questions I pose at the beginning of this chapter? Might human behavior change in some ways if we see that jays possess intelligence, consciousness, and emotions that exist on a continuum with humanity's possession of these things? As Marc Bekoff has pointed out, such an idea goes at least as far back as Darwin. "Darwin repeatedly stressed that the differences among species were differences in degree rather than differences in kind."[126] What might it mean to accept that humans only differ in degree from birds? If, as Bekoff writes, "thinking is no longer a feature of only some vertebrates," how should humans respond to a thinking blue jay?[127] And what role do science, literature, and art play in our ethical understanding of and interaction with other conscious beings?

Most obviously, science plays a large role. Scientific study of bird brains and behavior can offer empirical evidence of avian intelligence. But ornithology and ethology cannot fully answer the questions of nonhuman consciousness. Allen and Bekoff write in *Species of Mind* that "science is not likely to make complete contact with the nature of animal minds at any single point—many methods will be useful, and competing hypotheses should be evaluated."[128] They are mainly thinking about "many methods" in terms of various scientific approaches, but I see no reason why the methods of literature and art cannot play a role as well.

At the conclusion of his *Animal Minds*, Donald Griffin writes that "because mentality is one of the most important capabilities that distinguishes living animals from the rest of the known universe, seeking to understand animal minds is even more exciting and significant than elaborating our picture of inclusive fitness or molecular mechanisms."[129] Griffin is arguing for the importance of the work of cognitive ethology, but thinking of how animal consciousness works is by no means limited to the sciences. Through their explorations of an animal's mind, DeLillo, Formato, and Peterson imagine how a blue jay experiences the world. This imagining is by no means scientific. Nevertheless, all three foreground the ethical implications of taking nonhuman animal consciousness seriously. Wendell Berry, in a discussion of watching swallows fly over a river, shows how a literary exploration of animal consciousness can be considered an ethical endeavor. He writes, "I see also that every swallow is unrepeatedly what it is in each moment. We watch swallows with fascination because of our intuition that no swallow ever does twice quite the same thing that it or any other swallow has ever done. And this is because the swallows are living. . . . They are all only now, only instantaneously, living. This is an immense fact."[130] Berry calls this "immense fact" a "miracle" that cannot be fully understood by science. It is precisely because life cannot be completely comprehended that the human mind must try to do so within multiple registers. Berry writes, "To say that life is a miracle is to insist that life is not exclusively the concern of science and commerce, but is also, and *still* legitimately, the concern of religion, politics, and the arts—as appropriately and as needfully to be dealt with by prayer or policy or music or farming and by experimentation and trade."[131] Artistic and literary imaginings of what a blue jay might be seeing and thinking offer a way of beginning to understand interactions across species lines.

Dickinson, Thoreau, Audubon, DeLillo, Formato, and Peterson, all working in different milieus, provide a compelling picture of human attitudes toward blue jays. The more contemporary of these writers go a step further, and try to show what blue jays might think of humans. Indeed, for many of these writers and artists, thinking exceeds the bounds of the human; their blue jays are conscious, intelligent, and even emotional.

Nineteenth-, twentieth-, and twenty-first-century American science, art, and literature intersect at their consideration of the blue jay's mind. This intersection of science and art can create what the eco-philosopher Verena Andermatt Conley, following the work of Felix Guattari, calls "the tracing of new maps" of ecological thought.[132] Conley writes, "At the very limit of techno-scientific advances, the ways we perceive the world are being rapidly altered, though many inquiries in the human sciences lag behind. It is by incorporating these findings and by turning them toward humans and nature that ecological thinking and action can be oriented toward the future rather than a nostalgic past."[133] Conley argues that paying close attention to our perception of the world can be a fruitful endeavor for both the sciences and humanities. The multiple encounters with blue jays that I have mapped out in this chapter can point toward the kind of future that Conley envisions. Such a future, to paraphrase Dickinson, that leaves the blue jay out would be more than unfair, it would be diminished and unethical. Thankfully, unlike the red knot I discuss in chapter 3 (and unlike many other species in danger), the blue jay is in no danger of extinction. It is a mark of their adaptive intelligence that they thrive in human-altered environments. Humans and blue jays will remain neighbors for a long time, and maybe both will have a say in each other's respective future. Like the blue jay, the European starling, to which I turn next, is a close neighbor to humans. Since their introduction into the United States in the nineteenth century, the starling has become the most common bird in the country.

# 2   *Interpellation and Interiority*

## The European Starling

NOVEMBER 18, 2011: DES MOINES, IOWA

*Yesterday one starling chased a downy woodpecker from the suet. Today, a red-bellied woodpecker stayed and fought with a starling for a few seconds. After a few pecks and some scrambling for a foothold on the suet cage, the red-bellied flew off. Then another starling flew in; then another and another and another and another. Six starlings grabbed onto the five-inch square suet cage and ripped chunks off. A minute later, a few dozen starlings were on the ground, grabbing up the falling suet. At least twenty more perched on the telephone wires running over the yard and probably more than that were yelling in the trees. Even from inside the house, the squawking and squeaking were quite loud. Within ten minutes, the suet was gone. A few brave grackles and house sparrows looked for remnants on the ground, but the chickadees, nuthatches, and woodpeckers stayed away. I open the back door and every bird takes off, but only as far as the trees and the wire. As soon as I close the door, the starlings will come back, at least until they realize that all the suet is gone.*

At the end of his recent study of literary birds in British Romantic and contemporary Native American poetry, *Skylark Meets Meadowlark: Reimagining the Bird in British Romantic and Contemporary Native American Literature*, Tom Gannon writes, "The tempting (at least implicit) conclusion of many works similar to mine runs as follows: know other animals; know thyself better. The modern environmentalist version of this dictum tells us to save other species and the wilderness—for *us*, either for our own enjoyment or our own survival. But what an insult to other species that is, and what ultimately anthropocentric gall."[1] This notion of birds as either a means of appreciating nature or of understanding the human place in the world is a common thread that runs through the history of much American writing about birds, from Walt Whitman's claim in 1878 that, after listening to some birds sing for half an hour, "I have a positive conviction that some of these birds sing, and others fly and flit about here, for my especial benefit," to Henry David Thoreau's claim that he was "neighbor to the birds."[2] But perhaps it is John James Audubon, in both his *Birds of America* and his *Ornithological Biography*, who lays the groundwork for seeing birds as "for us."

Audubon published the first volume of his *Ornithological Biography* in 1831. The book described the habits of, and Audubon's interactions with, all of the bird species that Audubon painted for his *Birds of North America*. While Audubon was not the first to write about the life history of birds, the *Ornithological Biography*'s combination of natural history, emotion, and biography is unique. Part of the *Ornithological Biography* is "conscientiously packed with physical facts and measurements, close-up observations about how each bird hunted for food, chose its roosting place, fought, sang, played, courted, nested, and nursed its young."[3] For my purposes, the more interesting parts of the *Ornithological Biography* are those in which Audubon writes of his impressions of a bird's character and of his interactions with individual birds. Many of the accounts describe birds in terms of human values and emotions. The bald eagle is a "selfish oppressor" and "rank coward" with a "ferocious, overbearing and tyrannical temper."[4] The purple (common) grackle has "nefarious propensities" and is "full of delight at the sight of the havoc which he has already committed," to cite just a few examples.[5]

Audubon also writes anecdotally of his and others' encounters with individual birds, whether it's the bravery of an injured bird that has just been shot, or the character of birds kept as pets by Audubon or his friends. These stories seem to be a direct precursor of what could be called a more recent genre of "bird biography" in which a young, injured, or sick bird (or even an egg found in a nest) is raised in a human home. Margaret Stanger's *That Quail, Robert*, published in 1966, can arguably be seen as the modern beginning of the specific type of bird biography that I am interested in. *Robert* tells the story of a couple on Cape Cod who bring an abandoned quail egg into their living room. The egg hatches, and the bird becomes imprinted on the humans. She lives with them for many years and becomes a part of the family. This structure informs nearly all bird biographies. A wild bird—egg, nestling, just fledged, or injured—is brought into a home, named (fairly often given a male name and later revealed to be female), and becomes a part of the household—not quite as domesticated as a cat or dog, but not wild either. After *Robert*, one can read of *Peepers the Talking Starling*; *Arnie, the Darling Starling*; *A Hummingbird in My House: The Story of Squeak*; *Rosie: My Rufous Hummingbird*; *Jayson: The True Story of a 20 Year Old Blue Jay*; and *Wesley the Owl*. All of these books, to a greater or lesser degree, hinge on a dual recognition. Wild birds are brought into a human habitat and become domesticated. The newly domesticated bird rejects wild birds as a humanizing narrative takes shape. At the same time, the human moves toward the bird, seeking, but ultimately failing, to understand the bird's "nature." In short, Gannon's "anthropocentric gall" has been the dominant form of bird biography through the twenty-first century. This mode depends on the type of recognition and individuation that can be characterized as interpellation.

In bird biography, birds become subjects as they enter into a relationship with humans through what Louis Althusser calls interpellation: "a material ritual practice of ideological recognition in everyday life," such as a handshake or a statement like, "hello, my friend."[6] Through such "hailings," one "becomes a *subject*," an individualized body called into an ideological system.[7] Althusser, following Freud, writes briefly of "the specific familial ideological configuration" into which infants are born.[8] Two of the key means by which a newborn is interpellated are naming and sexing. As Althusser writes, "It is certain in advance that it [the infant] will bear its Father's Name, and will therefore have an identity and be irreplaceable." Likewise, the infant will "'become' the sexual subject (boy or girl) which it already is in advance." Both of these hailings are a key component of "the rituals of rearing and then education in the family" that transform an individual into a subject.[9] These rituals, so familiar within families that they might seem invisible, are, in fact, the narrative content of most bird biographies. That is, bird biography, as a genre, is all about the interpellation of birds: from an undifferentiated population of birds out there "in the wild," individual birds are called into human familial structures.

This strain of interpellation also runs through recent iterations of animal studies, as exemplified in the work of Jacques Derrida and Donna Haraway, two critics who problematize interpellation by pushing it to its limit on the border between the individual and the population. This line of thought points toward a way of thinking differently about animals, a mode of thought that Gannon also puts forward in his discussion of birds. Gannon seeks a way of encountering birds that does not view them simply as the unknowable other to a human self: "Yes, we can know that real crow poking outside in the garbage, shitting irreverently on our SUV. In fact, we *need* to know that bird, this animal, and know that we, too, are animals, however cursed we are by some tragic, speciesist, center-of-the-cosmos hubris."[10] Gannon presents a number of ways of producing this knowledge, mainly through a "critique of the literary use of birds as types and categories."[11] More specifically, Gannon argues that contemporary Native American poetry can "offer us the best opportunity" for communication that can "cross the border of species."[12] Perhaps the strongest example of interspecies communication in Gannon's study is his reading of Sherman Alexie's "Avian Nights," a poem Gannon calls "an amazing deconstruction of human and avian difference."[13] The section of the poem that Gannon analyzes

focuses on a group of European starlings that live in a family's attic
and are later exterminated. The poem concludes by asking a question:

Tell me: What is the difference between

Birds and us, between their pain and our pain?
We build monuments; they rebuild their nests.
They lay other eggs; we conceive again.
Dumb birds, dumb women, dumb starlings, dumb men.[14]

Gannon writes, "What is the difference, indeed? . . . Both are 'dumb,'
finally . . . humans and birds are just plain stupid, as earth-dwelling
organisms irrationally attached to their own."[15] The main difference
between starling and human here could be seen as one of embodiment. Earlier in the poem, Alexie writes, "But if God gave them
opposable thumbs, / I'm positive they would open the doors / Of our
house and come for us as we sleep."[16] The starling, of course, does not
have opposable thumbs, but it can make its voice heard. Both birds
and humans, for Gannon, are "inordinately prone to articulate that
attachment in songs of love, in songs of mourning. Birds and humans
are both inveterate users of *language*, finally."[17] Gannon hears the
starling speaking back to the human in a kind of dialogue.

I want to make a slightly different argument. The European starling, a bird that confounds easy categorization as either individual or
population, provides another way of thinking differently about birds.
Starlings, in their multiple ways of being in the world, exemplify
Felix Guattari's non-dialectic theory of subjectivity, from his *The
Three Ecologies*. Instead of thinking of the subject in terms of self
and other, Guattari writes of "existential refrains" that redefine "the
relationship between subjectivity and its exteriority."[18] The subject,
in this formation, finds its coherence as it responds to, and at the same
time reshapes, its surroundings. Listening to the starling's existential
refrain can provide a way of encountering a bird's point of view, and
lead ornithological biography, as a form of writing, away from interpellation and toward an understanding of bird subjectivity that sees
and hears all birds differently.

ORNITHOLOGICAL BIOGRAPHY

In his essay, "Audubon's *Ornithological Biography* and the Question of 'Other Minds,'" James W. Armstrong writes that the *Biography* works as a companion to Audubon's more well-known book of bird paintings, *Birds of America*, because it provides through writing a means of comprehending the interiority of birds that visual representation cannot alone achieve. He writes, "Audubon's need to portray the inner state of birds pushed him towards narrative, for he had to provide the context in which these interior states might arise and be exteriorized—and thus be recognized by us."[19] It is thus through narrative that Audubon hoped to show readers that birds were "not merely automatons . . . but subjects in the fullest sense of the term—beings with consciousness and volition."[20] In other words, Audubon employed narrative to call birds into a human framework in which birds, like humans, would be granted the special form of subjectivity that relies on a communicable interiority. Through his painting and writing, Audubon sought a way for humans to recognize birds as fellow subjects.

One prominent example of how Audubon used narrative to argue for the subjective experience of birds can be found in his discussion of what he calls "one of the most interesting of the birds indigenous to the United States of America," the wild turkey.[21] Audubon tells a story of a male turkey "which had been reared from its earliest youth under my care, it having been caught by me when probably not more than two or three days old." This bird "became so tame that it would follow any person who called it, and was the favorite of the little village." While tame, the turkey did not associate with the domestic turkeys at the house. Instead, it would spend the night alone on the roof. As the turkey grew, it would spend "a considerable part of the day" in the woods and "return toward night" to its roost. Eventually the turkey flew away and did not return. When it had been gone for several days, Audubon happened to be hunting near some lakes five miles from his home when he saw "a fine large gobbler cross the path before me, moving leisurely along." He sends his dog after the bird. "The animal went off with great rapidity, and as it approached the turkey, I saw, with great surprise, that the latter paid little attention. Juno was on the point of seizing it, when she suddenly stopped, and turned her head towards me. I hastened to them, but you may easily conceive my surprise when I saw my own favorite bird, and discovered that it had recognized the dog, and would not fly from it; although the sight of a strange dog would have caused it to run off at once." The turkey recognizes the dog, and unrecorded by Audubon, the dog seemingly recognizes the turkey, as Juno stops and turns to Audubon instead of seizing the bird. Audubon notes that he brought the live turkey home with him. He then tells how it was "accidentally shot, having been taken for a wild bird" the next year by someone who did not immediately recognize the turkey as Audubon's pet, that is, until it was brought to Audubon "on being recognized by the red ribbon which it had around its neck."[22] Reflecting on how the turkey recognized Juno, he asks: "Pray, reader, by what word will you designate the recognition made by my favorite turkey of a dog which had long been associated with it in the yard and grounds? Was it the result of instinct, or of reason—an unconsciously revived impression or the act of an intelligent mind?"[23]

Audubon never answers these questions. How to account for this recognition seems less important than the act of recognition itself. The turkey sees Juno; Juno sees the turkey. The turkey does not flee, and the dog does not attack. The man does not shoot. All of these acts go against instinct. And it is this moment of recognition that overrules instinct. The three actors—Audubon, Juno, and the turkey—all recognize each other as subjects. The turkey recognizes Juno as a specific subject, a dog not to be feared and fled from. Likewise, Juno recognizes the turkey as not just any member of the undifferentiated population of wild turkeys in the woods, but as a specific known subject. What seems astounding about this encounter is that the dog then seems to communicate this to Audubon, through a turn of the head. As Juno looks at Audubon, the mutual recognition, or hailing, is complete.

One cannot overemphasize the importance of mutual recognition here. Had the "favorite turkey" not been recognized, Audubon, who notes that he was hunting, would have most likely shot the bird, and Juno would have then "seized" it. But this does not happen. Even a casual reader of the *Ornithological Biography* will note that refraining from shooting a bird is an event of great consequence for Audubon, who continually notes the great pleasure of procuring one more specimen. But why does mere recognition prevent the bird from fleeing and the dog from biting? The dog saw the turkey as somehow different from other game birds. While it is not clear that the turkey is capable of reason, it seems to have learned something during its time as a pet. It knew, unlike other wild turkeys, that certain dogs and humans would not harm it. It learned to recognize individuals of those two species. It saw Audubon and Juno, and in a sense, interpellated them as subjects, even as friends who meant it no harm. The bird affirmed Audubon's existence, and Audubon spared the bird's life. Instead of a hunting story, Audubon tells an interpellation story.

This exact form of interpellation story can be traced through contemporary bird biographies. Margaret Stanger's *That Quail, Robert* is marked with many scenes of recognition and response. Soon after hatching in the kitchen of his caretakers, the fledgling northern bobwhite, "even at the age of about an hour . . . had followed the sound of human voices and found the first living creatures it was to encounter—two human beings."[24] From this moment of imprinting, the bird favors human company and rejects other birds. Many moments of interpellation follow. The bird is named, sexed (incorrectly, as is discovered a year later when "he" lays an egg), and banded so that "he was legally registered and perhaps protected for the future." After the banding, Stanger refers to Robert's "new status of ornithological citizenship."[25] The bird is house-trained, and "developed a feeling of complete security and confidence toward any and all humans."[26] Paired with his security around humans was a fear of birds. Robert either cowers in fear or completely ignores any birds he encounters on the front lawn of his house. Stanger writes that "on several of Robert's outdoor excursions his own quail family, all twelve of them, were often quite near him. There was never the slightest sign of recognition, much less reunion, on either side."[27] Stanger concludes, "Robert had repudiated her own kind in favor of her human environment."[28]

Stanger writes, "We should have realized earlier than we did that far from having a bird in captivity, we were helplessly and hopelessly ensnared and enamored." According to Stanger, who was a retired child psychologist, Robert had "spectacular" developments in vocabulary and personality. She notes the "distinctive chirps" that Robert made in different circumstances.[29] Perhaps most interestingly, she thinks of Robert as an individual, intelligent subject. In discussing Robert's behavior, Stanger asks, "Can there be any question as to her intelligence?"[30] Robert clearly recognized, remembered, and acted differently toward different humans. Some he seemed to think of as friends; some he disliked and avoided. In a sense, then, Robert and the multiple humans he encountered mutually recognized one another—human looks at bird and bird looks at human. The title of the book, *That Quail, Robert* sums up his relationship with humans perfectly. "That" marks him as a specific quail, easily recognizable and distinguished from the innumerable wild birds in his vicinity. "Robert" marks his naming, obviously, and also the fact that she is no longer just an anonymous member of a quail population living outside.

Robert and Audubon's "favorite turkey" exemplify the interpellative aspect of bird biography. But it is not only "game birds" like quail and turkeys that are subject to this form of narrative. Hummingbirds, robins, and owls have their own bird biographies. Narratives of domesticated animals, like ducks and parrots, also abound. Perhaps most interesting, though, are the biographies of a so-called invasive species that is sometimes seen as vermin and sometimes seen as a companion species: the European starling.

The European starling, *Sturnus vulgaris*, is the most common bird in America. An estimated 200 million European starlings live in North America, all descended from 160 birds released in New York's Central Park in 1890 and 1891. These birds were released by Eugene Schieffelin, a member of the American Acclimatization Society, which sought to establish American populations of every bird mentioned in Shakespeare's plays. These introductions failed to produce sustainable populations, except for that of the starling. European starlings quickly spread across America, partially due to their ability to adapt to, and thrive in, human-altered environments, especially cities and farms.

However, the European starling is also the most frequently extermi- nated bird in America because, in part, of this proximity to humans. In 2009, 1,703,697 starlings were "lethally controlled" by U.S. Wildlife Services.[31] Starlings tend to flock in agricultural areas, eating and spoiling cattle feed, spreading disease, and damaging crops. The star- ling is not protected by the Migratory Bird Treaty Act; most licensed wildlife rehabilitators will euthanize any injured starling brought to them. Starlings can also be a threat to other cavity-nesting birds, such as red-headed woodpeckers.

But, even as starlings are seen as little more than vermin in many contexts, their flocking behavior has inspired poets and mathematicians. Starlings are also one of the most common domesticated "wild" birds. Stories of pet starlings abound; they are named, cared for, taught, and loved. They are mourned when they die. Mozart had a pet starling; when it died, Mozart held a funeral and wrote a poem for it. He wrote, "my heart / is riven apart. / Oh, reader! Shed a tear, / You also, here."[32] Today, memorial web pages for deceased pet starlings are common.

And while most wildlife rehabilitators will not care for injured starlings, many humans have adopted starlings and raised them as part of the family. Izumi Kyle tells the story of "Kuro," a starling she rescued when she was twelve. "He was just a small, featherless hatch- ling that had fallen out of a nest at my primary school. Two children were teasing him, so I took him away from them and brought him home in a styrofoam cup." The Kyle family adopts Kuro, so that "our house was his home and our family lived in his cage!" Kuro learned to mimic familiar sounds: "He could say 'good bird!,' 'pretty bird!,' 'Kiss!,' 'Kuro stay!' and many combinations thereof, as well as whistle many tunes including the William Tell overture and 'Pop Goes the Weasel.'" Kuro lived for a record nineteen years; on his death, his family "was devastated and felt an incredible loss. . . . I still think about him often and remember all the wonderful experiences as if it was yesterday. I tear up at times thinking about him and have many dreams that he is still with us."[33]

*Arnie, the Darling Starling* was brought into the house of Margarete Sigl Corbo and raised as a member of the family. Corbo's book, written with Diane Marie Barras, hits all the interpellative notes of bird biography. Arnie is rescued from the wild when Corbo sees that he has fallen from his nest: "He stared past a conical, tightly shut infant beak, his darkly bright eyes insisting, 'Take me home. Immediately.'"[34] Corbo describes how she initially resisted giving the bird a name—"He's just a wild bird. He doesn't need a name . . . He does not get a name"— but then gave in. As she puts it, "I'd surrendered to the inevitability of Arnold as an appellation."[35] He is set free and returns numerous times.[36] He is described as a human infant and child throughout the text, until Corbo finally notes, "He was family."[37] Arnie ages, eventually dies, and is mourned. "Gently as a feather floating on a breeze, Arnie slipped from this life on February 11, 1983. He would have been four years old that May. His body rests beneath a lush canopy of daisies in Margarete's yard, but in the hearts and memories of the many people he touched, Arnie's spirit is vibrantly alive and as indestructible as dandelions—and starlings."[38] I will let these two examples stand for the stories of other named starlings such as Salem, Stormy, Jedda, Murphy, and Rudy. Clearly, these birds form strong bonds with humans. Humans who see starlings as companion species interpellate the birds into human society in the traditional way. Starlings, like other birds subject to biography, are sexed, named, raised as children, cared for in their old age, and mourned in death.

Ornithological biography, then, achieves its purpose of rendering birds as subjects. Bird biography attempts to find evidence of bird interiority and make this interiority manifest and communicable. Bird biography argues for, implicitly and/or directly, a place for birds as quasi-human subjects. Birds become companions to humans as they enter into human conceptions of the world. This relationship between birds and humans bears comparison to other human-animal pairings, such as the more common bond between humans and dogs. In *The*

*Companion Species Manifesto*, Donna Haraway famously writes of how she and her dog became companions. "We are training each other in acts of communication we barely understand. We are, constitutively, companion species. We make each other up, in the flesh. Significantly other to each other, in specific difference, we signify in the flesh a nasty developmental infection called love. This love is an historical aberration and a naturalcultural legacy."[39] What Haraway writes of her dog is also true for the companion relationship between starlings and humans who live together. That is, "love" seems to be the clearest definition of the basis for Corbo's affinity for Arnie, Kyle's for Kuro, and Mozart's for his starling. At the same time, though, many of these relationships are described in a manner that Haraway wants to resist. In her discussion of human-dog agility training in *When Species Meet*, Haraway writes that a dog is "not a furry child."[40] As I hope to have made obvious, bird biographers see their bird subjects precisely as feathered children. Perhaps something is lost in this humanizing of birds. In its many attempts to communicate the interior life of birds, ornithological biography takes its interpellative practice as natural, as something that does not call for any kind of reflection or analysis. But animals might have another way of living in the world. The developing discourse of animal studies can offer a means for thinking differently about human-bird companionship.

## DECONSTRUCTING BIRD BIOGRAPHIES

In *The Animal That Therefore I Am*, Jacques Derrida deconstructs the oppositional terms, as used throughout the history of philosophy, of human and animal. He shows how man has categorized, named, and made other the concept of "Animal." Derrida examines what this opposition hinges on, and he explores what thinking beyond this opposition might look like.

For Cary Wolfe, Derrida's book "is arguably the single most important event in the brief history of animal studies" precisely because of this deconstruction of the human/animal dialectic.[41] Through Derridean-inflected animal studies, according to Wolfe, "we are returned to a new sense of the materiality and particularity not just of the animal and its multitude of forms but also of that animal called the human."[42] That is, in deconstructing the human/animal binary, both terms can become reconfigured, as the dominant term, "human," is shown to depend on what Derrida calls the "subjection of the animal."[43] Derrida asks, "Is being-with-the-animal a fundamental and irreducible structure of being-in-the-world, so much so that the idea of a world without animals could not even function as a methodological fiction?"[44] The short answer to this question is "yes." And, as I will argue, starlings can offer proof that a world without animals cannot be thought.

Nonetheless, bird biographies implicitly buy into, and confirm, the humanist modes of "reading, interpretation, and critical thought" that Wolfe describes.[45] More importantly, in order to participate in these "humanist modes," ornithological biography buys into a humanist mode of being, embodied in interpellation and grounded in Derrida's "subjection of the animal."

The animal has no name and no ability to speak of itself, or of others for that matter. According to Derrida, "the animal is a word, it is an appellation that men have instituted, a name they have given themselves the right and the authority to give to the living other."[46] By naming other forms of life "animal," man places animals in a separate category. Likewise, philosophy denies animals language: "All the philosophers we will investigate say the same thing; the animal is deprived of language."[47] The animal cannot name itself; it cannot even respond to its naming by man. In short, the animal is seen as incapable of response. Animals become an other to be "subjected to farming and regimentalization at a demographic level unknown in the past . . . all of that in the service of a certain being and the putative well-being of man."[48] Philosophy and the production of meat for human consumption are linked by a belief in a man/animal dialectic that remains unmovable. Animals are not humans; humans are not animals. This is at the heart of what Derrida calls "this event—that is the *unprecedented* proportions of this subjection of the animal."[49]

Derrida coins the word *animot* (a combination of the French for animal and word) as a marker of how one might take apart the dialectic. "Animal words" might make clear that the concept of the animal is "neither a species nor a gender nor an individual, it is an irreducible multiplicity of mortals."[50] He goes on to write, "We have to envision the existence of 'living creatures,' whose plurality cannot be assembled within the single figure of an animality that is simply opposed to humanity."[51] How can this idea, as he suggests, be "envisioned"?

According to Derrida, "it would not be a matter of 'giving speech back' to animals but perhaps of acceding to a thinking, however fabulous and chimerical it might be, that thinks the absence of the name and of the word otherwise, as something other than a privation."[52] The absence of human language, then, is not a lack. Forgetting language for the moment, what becomes important is remembering the act of the cat looking. "The animal looks at us, and we are naked before it. Thinking perhaps begins here."[53] Bird biography pauses, like Derrida does, at this moment when the animal looks back, with its own point of view. But bird biography obscures this point of view precisely through interpellative acts. In order to be rendered as the subject of a biography, the bird's point of view has to be covered over through humanizing practices such as naming. Naming a bird erases its point of view. Robert, Kuro, and Arnie are cut off from any subjectivity outside of the human households in which they live.

According to Donna Haraway, this pause marks the limit of Derrida's thought. In *When Species Meet*, Haraway writes that "with his cat, Derrida failed a simple obligation of companion species; he did not become curious about what the cat might actually be doing, feeling, thinking, or perhaps making available to him in looking back at him that morning." From within the realm of philosophy that he deconstructs, Derrida cannot find a space for his cat to look back. Haraway writes that Derrida "did not seriously consider an alternative form of engagement either, one that risked knowing something more about cats and *how to look back*, perhaps even scientifically, biologically, and *therefore* also philosophically and intimately." In her reading of *The Animal That Therefore I Am*, Haraway argues that Derrida cannot imagine what his cat sees because of his focus. "He came right to the edge of respect . . . but he was sidetracked by his textual canon of Western philosophy and literature." As Haraway notes, "somehow . . . the cat was never heard from again in the long essay dedicated to the crime against animals." In short, Haraway locates the limit of Derrida's thought right in the cat's gaze that allows him to begin his inquiry. The shared gaze undermines the structure of Derrida's system—right from the start, as Haraway shows, he stops short of engaging an animal's otherness. Haraway writes that while "Derrida is among the most curious of men," in the face-to-face encounter with his cat he became "incurious."[54]

But just as Derrida's cat marks the limit of his thought, it is a bird, the Steller's jay, that marks a limit to Haraway's interrogation of the always-contingent "dividing line" that marks "life-and-death relations between human and nonhuman animals."[55] In a short chapter of *When Species Meet* called "Becoming Companion Species in Technoculture," Haraway describes her work with a group called "Forgotten Felines" to capture and sterilize and vaccinate a group of feral cats living in a barn in Sonoma County, California. The cats are then "released" with the understanding that the cats will be fed by humans for the duration of the cats' lives. The local raccoons and Steller's jays continually raided "the cats' food arrangements with aplomb" as the humans took part in an "arms race" to secure the cats' food. But the human-supplied cat food is not the only thing eaten in this multispecies encounter. One cat is found dead "with her front leg torn off, presumably by a raccoon."[56] And the cats, of course, do not stick to their human-supplied diet of cat food. Haraway hopes that the cats "will have a fine life keeping the rodents in check."[57] She also notes that the cats kill and eat some Steller's jays. She writes, "I don't care when I see Steller's Jays feathers littering their hunting grounds; those avian populations are not threatened by domestic cats around here."[58] The cats take precedence over the other animals—rodents, raccoons, and birds—living near the barn. Haraway writes, "Our loyalty seemed due the cats and not the jays and raccoons, because we had produced the food competition and invited—really engineered—the cats into semidependence on us."[59] How was this engineered semidependence produced? And to what effect?

A key step in this engineering is an "incuriosity" similar to the one Haraway found in Derrida's interaction with his cat. She writes, "I do remember the statistics of songbird kills by even well-provisioned pet cats in many places—enough to destabilize populations and add to the threat to already threatened species. I wish I knew the score in my region, but I do not."[60] Based on this missing information about her region, Haraway goes on to ask a series of questions. "Would I kill our feral cats if I learned they were a problem for the local quail or other birds? . . . Would I know if our dusky-footed wood rat or deer mice populations were in trouble? Does provisioning feral cats carry obliga- tions to follow through on questions of species diversity and ecological balance in microregions?"[61] Haraway is not interested in answering these questions here; rather, she uses these questions to establish the complexity of the "multispecies relationships" at work in this specific setting. She writes, "Nothing about the multispecies relationships I am sketching is emotionally, operationally, intellectually, or ethically simple for the people or clearly good or bad for the other critters."[62] For the semi-feral cats, this statement is true—it's not abundantly clear whether "Trap-Neuter-Release" (TNR) is good or bad—their lives may be better than those of the wholly feral cats, but it is certainly worse than that of indoor cats. Even the name of this practice is in dispute. While TNR is most common, Forgotten Felines defines its practice as the "TTVAR-M method of feral cat control. Trap, Test, Vaccinate, Alter, Return and Maintain."[63]

Haraway, in the questions she asks, shows the complexity of the issue for the people involved. For the rodents and birds involved, however, this situation seems a bit less complex, in that they are being killed. Some people have even called for the caretakers of feral cat colonies to be prosecuted under the Migratory Bird Treaty Act or the Endangered Species Act.[64]

Haraway's short chapter gestures at this complexity but does not address it. Her curiosity here is not strong. Of course, no writer can follow through on all the paths opened up by his or her work. Nonethe- less, I remain stuck on Haraway's remark that "I don't care when I see Steller's Jays feathers littering their hunting grounds." The choice to favor the cats over the birds and mice is the kind of choice that Haraway notes has to be made all the time in multispecies encounters. Clearly, not every species can win. But the alliance with the cats seems to violate at least two of three "tempting moves" Haraway calls for avoiding in multispecies encounters: "One must actively cast oneself with some ways of life and not others *without* making any of three tempting moves: (1) being self-certain; (2) relegating those who eat differently to a subclass of vermin, the underprivileged, or the unenlightened; and (3) giving up on knowing more, including scientifically, and feeling more, including scientifically, about how to eat well—together."[65] While she is not self-certain, her analysis does include the rodents as vermin, even as she parenthetically puts this categorization aside: "(I will leave unexamined the implicit category of vermin)."[66] More importantly, in not seeking answers to her questions about bird populations, Haraway has given "up on knowing more" about this "microregion."[67] My point here is not to point out a weakness in Haraway's argument. Instead, I want to draw a provisional parallel: Haraway's jays equal Derrida's cat equals Audubon's turkey equals Robert the quail, Arnie the starling, and all subjects of bird biography. That is, each of these specific animals marks the limit to a system of thought that seeks to engage the animal. And this limit is marked by interpellation.

In a short "philosophical postscript" on interpellation that Haraway appends to "Becoming Companion Species in Technoculture," she writes, "Today, through our ideologically loaded narratives of their lives, animals 'hail' us animal people to account for the regimes in which they and we must live. We 'hail' them into our constructs of nature and culture, with major consequences of life and death, health and illness, longevity and extinction."[68] I want to think about two reciprocal hailings that take place here: the humans' hailing of the cats and vice versa, and the humans' hailings of the jays and vice versa. This pair of reciprocal hailings highlights one important difference—the cats are interpellated into life, and the jays are interpellated into death. What can account for this important difference?

The cats are interpellated in multiple ways; they are familiarized with people, vaccinated, spayed or neutered, fed, and named. Haraway writes that the cats have "been interpellated into the modern biopolitical state" and have therefore "earned names to go with their historical identities and subject status." Readers are introduced to "Spike (black male), Giles (black male), Willow (dark gray tabby female), and Max (light gray tabby female)."[69] This naming and sexing, as Haraway notes, functions as a marker of the humans' ability to think of the cats as individual subjects with specific, historical identities. *When Species Meet* is rife with named, individual, human and nonhuman animals—Cayenne Pepper (dog), Bahati (dog), Donna (human), and even more abstractly, "Chicken Little" to stand in for domestic chickens in chapter 10.

The jays and rodents are never brought into this naming regime—the jays only have their species marker "Steller's," and the rodents are barely even described at the species level. They get interpellated into the human system as populations, where the life of one is interchangeable with the life of another, so long as the population is not endangered. Haraway writes, "Those avian populations are not threatened by domestic cats around here," so "I don't care" if the cats kill them.[70] One Steller's jay is no different from another. Any jay may survive by eating cat food or may itself become cat food. Likewise, the rodents might be "dusky-footed wood rat[s] or deer mice."[71] My provisional conclusion, then, is that naming as a process of individuation opens a path into an ethical multispecies relationship that is much more careful and nuanced than the relationship engendered when the species involved are not named beyond the species level. Cats, dogs, primates, and other individualized subjects become central to multispecies relationships, while birds and rodents (among others) become liminal and therefore much more easily endangered by these relationships. In her discussion of Derrida, Haraway argues that his approach cuts him off from "a mortal and finite knowledge that understands [in Derrida's words] 'the absence of the name as something other than a privation.'"[72] However, Haraway and Forgotten Felines have interpellated the jays and rodents into just this realm of name-absent privation. They have no names, and no means of encountering them except at the species level can be envisioned. In this case, Haraway's curiosity does not go beyond cats, specifically named cats. Unnamed populations are at the limit of individuation and subjectivity.

Bird biography, of course, does move past the species level as it grants certain privileges to named birds. As they enter into a family assemblage, bird subjects reach their limit as named and humanized—that is, interpellated—beings. In writing the life stories of birds, biographers bring birds into a human ethical framework. Birds become understood only as they are subjected to the human. Named, individualized, interpellated birds are separated out from an undifferentiated population. The only birds that bird biography sees and hears are the ones that are given human qualities. It is only through this biographical subjection that birds are heard. The European starling, though, a bird that speaks both metaphorically and literally, might provide a way of thinking past this limit.

STARLING SUBJECTIVITY

Humans seem to view starlings in two seemingly incompatible ways: as pests to be exterminated and as companion species to be cared for and learned from. Parts of this contradiction can perhaps be explained by starling behavior: as undifferentiated flocks, starlings become vermin when in proximity to humans; when flocks take to the sky, they become inspiring. Individual starlings mimic sounds and follow eye-gaze direction, so they seem to be interacting with humans on a one-to-one basis. From a human perspective, in face-to-face encounters, starlings seem to have two sensory aspects of subjectivity as they respond to sound and sight—they seem to see and hear other starlings, other birds, and humans. Huge flocks of starlings, on the other hand, are faceless, and thus awe-inspiring and/or threatening. Starlings exist as both undifferentiated population and individualized subjects.

In flocks, starlings follow a simple rule that produces complex results. In his essay "Going Parallel," which is about "the polarities of self/other within contemporary technoscientifically inflected culture," Brian Rotman describes the emergence of complexity from such simple starling behavior as "the fact of their flocking, the emergence of a routine or algorithm with a complex dynamical profile from the simultaneous, identical, and simple activity of individuals."[73] This complex, dynamic system flows from one simple rule: Each starling in a flock does what its six closest neighbors do. In this way, following Rotman, one can say that starling flocks are serial and parallel at the same time. Flocks exist in "two modes," as Rotman writes, "the *serial*, which consists of doing one thing after another (the whole flock forming itself and moving through time) and the *parallel* (each starling flying in concert with the others) doing many things at once."[74] A recent study suggests that starling vision is a key element of flocking behavior. That is, starlings do what their six or seven closest neighbors do by watching them. They act in a serial manner that is, in fact, also parallel. They are both individuals responding visually to their neighbors and a flock acting as a cohesive unit.

This flocking behavior serves an evolutionary purpose as it helps starling flocks confound predators such as peregrine falcons. This adaptive behavior produces a secondary effect from a human perspective: beauty. In his essay Rotman asks, "Do starlings have any inkling of how majestic and beautiful their flocking is? Is there a starling sublime?"[75] He cites Richard Wilbur's poem "An Event," which describes a starling flock as "like a drunken fingerprint across the sky!" Of course, it is these same sublime flocks that are often exterminated. A U.S. government "Fact Sheet—Controlling Starling Damage at Feedlots" notes the damage that starlings can do. They cause harm through "consumption of cattle feed" that "can be a significant economic hardship to producers"; their "fecal contamination of cattle feed and drinking water can create disease hazards for cattle, especially calves and pregnant cows. . . . Fecal contamination, nesting materials and bird carcasses on and in structures and farm equipment such as dispenser pumps, grinder/mixers, augers, and vehicle engines, can hamper farm operation, and cause costly property damage."[76] In urban settings, "problems can range from excessive noise to large quantities of excrement deposited on sidewalks, cars, and buildings. . . . Starlings have transmitted encephalitis and ornithosis."[77] It is also worth noting that in their native European habitat, starlings are seen as a food source for humans; in France, starling pate is readily available. In short, depending on the context, starling flocks are majestic, threatening, inspiring, eradicated, and eaten.

Starlings use vision to stay in flocks; another aspect of their visual ability might help explain their status as companion animals. Starlings can follow human eye gaze, and they seemingly understand what it means to be looked at. A recent study gives what the authors call "the first explicit demonstration of a bird responding to a live predator's eye-gaze direction."[78] As prey animals, starling flocks must be vigilant against predator threats. As eye-gaze direction is a common signal of intent for mammalian predators—which simply means that a mammal usually looks at its prey before striking—recognition of being looked at gives starlings a "competitive advantage" over birds that might not be able to read eye-gaze direction.[79]

Starling biographies often write of visual contact between bird and human. As I discuss above, Corbo's first encounter with Arnie is one of eye contact, as Corbo "reads a message in his darkly bright eyes."[80] Likewise, their last encounter is also visual. As Arnie is near death, "he gazed up at Margarete with love shining in his eyes, breathed a tired sigh, and rested his head against her chest."[81] While there is no scientific evidence linking an ability to recognize a predator's eye gaze and the ability to make eye contact, Corbo's suggestion that Arnie communicated with her visually is certainly plausible.

Starlings are also excellent mimics, to the point that they might seem to engage in conversation and respond vocally to human prompts. In their essay "Mozart's Starling," Meredith West and Andrew King have noted that companion starlings give humans "a sense of shared environment with another species, a sensation hard to forget" so that humans become "beguiled by the chance to glimpse a bird's-eye view of the world."[82] How close can humans come to understanding what the starling's point of view might be?

In striving to glimpse a starling's point of view, I do not want to pursue the question of whether or not a starling has a theory of mind. As Carter et al. point out in their discussion of the eye-gaze experiment, "while we do not deny the interesting possibility that starlings might have a cognitive appreciation of the knowledge state of their predator through recognizing the predator's visual perspective, this type of explanation may not be necessary. The starlings' responses in these experiments could be explained as a result of innate tendencies and conditional learning during their experience prior to the study."[83] A theory of mind is not necessary in order to understand the effects produced by starling eye-gaze recognition. Carter et al. write that the behavior works regardless of what the mechanism driving it may be: "Whether or not the responses involve some sort of mental attribution or theory of mind, and whether or not they are innate or acquired, the result is that starlings are able to discriminate the very subtle eye-gaze clues of a nearby live predator and adjust their anti-predator responses to fluctuations in predation risk in an adaptively beneficial manner."[84] In other words, the result does not explain what is happening in a starling's brain when it responds to the eye gaze of a predator. And such an explanation is unnecessary. Inferring a theory of mind from this behavior would be nothing more than conjecture. Likewise, ascribing a theory of mind, or even a clear reason to starling mimicry, seems impossible and unnecessary. So what do these starling interactions with their environments tell us about their point of view? In recognizing eye-gaze direction, do starlings know that a predator is looking at them? Do they know that the body attached to those eyes wants to consume them? In mimicking and "talking" to humans, do starlings know that they are engaging in conversation? In flocks, do starlings have a mental awareness of the simple, visually guided, rule of proximity that guides their collective behavior? Do they know that they are behaving collectively? Do they know they are flocking to avoid a predator? Do they know that their singular action benefits the individual and the flock? Do they know that their flocks are beautiful?

I think these questions are impossible to answer. But humans can understand *something* about a starling's point of view. We configure subjectivity as individual or collective, as serial or parallel, as named or unnamed, as pet or food, as person or nuisance, but there's no reason to believe that this configuration is correct; there's no reason whatsoever to believe that birds categorize the world in this way. Recognition is not in and of itself part of a self/other dialectic. Birds recognize others, but not necessarily *as* others. Tom Gannon writes: "I would contend instead that subject and object, self and nature, are false dualisms: when you can make the imaginative leap that 'you' *is* also a bird, another species, whether this is only metaphorically or mystically true, in the Western scheme of things, the world will be a better ecological place."[85] I agree with Gannon that "subject and object" does not provide a way for understanding bird subjectivity. But I want to emphasize something different than Gannon's important reminder that birds should not be perceived dualistically.

Birds do not exist in the traditional dialectic interpellative understanding of subjectivity. Humans certainly understand starlings this way, but that is no reason to assume that starlings see and hear things in the same way. In his work on how subject formation happens, Felix Guattari writes of "different ways of being" that he calls "existential refrains." Rather than seeking a theory of mind, or any evidence of interiority, Guattari bases his understanding of subjectivity on external effects. He writes, "It is less a question of having access to novel cognitive spheres than of *apprehending* and creating, in pathic modes, mutant existential virtualities."[86] To apply this understanding to starlings and other birds, one can say that bird-human relations should not be configured around a recognition of an interior consciousness that would provide evidence of subjectivity. Rather, interactions can be seen as a matter of "apprehension," of having an effect on. From this perspective, bird biography that interpellates birds as human subjects also serves to obscure what might be unique to bird subjectivity. Named, individualized birds might be thought to have a mind, but such an understanding says more about human perceptions of others than it does about birds. Guattari writes that "different ways of seeing and of making the world, different ways of being and of bringing to light modalities of being" can be found in listening to existential refrains.[87]

In "Mozart's Starling," West and King provide a way of thinking about a bird's point of view from a nonhuman perspective. They explore "the idea that hand-reared birds perceive their human companions in terms of the social roles that naturally exist among wild birds." That is, a hand-reared, or companion, bird might perceive the human other as bird in an act of orni-pomorphism. In a starling's eyes and ears, a human is a starling. As a bird's behavior changes over time, its interactions with other members of its species change too. West and King note that "in the case of captive birds, humans become the companions for all seasons, with the nature of the relationship shifting with the changing development and hormonal cycles in a bird's life."[88] That is, birds might see human-birds as parents, mates, rivals, flock members, and so on. This bird apprehension of humans runs parallel to the human apprehension of birds. To use the language of Deleuze and Guattari, this apprehension could be called a double capture: the becoming-bird of the human and the becoming-human of the bird. Such a becoming is not an imitation or even a similarity. Deleuze and Guattari write that "becoming is involutionary, involution is creative. . . . To involve is to form a block that runs its own line 'between' the terms in play and beneath assignable relations."[89] This formulation of becoming is not grounded in the subject; it is a movement between subjects that reconfigures both. Understood as an involvement or an apprehension, the varying nature of the becoming-bird of the human makes sense as humans are constantly reconfigured by birds.

From this perspective, starling mimicry may be more than just mimicry. West and King write that "for many birds, acoustic communication is as much visual as vocal experience."[90] In experiments, birds mimicked less in the company of only tapes. When exposed to living beings in a social environment, mimicry increased. Mimicry might be thought of, then, as a means of social interaction. West and King posit the following hypothesis: "We propose that some birds use acoustic probes to test the contingent properties of their environment, an interpretation largely in keeping with concepts of communication as process of social negotiation and manipulation. . . . Like bats or dolphins manipulating sounds to estimate distance, some birds may bounce sounds off the animate environment, using behavioral reverberations to gauge the effects of their vocal efforts. . . . [not] for self-reflection but instead a social sounding board with which to shape functional repertoires."[91] Mimicry is an affective interaction with the world. It's even a model for being in the world. Starlings manipulate their environment with sound and vision, responding to things near them, whether it's the six or seven nearest starlings in a flock, or the human

companion sharing living space. Starlings have a Guattarian notion
of being in the world—forming new alliances, or "mutant existential
virtualities," with every vocal or visual apprehension of the world. In
*A Thousand Plateaus*, Deleuze and Guattari write of mimic birds,
"Imitation may not be the best concept for these phenomena, which
vary according to the assemblage into which they enter . . . It is less
a question of imitating a song than of occupying corresponding frequencies."[92] Mimicry becomes a means of interacting with the world;
it becomes more of a call and response than an imitation. The starling
emits a sounds and the world responds. Interiority, in the sense of a
theory of mind, is not necessary to understand the world this way.
What counts are exterior effects—a starling's voice and sight alters the
world as he or she perceives it; what's inside the starling's head is less
important than the effects produced in the world. Subjectivity is more
of a moving outward than a looking inward. Guattari's non-dialectic
configuration of subjectivity is useful here, because it does not seem
limited, in the way an interpellative sense of self/other is, to human
subjectivity. All living things can be said to have an existential refrain.

In mapping these refrains, Guattari writes in *The Three Ecologies*
that "what we must emphasize here is that the work of locating these
existential refrains is not the sole province of literature and the arts—we
find this eco-logic equally at work in everyday life, *in social life at
every level*, and whenever the constitution of an existential Territory
is in question."[93] If one defines "social life at every level" as broadly
as possible, to mean any possible interaction that ever takes place, the
existential refrain of a starling can be seen and heard because it is clear
that starlings affect the world through their sight, hearing, and vocalizations. In a sense, it becomes impossible for something not to have
an existential refrain. Every thing is alive, in this sense, every thing is
affecting the world. Starlings, and all birds, are always apprehending
and creating, in pathic modes, ways of being.

A return to quails, and to Audubon, can help make this point. In
looking at how Audubon attempts to communicate bird subjectivity,
Armstrong looks closely at both Audubon's painting and writing about
bobwhite quails. He cites Audubon's discussion about his painting of

a group of quails under attack from a hawk: "The different attitudes exhibited by the former cannot fail to give you a lively idea of the terror and confusion which prevail on such occasions."[94] Armstrong questions whether readers and viewers will trust Audubon's representation of quail interiority, whether readers will believe that quails can indeed feel the terror that Audubon illustrates. Armstrong writes, "We do not necessarily trust him when he says he has got the interiority of his subjects right" because we are "rather inclined to dismiss such claims as examples of anthropomorphism." Armstrong rhetorically asks, "Do bobwhites feel terror?"[95] From his perspective we cannot answer this question because we cannot escape skepticism; we cannot access a quail's mind through Audubon's representations.

Armstrong's logic seems correct here. He argues that Audubon's painting and writing is evidence only that Audubon is "a thinking subject," who in turn asserts that the quail is too. Armstrong writes that "the presence of other minds—in this case, of the birds' minds or feelings—can only be asserted by the testimony of a thinking subject, as such a testimony is not a 'representation' of nature: it is rather more like a promise, or an affidavit."[96] From this perspective, readers and viewers have access to quail interiority only through Audubon's assertion that the quail does indeed have a mind. From an interpellative perspective, we can only see Audubon's dramatization of quail subjectivity: Audubon says that he saw bobwhite quails responding with terror, and thus becoming subjects, but the only evidence is Audubon's representation of this moment. One can never be fully sure that birds are responding to a human hailing in an understandable manner. What Audubon sees, and paints, as terror might be a marker of a completely different interior state. But the problem here is not Audubon's failure to create a completely convincing illustration of a bird's mind, which seems impossible. Rather, the problem is one of recognition within a specific way of understanding subjectivity.

As a question of recognition, the equation of expression that would make quail terror understandable in terms of human terror cannot help but fail. But rather than seeing Audubon's quail portrait as unconvincing evidence of an interior state of mind made manifest in the body, the painting can be considered as an illustration of affect. There is little doubt that a group of quail, or any prey species, under attack from a predator will react by fleeing. But this flight need not be seen as a reflection of an interior state of mind that would always remain inaccessible. Flight in response to attack does give evidence that something is happening; that the quails in Audubon's painting are responding to the diving hawk is beyond dispute. Audubon portrays what Guattari would call the quail's "capacity to be affected" by other things. Bobwhite quails respond to danger just as Robert the quail responded to his environment, just as Audubon's turkey responded to Juno, just as Arnie the starling responded to Corbo. My point is not that all of these responses are the same—they are, in fact, radically different—but that they are all reconfigurations of subjectivity.

Recognizing affective responses as forms of subjectivity should be a key task of animal studies. In her essay, "Literary Animal Agents," Susan McHugh sees "animal studies researchers as united by a commitment not so much to common methods or politics as to the broader goal of bringing the intellectual histories and values of species under scrutiny."[97] This configuration of animal studies would interrogate what exactly happens in interspecies interactions. Such interactions can be seen as what McHugh calls "markings of potentials for different orders of agency beyond the human subject."[98] Bird-human interactions can be one place where such "different orders" might be found, especially if these interactions are understood outside of a dialectic, interpellative understanding of subjectivity. Birds might be understood not as an other that reflects a human self, but as living beings acting in a world that is not dependent on a human definition of self-centered around the "I."

Derrida, in his discussion of Kantian ethics and animals, notes the importance of the "I," as well as its human-centeredness. The "I," according to Derrida, is what is denied the animal. Deprived of this "I," Derrida writes, "the animal will lack any 'I think' as well as understanding and reason, response and responsibility."[99] What is at stake here is where the animal resides in an ethical system—on what side of the life and death line it is likely to end up. Derrida writes that there is no simple way to include the animal within a Kantian (or, more broadly, any philosophical) system. He writes, "It is not just a matter of giving back to the animal . . . the I of *automonstration*. It is also a matter of questioning oneself concerning the axiom that permits one to accord purely and simply to the human or to the rational animal that which one holds the just plain animal to be deprived of."[100] To encounter animal, or more precisely for my purposes, bird, subjectivity would mean an abandonment of the whole system that relies, at base, on the assumption that humans have an "I" that all other animals lack. Derrida offers no way to move beyond this "giving back"; he notes the complications involved when he writes that "one could go a long way in multiplying these indices and examples, something I don't have time to do."[101] Derrida's gesture here, though, implies that it is the exclusive ascription of the "I" that cannot hold up to close scrutiny. In short, there is no clear dividing line between the human, rational animal that is given an "I" of self-awareness, and the "just plain animal" lacking both an "I" and rational thought.

In a different register, cognitive ethologist Marc Bekoff, who, according to Haraway, has "met the gaze of living, diverse animals and in response undone and redone [himself and his] science,"[102] offers a means for understanding animal subjectivity that does not depend on the presence or absence of an "I." In *Minding Animals: Awareness, Emotions, and Heart*, Bekoff succinctly asks, "Should we be more concerned with species and their survival than with individuals and their well-being?"[103] He offers no easy answer. He writes that "once an individual animal has been identified and named, there is an immediate change in the way he or she is perceived."[104] But Bekoff is not talking about a lost objectivity; such a thing does not exist. He continues, "I do not have any problem naming animals, and I know of no evidence that unequivocally shows that naming animals produces less reliable scientific results than referring to animals with numbers."[105] Here, Bekoff is discussion how naming affects human understanding of animals in the realm of scientific study. His endorsement of "biocentric anthropomorphism" provides access to "other animals' behavior and emotion." At the same time, Bekoff does not think that naming (and other forms of anthropomorphic language) "force us to discount the animals' point of view."[106] His formulation of what an animal's point of view might be resonates with a non-interpellative understanding of bird subjectivity. He writes that "perhaps some animals simply do not need to know who they are" in the way that humans do. Instead of a dualistic self/other mode of bodily awareness, Bekoff posits another way of thinking about individuation. "While individuals surely need to know that they are not another individual, this does not mean they need to be self-aware. Rather, it is necessary and sufficient only that they have a sense of their own bodies and body awareness. . . . Knowing who you are is not necessarily 'better' than knowing you are not another individual." Bekoff's decoupling of bodily awareness and self-awareness is key. The ability to be an actor in the world does not depend on a human theory of interiority. One does not need to be an "I" to respond. Bekoff writes that "animals do not have to write autobiographies."[107] It is precisely in this *not* writing that bird subjectivity is most apparent. In not writing autobiographies, birds offer evidence that they are not, to return to Gannon's formulation, "for us." Leaving behind "anthropocentric gall" might require leaving behind the dialectic, interpellative "I" that grounds a widespread understanding of human and nonhuman subjectivity in both bird biographies and animal studies.

HUMANS AND STARLINGS

In her essay, "Naming Names—Or What's in It for the Animals?," Lynda Birke asks some important questions, often ignored by practitioners of animal studies, about the relationships between humans and animals. She writes, "Whenever I review papers for journals, or read much of the published literature, or do my own research in human-animal studies, I often find myself thinking—but what's in it for the animals? How could/might they benefit? Do they? Does this research I read about take seriously the animals' points of view—or only the viewpoint of the humans thinking about animals?"[108] Birke's questions draw attention to the actual animals being researched and written about. I want to attempt to answer her questions as they apply to the relationships between humans and starlings. How might star-lings benefit from animal studies? What can animal studies learn from starlings?

Birke writes that animal studies has "the potential to contribute to sociocultural change, to enable us to take nonhuman animals more seriously as conscious, sentient beings. In that sense, it could be said to be beneficial for animals in a generalized way, in that it gets a few more humans on their side."[109] Certainly, starlings might benefit in this way. Studies have shown that starlings have a mind, that they communicate, that they have an awareness of others. Such knowledge, though, probably will not lead to concrete benefits for starlings. To be blunt, animal studies can do little to benefit starlings. A feedlot damaged by starling excrement will not change its extermination practices based on knowledge that starlings probably have some sort of consciousness. But, as a species, starlings have already greatly ben-efited from human actions. Their entire North American population exists because of human intervention—from their nineteenth-century introduction in New York, to human alteration of habitat. Starlings thrive in human-altered environments. Farms and feedlots provide them ample food and habitat, as do urban and suburban environments. Starlings inhabit every state in the continental United States. Their estimated U.S. population of 200 million is not too far behind the human population of the same area. In short, starlings are incredibly common. One might say that they are the ultimate companion species, sharing every environment that humans have created in America.

But what of a starling's point of view? I have argued that one can-not know what is happening in a starling's mind. But I also want to emphasize the idea that starling subjectivity does not depend on a human understanding of interiority. Starlings do not live dialectically, and animal studies can learn something from this. Another of Birke's questions proves useful here. As she seeks "to examine the relationships between people and animals and how those are experienced by either partner," Birke asks, "How can we go about examining the processes of enmeshing, of coming together, that create a relationship?"[110] To apply this question to my research, I ask: What does the human-starling relationship of the last two hundred years in America tell us about how humans and starlings inhabit the world as companion species?

In her "Animals, Anomalies, and Inorganic Others," Rosi Braidotti argues that human-animal relationships are essentially a matter of what she calls "affirmative ethics."[111] Braidotti rejects human-animal relationships that are grounded in metaphor and dialectic thought. For Braidotti, "animals are no longer the signifying system that props up humans' self projections and moral aspirations."[112] The sly fox, the brave eagle, and other animal symbols obscure the actual lived experiences of both humans and animals. Braidotti argues that animals bypass the "dialectics of otherness" that has served to create a human-centered "normativity." If we "relate to animals as animals ourselves," Braidotti writes, a new "bioegalitarianism" might be brought into existence.[113] Starling-human relationships provide one way of understanding this worldview. Braidotti calls for "the recognition of transspecies solidarity on the basis of our being in this together—environmentally based, embodied, embedded, and in symbiosis."[114] Humans and starlings are the perfect embodiment of this transspecies relationship. The symbiosis between humans and starlings was not designed by either species; nonetheless, it is so firmly entrenched in America that one can hardly find one species without the other in close proximity. From Braidotti's viewpoint, such proximity creates the necessity of an ethical relationship. "The ethical relation is essentially a matter of affinity: being able to have positive encounters with another entity. . . . By entering into affirmative ethical relations, becoming animal . . . engenders possible futures. They construct possible worlds through a web of sustainable interconnections."[115] Humans and starlings have created a world. Where there are starlings, there are humans. Where there are humans, there are starlings.

Thinking about the vastness of this specific companion species relation can lead to new ways of understanding consciousness itself. Braidotti writes, "Consciousness is an unfolding of the self onto the world and an enfolding within the self of the world. What if consciousness were, in fact, just another cognitive mode of relating to one's environment and to others?"[116] From this perspective, human consciousness and starling consciousness are not all that different. Both can be understood as a means of being in the world. That is, starlings interact with and respond to the world just as humans do. Such an understanding of the world does not privilege human interiority; interpellation is not the only way of being a subject in this world. The starling-human world shows just how common and widespread companion species relationships are.

At the end of *When Species Meet*, Donna Haraway writes that "animals are everywhere full partners in worlding, in becoming with. Human and nonhuman animals are companion species, messmates at table, eating together, whether we know how to eat well or not."[117] Starlings are a literal embodiment of this claim. Companion species encounters constitute the world in mundane, everyday ways. Haraway writes of "the ordinary knots of daily multispecies living in a particular place and time"; the human-starling companion species relationship is a perfect example of just such an embodied, historically specific, and common relationship.[118] The human-starling relationship in twenty-first-century America grew from its textual roots by historical accident—they are the only species introduced by Eugene Schieffelin that established a thriving population in America—and has become a daily marker of the enmeshed, embodied companion species relationships that exist everywhere.

Human experimentation, beginning with Schieffelin's starling release in New York, started an explosion of the starling population across America so that, today, starlings live nearly everywhere in the country. More recent studies have focused not on starling populations, but on how starlings learn and use song at the social, individual, and neurobiological level. Some of this work forges tentative connections between human and avian experiences of the world. In "Mechanisms of Song Perception in Oscine Birds," Knudsen and Gentner write of "the fact that birds and humans share a similar perceptual representation of the acoustic world," or, as they more colloquially put it, human and songbirds "hear the same world."[119] Starlings, like humans, "use auditory feedback to learn their vocalization."[120] Both humans and starlings use vocalization to communicate in complex ways, and both "possess multiple mechanisms for extracting behaviorally relevant information from communication signals."[121] That is, humans and starlings are both able to separate the signal from the noise as they listen to their environments. Isolated starlings that learned songs only through tape recordings did not develop the repertoire of paired starlings, showing that "social interaction can exert a powerful influence on the learning process" for starlings as it can for humans.[122] Starlings, again like humans, also use multiple aspects of vocalization to distinguish one starling from another. Perhaps most interestingly, Gentner et al. have argued that starlings are able to make certain grammatical classifications. "European starlings (*Sturnus vulgaris*) accurately recognize acoustic patterns defined by a recursive, self-embedding, context-free grammar. They are also able to classify new patterns defined by the grammar and reliably exclude agrammatical patterns."[123] In other words, starlings can distinguish between novel configurations of song that follow certain grammatical rules and those that do not follow such rules. Chomskyan linguistics holds that recursive grammar is uniquely human; against this claim, Gentner et al. posit that "the capacity to classify sequences from recursive, centre-embedded grammars is not uniquely human."[124] In short, recent studies of starling vocalizations have clearly demonstrated the complexity of starling auditory learning and communication.

For many researchers, this complexity points toward ways of understanding how song works in the bird brain, and perhaps how language works in the human brain. Scientists have located the areas of bird brains, called the auditory telencephalon, where song is recognized and processed.[125] By studying "the robust neural substrates," researchers have identified how specific neurons in bird brains respond to familiar and unfamiliar songs.[126] Knudsen and Gentner note the "promise" of birds and humans hearing the same world, because "there may be common neural and behavioral mechanisms adaptive for processing signals within this shared acoustic space." While noting that bird song is worth studying in and of itself, they continue, "The parallels to human perception make it an excellent model for investigations for higher-level auditory processes, and enable a full range of neurobiological and behavioral techniques that are difficult to use in humans."[127] Likewise, Prather and Mooney call bird neurology an "unusually attractive model system in which auditory processing of complex natural acoustical objects can be explored."[128] In other words, examining how bird brains respond to song might tell us something about how human brains respond to language. Gentner et al. argue that species difference might be more fruitfully thought of "as quantitative rather than qualitative distinctions in cognitive mechanisms." Thinking of birdsong and human language as different in degree rather than kind leads to the claim that "there might be no single property or processing capacity that marks the many ways in which the complexity and detail of human language differs from non-human communication systems."[129] To return briefly to Braidotti's language, starling and human speech provide one more example of "affinity" between species. Starlings and humans hear the world the same way, and they might vocally communicate within it in similar ways.

This point of affinity can be illustrated in another way, too. In his science fiction novel *Perdido Street Station*, China Mieville writes of the "weaver," a multidimensional giant spider that perceives the "metaphysical substance" of the universe as a series of knots in a web. The weaver allows a human being access to this web, and he sees "the crawling infinity of colors, the chaos and textures that went into each strand of that eternally complex tapestry . . . each one resonated under the step of the dancing mad god, vibrating and sending little echoes of bravery, or hunger, or architecture, or argument, or cabbage or murder or concrete across the aether. *The weft of starlings' motivations* connected to the thick, sticky strand of a young thief's laugh."[130] "Starlings' motivations," here, then, are one among a multitude of nearly infinite nodes of mundane existence. What I find most interesting about this passage is the uncommented-on idea that starlings have motivations. If motivation can here be thought of as a way of living in the world—of singing, listening, responding, gazing, flying, and so on—then Mieville's fiction takes a step that scientific experiments cannot. The narrator's ability to see these motivations implicitly argues that starlings, like humans and other things (even cabbage and concrete) have a way of being in the world. Starlings exist. In fact, there are starlings in my backyard as I write this. I can hear them and see them if I look out the window. If I go outside, they will probably fly off, and then come back. They are alive. And if I have a point of view, they do too.

Blue jays and starlings tell us about how avian and human intelligences interact. In the next two chapters, I will look more closely at birds in their environments as I consider how public policy affects both an endangered subspecies—the *rufa* red knot—and an abundant one—the resident Canada goose.

# 3   *Capital and Conservation*

## The Red Knot

MAY 15, 2003: DELAWARE BAYSHORE

*Seen with only the naked eye, they look like a bunch of light brown spots moving around on a dark brown field. With a pair of binoculars, or better, a spotting scope, they resolve into fifty or so discrete birds feeding in a muddy tidal zone. Since this is May and the birds are thus in their breeding plumage, the red knots and short-billed dowitchers are easy to identify: the knot with its bright red breast and the dowitcher with its black belly feathers. The semipalmated plover is easy to identify, too: it is the only plover species there, so it has a shorter beak and different body shape than the others. Those three species account for about 75 percent of the birds present; all that's left to identify is what are collectively known as the "peeps," a group of sandpipers of similar size and coloration that can be difficult to distinguish from one another, especially by an amateur: the least, semipalmated, and western. Before considering plumage and shape, the place and time of year—the Delaware Bayshore of New Jersey, May 15—tells you it is very unlikely that western sandpipers would be here. So it is down to the least and the semipalmated. It is not very likely that the slight webbing between the toes that gives the semipalmated its name will be visible; the yellow legs that would distinguish the least from the grayish-black-legged semipalmated are covered with mud that makes all their tiny legs look an indistinct brownish-grayish-blackish color. The semipalmated feeds in slightly deeper water than the least, so the birds closest to shore are probably semipalmated. To be certain, though, you can compare their beaks: the least's is slightly thinner, with a finer tip and a slight droop at the end. The least is a darker chocolatey brown, the semipalmated a bit plainer. In combination all of this information allows you to semi-confidently separate least from semipalmated.*

*All of the birds on the mudflats have been identified and described on this year's list. But so what? What kind of interaction is this? If the birds have any awareness of you, it is as a vague threat in the distance, to be fled if you get any closer. This act of looking seems to have little tangible effect on either the human looking or the birds being looked at, besides, respectively, a sense of satisfaction and pleasure on the human side and a vague sense of increased stress for the birds. Nonetheless, this kind of act gets repeated all the time. It must have some effect on its participants.*

The aural and visual encounter between humans and birds, which has been going on since both forms of life have existed, began to solidify into a hobby, into something that a middle-class citizen of America might spend a morning doing, at approximately the turn of the nineteenth century. Certain technologies—optics (binoculars), field guides, and later, automobiles—helped to enable this pursuit. In the twentieth century, bird-watching became an immense industry. At the beginning of the twenty-first century, one report claims that in America "an estimated 70.4 million people now go out-of-doors to watch birds one or more times per year."[1] Many have noted a certain irony here. As the number of bird-watchers has increased, the number of birds has decreased. Populations of birds in America have been declining at an alarming rate.

This growing awareness of birding comes at an odd time; birds are in jeopardy. According to thirty-five-year-trend data (1966–2001) from the U.S. Geological Survey, almost one-in-four bird species in the United States show "significant negative trend estimates." This decline is attributed primarily to the degradation and destruction of habitat resulting from human population growth and shortsighted environmental practices such as the razing of wetlands needed by migratory birds.[2] The large number of bird-watchers in America could constitute a political and economic force for conservation. As Cordell and Herbert note, "Birders can be a very powerful force in helping to assure the future of all bird species. Increasing numbers of birders and of interest in birding should reflect more people willing and eager to be active in the stewardship of this most precious of natural resources."[3] A recent study by the U.S. Fish and Wildlife Service, "Birding in the United States: A Demographic and Economic Analysis," states that "the higher the income and education level the more likely a person is to be a birder."[4] According to this report, bird-watchers were responsible for $82 billion of economy activity in 2006, including the creation of 671,000 jobs and $11 billion of tax revenue on the local, state, and national level.[5]

Despite these numbers, the connections between bird-watching, conservation, and capital are not as strong as one might think. The spring migration of shorebirds through the Delaware Bay area serves as a perfect example of the inverse relationship between the growing population of bird-watchers and the declining population of birds. As I note above, the differences among the various shorebirds at the bay would still exist without encountering human consciousness. The least sandpiper and the semipalmated sandpiper would still have their differences; they would fill different niches, they would not interbreed, they would have other, different behavior patterns, but they probably wouldn't be on the verge of being endangered. This chapter, by looking at the case of a particularly imperiled shorebird, the red knot, will map out how bird-watching, conservation, and capital intertwine to affect both birds and humans in twenty-first-century America.

## THE RED KNOT AND DELAWARE BAY

Ninety percent of the Western Hemisphere population of the red knot passes through the Delaware Bay area each spring to feed on horseshoe crab eggs. Starting in the late 1970s, and increasing dramatically since then, horseshoe crabs in the Delaware Bay have been harvested in increasing and unsustainable number, to be used as bait to catch eel and whelk, which can then be sold on a growing world market. Since 1990 there has been a "nearly 10-fold decrease in horseshoe crab egg density on bay beaches."[6] The effect on red knots has been dramatic: in "20 short years, maybe only two or three generations of Red Knots, the birds have declined by more than 66 percent on Delaware Bay, and by 57 percent at their principle wintering grounds near Tierra del Fuego."[7] There are no signs that this alarming trend is reversing itself. In August 2006 the *rufa* subspecies of the red knot was "designated a candidate species for possible addition to the Federal list of endangered and threatened wildlife." Because of "higher priority listing actions,"[8] the red knot remains a candidate for inclusion on the list, but it has not been included as of 2012. The Department of Environmental Protection of New Jersey listed the bird as an endangered species in the state as of February 23, 2012. Even with a moratorium on the harvest of female horseshoe crabs in Delaware, and on all horseshoe crabs in New Jersey, the horseshoe crab harvest "still exceeded production,"[9] and a 2007 report predicted that the *rufa* subspecies might go extinct within ten years, as the knot's "population has fallen from 100,000–150,000 in the early 1980s to around 17,200 in 2006."[10]

Neither economic nor political logic can explain this decline. "The ecotourism value of the bird and crab aggregation alone" has been valued at $34 million.[11] Another study "calculated the aggregate seasonal value of birding during the annual spring migration at near $263 thousand" for just the Delaware Bay region.[12] The value of horseshoe crabs on their own does not compare. While some conservationist actions have been taken, many say that these steps will stop neither the decline nor the eventual extinction of this population of the red knot, as the entire harvest is estimated to be worth only $11 million per year.[13]

One expert on the situation asks what I think is a key question regarding the shorebird migration issue: "With ecotourism clearly on the rise, and crabs plainly on the decline, why isn't it a no-brainer that the horseshoe crabs that underpin the entire phenomenon should be protected?"[14] Economic data, for some reason, remains unconvincing to policy makers. One government report notes that "although there is a certain irony in people becoming enthusiastic about birds as they disappear, it also presents an opportunity" in that birders might act as conservationists.[15] Another way to state this irony would be to say that bird-watching is an observation of the progress of extinction brought on in large part by the activities of the species doing the watching.

## BIRD-WATCHING AND CONSERVATION

The introduction to "Birding in the United States" makes a claim about the efficacy of the demographic and economic information contained in the report. "By understanding who birders are, they can be more easily reached and informed about pressures facing birds and bird habitats. Conversely, by knowing who is likely *not* a birder, or who is potentially a birder, information can be more effectively tailored. The economic impact estimates presented here can be used by resource managers and policy makers to demonstrate the economic might of birders and, by extension, the economic impact of birds."[16] The report, then, makes an explicit link between bird-watchers, conservation, and capitalism. The link starts with the economic fact that bird-watchers spend money on bird-watching. Because of this fact, the report reasons, if bird-watchers are informed about conservation issues, they are likely to monetarily support conservation. Thus, both birds and bird-watchers have economic force that can be used to serve conservation needs.

The link between bird-watching and conservation might be more tenuous than this, though. In his *Binocular Vision: The Politics of Representation in Birdwatching Field Guides*, Spencer Schaffner shows just how and why one cannot assume there is a strong connection between bird-watching and conservation. While noting the important fact that "there is no doubt that bird-watchers have contributed actively to environmental conservation on many levels," including legislative and economic levels, Schaffner argues that "most birdwatchers use field guides and many birdwatchers are conservationists, but clear causal relationships between field guides, birdwatching, and conservationism are based on shaky suppositions."[17] Schaffner interrogates these "shaky suppositions" through a careful rhetorical analysis of birding field guides in the nineteenth and twentieth centuries. He shows that, far from being ahistorical texts meant simply to aid in identifying birds, field guides are infused with the ideological interests of their authors and times. For him, field guides "are political texts that are involved in much more than simple acts of identification."[18] The use of field guides by bird-watchers, then, can help forge a specific way of seeing birds, humans, and their respective places in the world, even as the field guides themselves make an argument for conservation.

As bird-watching connects human subjectivity to bird existence primarily through binoculars and field guides, the role that field guides play should not be underestimated. Bird-watching is a kind of visualization technology that produces specific ways of seeing the world that, in turn, produce specific ways of both living in and valuing the world. Bird-watching accommodates birds to a human visual apparatus, to allow bird-watchers to differentiate birds by species (and subspecies and population), age, and sex. With these differentiations in hand, twenty-first-century bird-watchers can know more about birds than nineteenth-century ornithologists could have dreamed of.

In the twentieth century improved optical technology led to binoculars replacing guns as the primary tool of bird-watching. The collecting guides of the nineteenth century have become the field guides of today, which provide detailed illustrations and descriptions that give readers, as David Allen Sibley says in *Sibley's Birding Basics*, "an understanding of how our impressions of the birds are shaped by the environment and the birds' behavior. This understanding will allow you to identify the common species with greater speed and confidence, tackle some of the really difficult species, and enjoy a greater appreciation of the birds themselves."[19] Most field guides today also include at least a short section on ethics and conservation. For instance, *The Sibley Field Guide to Birds of Eastern North America* says that bird-watchers "must first consider the welfare of the bird . . . Tread lightly and encourage others to do the same."[20] Roger Tory Peterson's *Peterson Field Guide to Birds of Eastern and Central North America* has a "conservation note." "Birds undeniably contribute to our pleasure and standard of living. But they are also sensitive indicators of the environment, a sort of 'ecological litmus paper,' and hence more meaningful than just chickadees and cardinals to brighten the suburban garden, grouse and ducks to fill the sportsman's bag, or rare warblers and shorebirds to be ticked off the birder's checklist. The observation of birds leads inevitably to environmental awareness."[21] This change from collecting guides to more ecologically sensitive field guides is clearly part of a larger movement, over the last hundred years or so, away from the study of individual specimens and toward the study of ecology and ethology. As Peterson's "note" shows, the value of birds can be determined in multiple ways, from ecological indicators, to objects of aesthetic appreciation, to prey, to catalysts for "environmental awareness."

It is worth noting that most discussion of conservation and ecology gets presented in the front matter of field guides. The actual "meat" of most field guides limits text to words that will aid in bird identification, for the obvious reason that a bird-watcher wants to identify birds as simply and quickly as possible, and large blocks of text would impede this. These representations, though, usually present birds outside of any specific environmental context. As Schaffner writes: "Instead of representing birds as enmeshed in multidimensional networks including environmental issues and problems, mainstream field guides sanitize representations of birds and the worlds they live in, representing birds as living apart from one another and from the consequences of human intervention. In this way, field guides are strong promoters of what I call binocular vision, a taxonomic, focused way of seeing and thinking about individual parts of 'nature' as disconnected from one another and from humans."[22] This out-of-context representation of birds effaces conservation in the service of identification. For this reason, field guides will help a bird-watcher to differentiate the numerous species of shorebirds feeding in, say, the Delaware Bay beach. Field guides will not, at least on their own, cause a bird-watcher to understand the human-created danger to the very existence of the birds being identified. Nor will this act of identification necessarily lead a bird-watcher to take a more active role in bird conservation or to give money to causes that support conservation.

The red knot situation points to the shaky connection between bird-watching and conservation. Many conservation groups, such as New Jersey Audubon, the South Jersey Bayshore Coalition, and Friends of the Red Knot, are working doggedly to protect the red knot and other shorebirds. But, as Lawrence Niles, one of the lead scientists in red knot research, points out on his blog, the situation for the red knot continues to worsen. For Niles, part of the problem is that "the people who care for shorebirds have no substantive voice (or choose to not speak loudly)."[23] It is important to note here that Niles and other scientists have laid out a straightforward plan for restoration of the *rufa* population. "Our analysis shows that the best chance for halting and reversing the decline of the Red Knot would be through restoration of horseshoe crabs and their eggs to levels prevailing in the early 1990s."[24] Even with knowledge of how to save the red knot and with people who care about the birds, its extinction seems imminent. Why?

On his blog, Niles asks such questions and proposes some solutions. He notes that many bird-watchers "pay for expensive equipment and extravagant tours or adventures, and often travel great distances to make it all happen." He cites statistics that show one-third of U.S. residents engage in some kind of wildlife watching. In light of this evidence that people do care about wildlife, he asks: "Why is this massive group of people not involved in solving these very solvable problems and why are they not challenging our conservation system to do a better job?"[25]

He offers two answers, one concrete and one more abstract: corporate interests and lack of will. Using blunt language that would be foreign to his scientific articles, Niles calls out the "industrial fishing concerns that dominate the ASMFC [Atlantic States Marine Fisheries Commission]" and who support "the corporate harvest of horseshoe crabs" at the expense of shorebirds and any other environmental concerns. Niles argues that the ASMFC has a long history of "depleting fisheries for the sake of a strong commercial interest." It is important to note here that this issue is not simply one of economics. As I discuss above, the economic value of ecotourism in the region is roughly three times that of the economic value of horseshoe crabs alone. All of this information leads Niles to conclude, "It's the lack of will that allows corporate interests, and the politicians that serve them, to rake in profit at the expense of the long-term prospects of fish and wildlife."[26] In short, then, public will, at least in this case, cannot overcome the force of corporate interests. Niles offers some concrete plans for changing public will, and I will address these later in this chapter. Niles's critique, though, raises a larger issue that is worth exploring in more detail: the relationship between birds, humans, and capitalism.

## BIRD-WATCHING AND CAPITALISM

In *Binocular Vision*, Schaffner writes that late nineteenth century field guides worked as tools for conservation. Guides such as Florence Merriam's *Birds through an Opera Glass* (1889) and Mabel Osgood Wright's *Birdcraft* (1895) encouraged bird-watchers to enjoy looking at birds even as many bird populations were in steep decline due to overhunting for the fashion trade. These guides tried "to infect a readership with an infatuation for birds that would transform consumers of birds and bird feathers into their caretakers."[27] Merriam and Wright encouraged readers to study and classify birds as a leisure pursuit, rather than wearing dead birds as ornaments. As Schaffner writes: "Coordinating with other organized efforts to save birds at the end of the nineteenth century, field guides were instrumental in sustaining ways of thinking about and relating to the environment that played a part in altering social, economic, and environmental landscapes."[28] Schaffner discusses the myriad rhetorical techniques used by these field guides to make a conservationist argument. He also situates these guides historically at the origin of bird-watching as a hobby and at the origin of what today is called "citizen science."

As I discuss in chapter 1, much nineteenth-century writing about birds was strongly anthropomorphic, as writers such as Audubon understood bird behavior through the lens of human morality. Schaffner shows that early field guides deployed anthropomorphism in the service of conservation. That is, writers such as Merriam sought to make people form an emotional attachment to birds. "Merriam's birds were not to be saved because they were an integral part of fragile ecological systems, as later environmental writing would have it, but because killing birds disrupted human spheres of value."[29] Portraying birds as emotional agents allows one to argue for empathy between humans and birds, which in turn can lead to a conservation ethic based in caring for specific species of birds that exemplify positive human values. Through such practices as narrative and the naming of individual birds, birds came to be seen as "emotionally charged objects or catalysts" for conservation.[30] In short, birds were presented as like humans, and thus as worthy of human valuation and protection.

Central to this human valuation was the act of identification and classification. Schaffner writes, "These books assume that anthropomorphism, discerning birdwatching, and strong emotional feelings about birds can only be achieved once a species is identified and named."[31] In order to render birds within the human realm, the discerning human had to know what he or she was seeing when looking at birds. Thus, early field guides worked to draw the parameters of bird-watching as both a hobby and as a form of amateur science.

As hobbies became seen as "a productive use of free time" in the late nineteenth century, they served to reinforce the values of a capitalist society.[32] Likewise, bird-watching, with its diligent list making, could be seen as "a mode of accountancy that puts birdwatching in sync with the task-oriented workplace and well-managed home."[33] Bird-watching, with its required tools of binoculars and field guide, became both a hobby and a form of amateur science, as early guides established classification as the baseline of the hobby. That is, one had to learn how to reliably classify the birds that one was looking at in order to get any enjoyment or knowledge from the act of watching. Such classification and listing were central to nineteenth-century ornithology, so "to the extent that it [bird-watching] involved the careful practice of assigning individual birds to taxonomic categories," bird-watching was a form of amateur science.[34] In many ways, then, bird-watching was a perfect capitalist hobby. Bird-watchers classified, categorized, and assigned difference to what must have seemed like an undifferentiated mass of avian life to the non-bird-watcher. Bird-watching, in its very essence, seemed to function as a means of valuation.

Schaffner argues that the valuation of birds should not be viewed entirely as a function of industrial capitalism. "Early formulations of birdwatching were also an affront to aspects of commodity culture that resulted in the deaths of many birds. Furthermore, the spiritual and aesthetic connections many birdwatchers have established with birds run counter to a strictly capitalist valuation of nature based on use value."[35] The very fact that such birds as the snowy egret were not completely eradicated in the nineteenth century points to the truth of this claim. Without the formation of the conservation movement, the simple use of bird feathers as fashionable adornment would have led to the extinction of many species. Nonetheless, nineteenth-century ornithology could not help but classify birds according to their use value.

Since the nineteenth century, bird-watching and ornithology have been linked "via the common concern of species identification."[36] Of course, the means of identification and classification differ. Comparing early field guides to early ornithological manuals, such as Elliott Coues's *Key to North American Birds* (1872), reveals one key difference. The bird-watching hobbyist only looked at birds; the ornithologist collected, that is, shot and mounted, birds for more detailed study and classification.[37] While field guides gave "participants an accessibly challenging set of tasks to accomplish," works such as Coues's described, in detail, the labor of practicing ornithology.[38] Coues's book is divided into three parts: "Field Ornithology," "General Ornithology," and "Systematic Synopsis of North American Birds." "General Ornithology" instructs readers on the "Principles and Practice of Classification" and "The Topography of Birds"; "Systematic Synopsis" offers descriptions of every North American bird species known at the time.[39] While ornithology has obviously developed as a science since the late nineteenth century, a twenty-first-century reader of these two sections would find them quite familiar. It is the first section, "Field Ornithology," that would seem foreign to most contemporary readers.

"Field Ornithology" describes, over fifty-nine pages, how to collect birds and how to prepare birdskins for study. Coues defines his purpose by writing that his instructions, if followed well, will "enable anyone who has the least taste or aptitude for such pursuits to become proficient in the necessary qualifications of the good working ornithologist."[40] The instructions that follow make it clear that ornithology, as described by Coues, is vastly different from the hobby of bird-watching.

Coues instructs readers on what kind of gun to use, how a dog can be helpful for collecting, the best practices for shooting birds, what instruments are needed to prepare birdskins, and "ornithological book-keeping."[41] In a brief section called "What is a 'good day's work?,'" Coues quantifies what an ornithologist should strive for. "Fifty birds shot, their skins preserved, and observations recorded, is a very good day's work; it is sharp practice, even when birds are plentiful. . . . You will do very well if you average a dozen a day during the seasons. . . . The greatest number I ever procured and prepared in one day was forty, and I have not often gone over twenty. Even when collecting regularly and assiduously, I am satisfied to average a dozen a day during the migrations, and one-third or one-fourth as many the rest of the year."[42] Clearly, collecting involves a lot of work. Traveling into the field, finding, shooting, and then preparing specimens for study is not something the hobbyist would ever have time or inclination for. Coues's "good day's work" is not a walk in the park with field guide and binoculars. His work produces something much more material than a list of species seen, namely "birdskins."

It is precisely in these well-prepared and preserved birdskins that Coues locates the value of birds. He asks, "How many birds of the same kind do you want?," and answers "all you can get—with some reasonable limitations; say fifty or a hundred of any but the most abundant and widely diffused species."[43] Coues notes that this might seem like greed to non-ornithologists, but he argues that "birdskins are capital; capital unemployed may be useless, but can never be worthless. Birdskins are a medium of exchange among ornithologists the world over; they represent value,—money value and scientific value. If you have more of one kind than you can use, exchange with someone for species you lack. Both parties to the transaction are equally bene-fitted."[44] Birdskins, then, for Coues, embody three kinds of value: exchange value, money value, and scientific value. Coues's ultimate value seems to be the scientific knowledge embodied by birdskins. The exchange of birdskins becomes an exchange of knowledge; the entire field of ornithology benefits as more scientists produce a larger body of knowledge, and as they share this knowledge amongst themselves.

Birdskins, in this understanding, become knowledge. Coues champions "the true ornithologist," who kills birds "simply because that is the only way of learning their structure and technical characters. There is much more about a bird that can be discovered in its dead body,—how much more, then, than can be found out from its stuffed skin."[45] One can make a useful continuum of scientific value here. Live birds hold the least value/knowledge for ornithologists; a "dead body" has a bit more value/knowledge; a "stuffed skin" produces the most value/knowledge. As a further parallel between scientific value and monetary value, Coues condemns "the man who only gathers birds, as a miser money, to swell his cabinet," as he champions the naturalist who participates in the marketplace of birdskin trading.[46]

Coues draws no real distinction between value and knowledge. Birdskins are valuable because they contain knowledge to be discovered by the ornithologist interested in producing a systematic understanding of bird life. In "Beyond Birds: Biopower and Birdwatching in the World of Audubon," Timothy W. Luke makes a compelling argument that this nineteenth-century focus on systematics is a disciplinary maneuver that goes hand in hand with the rise of American capitalism and consumer culture. He claims that naturalists like Coues "imported the mental habits of control and the moral acceptance of commodification into birding through the cult of collecting."[47] Indeed, Coues notes the "sad destruction" of collecting that can only be overcome by the "worthiness of motive" of the collector to produce and share knowledge.[48] Luke characterizes such "worthiness" as "the credos of exhausting analysis, careful examination, and hierarchical judgment so dear to the national bureaucratic regimes rising around the woodlands and marshes where birds and their eggs were found."[49] In other words, the systematic killing, collecting, and ordering of birds valued by collectors embody what Luke calls "the essence of modern consumer capitalist societies": the regulation of bodies.[50] The preparing of birdskins, then, can be seen as a literalization of this kind of regulation.

For Luke, though, the nineteenth-century shift from shooting birds to looking at birds is not a story of conservation; rather it is an intensification of the disciplining of human and bird bodies in the service of capitalism. The change from collecting to watching is merely a shift from one kind of consumption to another, "from the primitive accumulation of things to the manufacture of experience." Luke views the rise of bird-watching as a response to the threats faced by birds in the nineteenth century. "To eliminate bird, egg, and feather collectors, American nature consumers had to be given new products to consume, new behaviors to perform, new values to espouse."[51] The experience of bird-watching itself then, with its systematic listing and classifying, replaces collecting. The wider scale of bird-watching, though, intensifies its regulatory function. Rather than a small group of dedicated collectors, America now had a multitude of watchers armed with field guides and binoculars. While these bird-watchers helped to remove birds from the direct markets of fashion where value equaled feathers taken from shot birds, they did not remove birds from the field of capitalist exchange. Bird value shifted away from the dead bodies of birds, and toward the live experience of viewing birds in the field.

In *Downcast Eyes: The Denigration of Vision in Twentieth-Century French Thought*, a wide-ranging study of visuality, Martin Jay writes that the development of "exosomatic organs" such as telescopes and cameras has enabled the human eye "to accomplish its tasks at a far greater remove than any other sense, hearing and smell being only a distant second and third."[52] With this "expansion" of the ability to see, technologies of visuality, Jay writes, have "been linked in complicated ways to the practices of surveillance and spectacle, which they often abet."[53] In other words, the technology-aided increase in the power of the eye leads to much more than the ability to simply see more of the world. Vision becomes a vector of knowledge and values situated in specific historical and cultural frameworks.

The growth of bird-watching from the nineteenth to the twenty-first century goes hand in hand with the growth of capitalism over the same period. Jay argues that "the placement of objects in a relational visual field, objects with no intrinsic value of their own outside of those relations, may be said to have paralleled the fungibility of exchange value under capitalism."[54] Jay is not talking about bird-watching here. Nevertheless, he presents an interesting way of thinking about the history of human-avian interaction. Bird-watching, considered as an industry, creates economic value out of birds precisely by placing them in a "relational visual field." That is, the primary tools of bird-watching—field guides and binoculars—serve precisely this function. Viewing birds in the twentieth and twenty-first centuries attaches economic value to them, just as collecting birds attached economic value to them in the nineteenth century. In this sense, bird-watching functions, as one element among many, to strengthen the connection between capital and nature.

This relationship between capital and nature has certainly intensi-fied through the twentieth century and into the twenty-first. As Michael Hardt and Antonio Negri point out in *Empire*, "it is quite clear that capitalist expansion continued at an increasing pace in the latter half of the twentieth century."[55] Bird-watching, measured by its economic force alone (as I discuss in the opening paragraphs of this chapter), has mirrored this expansion. Hardt and Negri write, "Through the processes of modern technological transformation, all of nature has become capital, or at least has become subject to capital."[56] While this claim is obviously much broader in scope than my focus here, it can readily be applied to birds in twenty-first-century America, so that one may conclude: *All birds have become capital.* When Luke asserts that "birding has changed into a type of govermentalizing biopolitics," he seems to be making just that argument. He argues that the National Audubon Society exerts a "quite managerial and manipulative" power over avian life.[57] Luke notes that groups like Audubon have little choice in the matter, as they must "organize themselves to survive in the mainstream environments of American society, which have been, in turn, defined by industrial democracy, suburban consumerism, and scientific realism." Nonetheless, his critique only broadly gestures toward other possibilities, such as when he concludes by contrasting the "exciting world of Audubon" that is "centered upon human needs and interests" with a "selfless concern for Nature as such."[58]

What this selfless concern might look like is unclear, but it seems to do rhetorical work as a means of opposition to a "managerial and manipulative" relationship to birds. But, if indeed all birds have become capital, there seems to be little choice but to attempt to manage them, especially as populations of birds such as the red knot become endangered.

## THE RED KNOT AS CAPITAL

Numerous studies have attempted to place a monetary value on human interactions with birds, whether by measuring the economic effects of ecotourism, the "willingness to pay" (WTP) for certain wildlife-watching experiences, or the use value of *rufa* red knots for bird-watchers. Two recent studies have estimated "the recreational use value of household trips to view shorebirds during the annual horseshoe crab/shorebird migration on the Delaware Bay." Myers et al. conclude that the "willingness to pay" (WTP) for recreational birders on the Delaware Bay in 2008 was "$66–$90/household and for an overnight trip about $200–$425/household."[59] Edwards et al. estimated that 3,336 households (made up of 5,583 persons) visited the Delaware Bay to watch the shorebird migration, for an estimated use value of $215,000. These WTP estimates focus only on the value people place on watching the birds; they ignore "nonuse values and values related to other uses of the resource," such as the larger ecotourism values to the region, which have been estimated at $34 million, as I discuss above.[60]

Both of these studies briefly discuss the value of their economic measurements. Myers et al. note, "Individuals who engage in wildlife watching have measurable welfare resulting from their experience, and government action can play an active role in affecting this experience."[61] Edwards et al. write, "Our goal was to provide a set of estimates that may be useful in damage assessment and benefit-cost analysis."[62] In other words, the hope is that these economic valuations will be a factor in public policy decisions regarding horseshoe crabs and migrating shorebirds. Neither study advocates any specific policy, nor does either focus on theoretical aspects of the economic valuation of bird-watching.

A study done on the sandhill crane migration along the Platte River in Nebraska does address some of these questions. Stoll concludes that "birders were estimated to place a $413 value on maintaining the current *status quo* situation in terms of species diversity and size of the crane population."[63] Like Myers and Edwards, Stoll hopes that his research can influence policy, as he writes, "No longer must conservationists enter the policy arena and debate without economic tools at their disposal."[64] At the same time, he notes that the value of the Platte River migration is not merely economic. "Besides resource values that are reflected in markets, there are others that are not so easily recognized such as contributions to the gene pool and other arguments made by ecologists. Also, there is the matter of monetary values as exhibited by markets or measured with nonmarket techniques and the recognition that they may not capture everything one would like but at least they put the resource into the currency used in benefit/cost policy debates."[65] While economic valuations might efface ecological, aesthetic, spiritual, and other valuations, they nonetheless can provide a concrete means of arguing for conservation that might in turn preserve other values. By showing that bird-watching can function as an important aspect of capitalism, economic valuations make an argument for bird conservation. From this perspective, birds are capital, and should be managed in a way that preserves them as capital. In short, if the *rufa* population disappeared, so would the economic benefits that they embody.

In *The Ecology of Commerce: A Declaration of Sustainability*, Paul Hawken argues that just this kind of economic valuation is missing from discussions of conservation and capitalism: "The single greatest flaw of modern accounting is that the cost and losses of destroying the earth are absent from prices in the marketplace."[66] Hawken is perhaps the most well-known proponent of the argument that contemporary capitalism can and should shift toward what he calls a "restorative economy." Such an economy would not focus purely on profits and growth; instead, it would focus on "the ability to integrate with or replicate cyclical systems in its means of production and distribution." In a restorative economy, business becomes more like nature and nature becomes more like business. As Hawken writes, "In such an economy, there is the prospect that restoring the environment and making money would be the same process. As in nature, business and restoration should be part of a seamless web."[67] From this perspective, a restorative capitalism would find solutions to ecological problems, via "'ecopreneurs' dedication to restoring the world around them for the world that comes after."[68] Business would solve the problems that it created.

In a roundtable discussion published in *BioScience* in 2000, Hawken and others provide a concise overview of this strain of environmental thought. Put simply, they argue that the environment should be "owned and managed like a private firm or like a portfolio of private financial assets" precisely because nature is a "productive asset shared by all of humanity."[69] Many critics have noted that this view has come to dominate conservationist thinking in the twenty-first century to the point that it has become hegemonic. Brockington and Duffy write, "The idea that capitalism can and should help conservation save the world now occupies the mainstream of the conservation movement."[70] This idea underlies such "green" capitalist areas as the ecotourism industry and "ethical consumption."[71] It also pervades the work of nongovernmental organizations (NGOs) that focus on international biodiversity, by, in part, building corporate partnerships.[72] Igoe, Neves, and Brockington show how this ideology serves capitalism through the "pervasive and implicit message that saving the planet is ultimately best achieved by consumption, albeit of particular kinds."[73] Before exploring some of the potential problems with the "capitalism as environmental solution" view, I turn now to how this viewpoint has influenced red knot conservation efforts.

MARKETING THE RED KNOT'S CAPITAL

The economic value of the *rufa* red knot population has been established. What I have not discussed yet is how the red knot gets marketed. That is, I turn now to consider how conservationists have worked to promote the market value of the red knot. Most prominently, the *rufa* red knot now has a social marketing campaign organized by a nonprofit group, the Manomet Center for Conservation Sciences. Manomet clearly situates itself within the new mainstream environmentalism that sees capitalism as part of the solution. Its website claims, "We have a record of success in bringing groups together—conservatives and liberals, businesses and environmentalists, urbanites and farmers. This is the way to solve big problems for the long term."[74] Manomet defines itself as a "backbone organization" that provides "quiet leadership in creating a common agenda, shared measurement systems, mutually reinforcing activities, and continuous communication." Manomet works with scientists, conservationists, and other stakeholders to produce comprehensive, sustainable conservation plans.[75] Manomet's goals for its "Recovery of *Rufa* Red Knots" program include "building the science foundation for knot recovery," conserving habitat across the knot's range, and developing a social marketing campaign for the knot.[76]

The Facebook page, "Celebrate Delaware Bay," went live on April 1, 2011.[77] The page offers links to lots of information about related organizations, meetings, news, and book reviews. In short, it serves as a clearinghouse of information about the status of the red knot and what's being done to improve it. Manomet has also posted a series of YouTube videos about the Delaware Bayshore. While this social media work might seem to pale in comparison to the importance of scientific research, Manomet makes clear that social marketing is a key component of their recovery plan. Defining "social marketing" as "the systematic application of marketing and related techniques to achieve behavioral goals for a social good," Manomet strongly links a tool of capitalism to a conservationist goal. "Through 'marketing' the excitement, social and economic opportunities that shorebird habitats provide to their host communities, we find the prospect of increased visibility and public support for conservation."[78] And the *rufa* red knot has indeed experienced increased visibility. A "kid-driven" conservationist group, "Friends of the Red Knot," gathers and shares information as part of its goal to "get the Red Knot *rufa* protected from extinction."[79] The state of Delaware has started "the Delaware Bayshore Initiative" to promote conservation through "low-impact recreation" and economic growth through "ecotourism and new retail/hospitality business opportunities." The press release for the initiative strongly links conservation and economic activity: "[We] will build upon existing efforts and marshal new resources to drive habitat protection, promote tourism, and strengthen local economies."[80]

In addition, two recent books focus on conservation, migration, and the Delaware Bayshore. *Life Along the Delaware Bay: Cape May, Gateway to a Million Shorebirds* aims to educate a wide, but specific, audience of "conservationists, ecologists, and political and policy professionals, as well as the general public, looking for guidance on bay-wide conservation."[81] The book addresses "threats and conservation issues" in its last chapter. Before that, it details, in photographs and narrative, the history of the area, as well as providing detailed information about the bird species that make use of the Delaware Bayshore. *Moonbird: A Year on the Wind with the Great Survivor B95* works from a different perspective, as the book personalizes red knot migration by focusing on one specific banded bird's migration from the tip of South America to the Delaware Bayshore, to the Arctic, and back again. *Moonbird* asks, "Will B95's and *rufa's* days of flight soon come to an end?"[82] *Moonbird* also profiles some of the scientists involved in red knot conservation. Despite their different approaches, both books strive to raise awareness of the extinction threat.

It is clear that concerned people have done a lot for the *rufa* red knot. Scientists have developed a feasible conservation plan. Economists have shown that the red knot migration is more valuable than the horseshoe crab harvest. Governmental and nongovernmental organizations have worked to increase awareness. Writers and photographers have documented the value of these birds. A nonprofit agency has organized a social marketing campaign to publicize the extinction danger. Yet, on May 14, 2012, Lawrence Niles noted on his blog that horseshoe crab numbers have not increased. "Moreover," he wrote, "the survival models developed for horseshoe crab and Red Knots developed by a team of scientists, including me, suggest a recovery period of decades. In the meantime Red Knots, one of many shorebird species that rely on the horseshoe crab's eggs, are fast heading towards extinction and the listing of the knot is imminent. . . . These birds cannot wait for an anemic approach to restoration."[83]

So why is the management plan for the red knot not working? Is the linking of capitalism and conservation partially to blame? In their argument that this link has become hegemonic, Igoe et al. argue that "when it is so systematically and extensively promoted ... it acquires the appearance of being *the only* feasible view of how best to pursue and implement conservation goals."[84] In short, viewing capitalism as the solution to conservation issues obscures the point that capitalism is the cause of most of these issues. Timothy Luke, in his critique of the "Audubonizing" of nature, bluntly states, "The real threat to bird life in nature today is the waste and wealth produced by American capitalism."[85] This blatantly obvious point can easily be forgotten when capitalism and conservation are seen as allies. Corson argues that such amnesia can prevent structural changes, as it leads to a rigidity of thought that has "reinforced the separation of environmental concerns from their broader political economic drivers. It has allowed for the conceptualization of environmental goals without changes in existing political institutions."[86] In other words, this line of critique sees conservation as co-opted by capitalism to serve the goals of capitalism. Nature gets defined by its exchange value, and other, noncapitalist values get forgotten. For Igoe et al. this view leads to "the possibility of imagining the Earth as a virtual ledger, on which it is possible to carry out a quantitative balancing of environmental goods and bads."[87] The authors' point here seems inarguable. The ultimate logic of a capitalist valuation of nature leads to just this "virtual ledger" of equivalencies.

Situating the red knot, or any bird species, within such a virtual ledger is a risky experiment. If birds have been totally assimilated by a capitalist point of view, then the survival of birds becomes purely a matter of economics. To use Coues's nineteenth-century term, the "money value" of birds becomes the ultimate determining factor in conservation decisions. Adaptation into a system of equivalent value seems like a risky strategy for survival—of course, this is a strategy that the birds have no say in. If land development pressures assert a more stable and more easily quantifiable monetary value, or if, in the red knot's situation, a new value for horseshoe crabs appears, or if ecotourism falls off, economic analysis would then devalue birds. Such a devaluation could easily lead to the extinction of this population of red knots. Simply put, if the red knot becomes a commodity, it is subject to the risks inherent to capitalism. As Jeff Nealon succinctly notes in a discussion of Nietzsche and capitalism, "markets are sites of struggle and risk."[88] The U.S. economy has recently seen the results of some of these risks, but while economies can eventually recover, bird populations might not be able to. No amount of capital investment can reverse extinction once it happens.

Nealon, following the work of Deleuze and Guattari, emphasizes that one does not get to choose whether or not to enter into this system of risk. "One doesn't get to decide to denounce capitalism or appreciate it," he writes, because capitalism has become axiomatic, a set of rules that we have no choice but to engage with in the contemporary world.[89] You cannot simply accept or reject capitalism, "but you do have to respond to it, insofar as capitalism is all about axiomatic deployments of force. . . . Contemporary capitalism . . . is not the sort of thing that hides—it's everywhere, all the time." In other words, and in relation to the red knot, to say that capitalism is either the problem leading toward, or the solution to, the red knot's imminent extinction does not get one very far. Both claims seem too focused on the idea that one can either reject (capitalism kills birds) or accept (capitalism will save birds) the all-pervasive system of valuation inherent in "the totalizing situation of globalized consumption capital."[90] Hardt and Negri sum up this view when they write, "Capital has become a world. Use value and all the other references to values and processes of valorization that were conceived to be outside the capitalist mode of production have progressively vanished."[91] Those who care about the red knot have no choice but to work to establish the bird's value within capitalism. Yet, even as this work is being done, it does not yet seem to be helping the red knot.

Felix Guattari's work on capitalism and nature can help to illustrate exactly how difficult it is to bring about the kinds of change that would protect the red knot. In *The Three Ecologies*, Guattari writes, "The earth is undergoing a period of intense techno-scientific transformation" so that "if no remedy is found, the ecological disequilibrium this has generated will ultimately threaten the continuation of life on the planet's surface."[92] This transformation is a direct result of global capitalism, or what Guattari calls "Integrated World Capitalism."[93] For Guattari technology and science are one component (others include the economic and the juridical) of a worldview that became dominant late in the twentieth century. Guattari points out how such a "capitalist subjectivity" limits the ability to think in a different way: "Capitalistic subjectivity seeks to gain power by controlling and neutralizing the maximum number of existential refrains."[94] "Capitalist subjectivity" places value only on one way of viewing the world. Other "existential refrains," such as those that might focus on, for example, ecological, aesthetic, or evolutionary values, are granted little importance. Capitalist subjectivity gives no credence to "the ecological role and the sheer beauty and mystique of birds," precisely because these things are difficult to quantify monetarily.[95] And when these things do become quantified, according to Guattari, this worldview "destroys specific value systems and puts [them] on the same plane of equivalence: material assets, cultural assets, wildlife areas, etc."[96] Capitalist subjectivity views the "earth as a virtual ledger," as Igoe critiques and Hawken celebrates, thus flattening out all value so that anything becomes exchangeable for anything else. Wildlife areas, to use Guattari's example, would be no more or less valuable than the material assets that they represent. Watching a *rufa* red knot might have no more value than any other bird-watching experience, or even any other nature-related experience.

For Guattari this transformation is affecting much more than the earth and the environment. He writes that "it is the relationship between subjectivity and its exteriority that is compromised" by the contemporary world.[97] He warns against "the entropic rise of a dominant subjectivity" that would be "subject, in perpetuity, to the seductive efficiency of economic competition."[98] Guattari worries that capitalism creates and reinforces a way of being that wipes out any form of nonmonetary value. But, despite the seemingly monolithic power of capitalism, Guattari's work is optimistic. He calls for a creative reconfiguring of subjectivity, and of ways of valuing the world. Interestingly, Nealon, as well as Hardt and Negri, locates the possibility of transformation in the same place.

Even as Nealon highlights the pervasive force of capitalism, and the fruitlessness of either celebrating or condemning it, he, like Guattari, notes that subjectivity can transform what gets valued in the world. Nealon, following Nietzsche, notes that value itself is not inherent. "A thing's value is enforced not by the thing itself, but from elsewhere, from a relation of social force and strife."[99] And it is precisely in these struggling relations that transformation can take place. Nealon's description of human subjectivity within capitalism resonates with Guattari's. "Humans are reactive pockets of consumerist interiority," he writes, because this way of being is precisely "the style of subjectivity that capitalism has produced, selected for, and rewarded."[100] Like Guattari, Nealon locates the possibility of change in a transformation of this "style of subjectivity." "We have to become something else if we are to be capable of transvaluing values."[101]

Likewise, Hardt and Negri emphasize that, while world capitalism is a dominant force, it is not a natural inevitability. They want to resist the "widely propagated illusion that the capitalist market and the capitalist regime of production are eternal and insuperable. The bizarre naturalness of capitalism is a pure and simple mystification, and we have to disabuse ourselves of it right away."[102] It is only through "the singular and creative processes of the production of subjectivity" that the seeming naturalness of capitalist subjectivity can be overcome. For Hardt and Negri, "the fundamental productivity of being" itself is a baseline principle of great force that is capable of a strong response to the constant crises created by capitalism.[103] As they write variously of "generation," "biopolitical becoming," "desire," and "collectivity," Hardt and Negri argue that "concrete production, human collectivity in action" is the "basis and motor of production and reproduction."[104] Underlying capitalism, then, is the basic ontological force of human activity. Such activity can become rigid and reinforce the dominance of capitalism, or it can work to create different pathways of value. Hardt and Negri do not write about environmentalism and conservation per se, but their emphasis on the power of the multitude of human productivity coincides with Guattari's call for other "universes of value" that can lead to "an environment in the process of being reinvented."[105]

In *The Three Ecologies*, Guattari argues that "ecology must stop being associated with the image of a small nature-loving minority or with qualified specialists" if it is to bring about a change in the ways humans interact with the world.[106] The specific encounter between the population of the red knot that migrates through the Delaware Bay and the humans that observe and study this migration has clearly affected the humans involved. Can this change in understanding broaden to affect a significant portion of the human population that has little interest in birds and bird-watching? Can bird-watching act as a technology that alters human subjectivity? In *Chaosmosis: An Ethico-aesthetic Paradigm*, Guattari asks a question that he says "returns with insistence": "How do we change mentalities, how do we reinvent social practices that would give back to humanity—if it ever had it—a sense of responsibility, not only for its own survival, but equally for the future of life on the planet?"[107] Might all of the interactions between humans and red knots become a vector for just such a large-scale change in human understanding and valuation of the world?

This is obviously not an easy question to answer, and Guattari points to the difficulty of creating different ways of valuing the natural world. "Wherever we turn, there is the same nagging paradox: on the one hand, the continuous development of new technoscientific means to potentially resolve the dominant ecological issues and reinstate socially useful activities on the surface of the planet, and on the other hand, the inability of organized social forces and constituted subjective formations to take hold of these resources in order to make them work."[108] Guattari's "nagging paradox" enlarges the scale of the question asked by Lawrence Niles when he wonders why there is "a lack of will" to protect the red knot and the Delaware Bayshore. In other words, ornithologists and interested bird-watchers know exactly what should be done to ensure the continuation of the *rufa* red knot population. At the same time, these solutions have not been fully enacted. Guattari broadly argues that this paradox is at the heart of ecological crisis. The means exist to solve problems, yet the force to bring about these changes is missing. Paul Hawken makes a similar point in *The Ecology of Commerce*, where he writes, "The ideas and much of the technology required for the redesign of our businesses and the restoration of the world are already at hand. What is missing is collective will."[109] Whether Guattari and Hawken are overly optimistic about environment-saving technology is debatable, and somewhat beside the point here. The "lack of will" that Hawken mentions and the "inability" to bring about change noted by Guattari seem less debatable. And indeed, this absence of will to bring about ecological change resonates strongly with what Niles says about the red knot and the larger ecological prospects of the whole Delaware Bay region: "With care and public will, the bay could easily be turned around. Unfortunately, the care part is more easily achieved than the will. . . . The lack of will is a great mystery to the bay's conservationists."[110] In short, one of the primary difficulties of conservation and ecology seems to center around the question of will.

Guattari helps to show why this question is a difficult one to address, as he addresses what he sees as the key "problem" for ecologists. "Their problem today is . . . how to rebuild politics on different bases, how to rearticulate transversally the public and the private, the social, the environmental and the mental. In order to move in this direction, new types of dialogue, of analysis, of organization will have to be tested."[111] Ecology, then, cannot just focus on science and technology. According to Guattari, it must be concerned with multiple levels of human subjective interaction, from politics, to social issues, to human will itself. Ecology must create new means for understanding the relationship among all of these realms. Simply put, that's a lot to do.

Guattari's argument here is abstract, in that he is not referring to a specific ecological issue. Lawrence Niles, though, offers what adds up to a specific plan for engaging with the political, social, and environmental issues centered on the red knot and Delaware Bayshore. As well, he addresses the question of how to build up the will to make these changes. As I discuss above, Niles's and others' research has mapped out a conservation plan, which, if followed, would help to increase the population of *rufa* red knots. On his blog Niles writes about other work that he is doing for these conservation efforts; as well, he writes about political, economic and social issues pertinent to the Delaware

Bayshore, as he considers ways to create new forms of value. Niles has written, and continues to write, a lot about the red knot and the Delaware Bayshore. I will focus on what I see as three key ideas he presents for thinking and acting differently about conservation: raising awareness of the Delaware Bayshore and the plight of shorebirds that rely on it; creating value for the community living on the bayshore; and involving people with nature in direct, concrete ways.

Outside of the relatively small conservation and bird-watching communities, most humans probably do not know that a species of bird called the red knot even exists; certainly, knowledge that the red knot and other shorebirds are imperiled is not widespread. The social marketing campaign that I describe above strives to bring this awareness to a wider public. Niles notes that this campaign goes hand in hand with a movement to raise awareness of the Delaware Bayshore itself as a place of value. He notes that Manomet's shorebird project will work "to create a new social marketing campaign to lift people's opinions of the bay. Biologists and conservationists recognize its value, why not the people who live here?"[112] Establishing the value of the bayshore from the point of view of biology and conservation is relatively straightforward. Researchers have mapped out migration routes and established the density of horseshoe crabs that red knots need to refuel for their migration. Establishing the value of the bayshore from other perspectives is more difficult.

Niles notes that the bayshore "region is among the poorest in the state" of New Jersey. Because of this poverty, "you can't blame people fighting to stay solvent for not valuing the ecological treasure that literally laps at their feet." Niles says that revitalizing the area is just as important as preserving the habitat and managing the horseshoe crab harvest. Niles argues that local agriculture needs to be revamped, away from "low profit grains" and back toward "high-profit vegetables." Such vegetables could be "branded," like "Jersey tomatoes" produced in other parts of the state have, both to increase their value and to create recognition of the bayshore as a defined agricultural region. Likewise, he notes that bayshore towns like Fortescue would benefit from new infrastructure and from marketing, so that they could compete with nearby tourist destinations like Wildwood and Cape May. He writes, "Fortescue is a true American original, as NJ as NJ gets, a seaside town devoted to working people, one of the few left on America's Atlantic coasts." In addition, the area has "diverse abundant wildlife" and "gorgeous Delaware Bay sunsets." Yet, as Niles goes on to write, the town lacks infrastructure—it has no water or sewage system and its beachfront is eroded. The town is trapped by its poverty; according to Niles, even as it could become a vibrant place, it "doesn't merit the generous subsidies we lavish on the seaside haunts of the wealthy on the Atlantic Coast."[113]

Niles also calls for a rewriting of numerous environmental regulations, covering everything from land use to fisheries management. Niles and Rick Lathrop, the director of the Rutgers Center for Remote Sensing and Spatial Analysis, have proposed "a new municipally-based system for protecting wildlife habitats" that places specific values on habitat and calls for "no net-loss" of habitat value. In addition, Niles calls for local oversight of the bay's fishery in order to produce "a truly effective management system that rewards sustainable ventures, not boom-and-bust industrial exploitation." As he bluntly puts it, "the 'money' is in wise resource use" that would manage both the commercial and recreational harvests of blue crabs, weakfish, sturgeon, and even horseshoe crabs. In short, Niles calls for a new way of looking at conservation: "A new policy initiative that creates wealth for local people would inspire conservation from the bottom up. In the end, this may be the best path toward sustainable conservation."[114] Protecting the *rufa* red knot, then, is not just a matter of regulating the horseshoe crab habitat and conserving the beaches that the knot uses during migration. It also requires new ways of creating value for and in the local community; it calls for working within capitalism to produce agricultural and property values. And, it calls for reenvisioning the way the general public thinks about conservation.

According to Niles, over the past thirty years, "there has been a sea change in how people are involved in wildlife and their conservation. This change has reshaped the public's relationship with wildlife." While attributing some of this change to increased urbanization and other factors, Niles attributes a large part to the fact that most people interested in wildlife and conservation have few "direct, 'hands-on' experiences with wildlife." Compared to those who hunt and fish, and by definition have a "hands-on" relationship with animals, bird-watchers rarely, if ever, get close enough to touch a bird. The very visual technologies that underlie bird-watching are designed to allow visual identification at a distance. Niles cites the decrease in "amateur" bird banding and wildlife rehabilitation as another symptom of this distance from wildlife. Niles writes, "Decades ago bird banding was a pursuit of a small but dedicated group of people, who were not professional wildlife scientists, but smart people who cared about birds." Today, though, it is impossible for those who want to band "for fun" to get a permit without a valid scientific rationale. Niles notes that this policy makes a certain amount of sense, as it eliminates "bad actors" who might harm birds. At the same time, though, rules on banding "separate the bird loving public from this often inspiring but always tedious work." Likewise, according to Niles, those interested in wildlife rehabilitation have to acquire permits "so onerous few have the wherewithal to satisfy the many requirements." Because of this a "passionate endeavor for people who cared for wildlife as much as others care for pets" has diminished markedly.[115]

What Niles seems to be talking about here is a kind of investment on the part of those interested in wildlife. Making it next to impossible for amateur bird banders or wildlife rehabilitators to be licensed prevents the kind of "hands-on" interaction with animals that might spark an active involvement in conservation. In some ways the "hands-on" approach that Niles champions harkens back to the nineteenth-century notion of the amateur ornithologist who was the audience for guides such as Elliot Coues's *Key to North American Birds*. Coues's guide, as I discuss above, requires time and dedication from the prospective ornithologist. But it is worth noting that those are the primary requirements for following Coues's instruction. In his first paragraph, Coues makes clear that his audience is "any one who has the least taste or aptitude for such pursuits to become proficient in the necessary qualifications of the good working ornithologist."[116]

Times have certainly changed. It is impossible to imagine Coues's work in a twenty-first-century context of "citizen science." Part of the difference between then and now is obviously one of conservation. Bird populations are so much smaller across the board today that they could not be sustained if amateur ornithologists were to "collect" specimens. But just the thought itself of heading out into the field to shoot birds and then prepare their skins, regardless of conservation issues, would seem entirely strange to present-day bird-watchers. This obviously is not a bad thing. Nevertheless, it does point to a radically different sort of relation between humans and birds. In short, twenty-first-century bird-watching is not at all a "hands-on" experience. Birders and birds keep a physical distance from one another. Birds are protected, as they need to be for conservation reasons. Whether this distance between birds and bird-watchers has led to a lack of interest in conservation is an interesting, if unanswerable, question.

Niles writes about another way humans might have a more hands-on experience with wildlife that would produce benefits for people, horseshoe crabs, and red knots. While noting that he is "deeply involved" in the fight over horseshoe crab harvest, Niles also claims that there is "a better way." He asks a series of questions that point to the power that an organized group of people can have. "What if thousands of people were inspired to come to the bay and save the lives of horseshoe crabs hopelessly caught in between bulkheads or in the crevasses of rocky groins? What if people were organized into a great effort to right overturned crabs, flipped by Delaware Bay waves? Would the crab recovery go from decades to years if thousands of crabs' lives were saved by well meaning people each year?" While the thought of a multitude of people flipping over horseshoe crabs might not seem revolutionary in any way, it can be seen as a direct and specific proposal for creating Guattari's "other universes of value" through the force of Hardt and Negri's "human collectivity in action." In addition to saving thousands of egg-producing crabs, Niles argues that such a collective action might lead to "conservation, and the science on which it is based" being "re-seen as recreation."[117] Such a re-seeing could lead to new ways of engaging with the world. The physical act of picking up horseshoe crabs might just lead people to a new understanding of the value of the Delaware Bay for humans, horseshoe crabs, and migratory birds.

Even as Niles and others develop a very specific conservation plan for the red knot that includes science, conservation, recreation, public policy, and multiple kinds of economic valuation, the *rufa* red knot's future remains in doubt. But, all of the efforts to conserve red knots do illustrate how conservation can work in the twenty-first century. There seems to be no choice but to attempt to communicate the red knot's value and then capitalize on that value; that is, the choice might be as simple as this: sell the red knot as a valuable commodity and hope people are willing to buy, or watch as the red knot goes extinct. To say that capitalism is a conservation problem to be overcome does little for birds. Likewise, to claim that capitalism will solve all conservation issues is overly simplistic.

It is certainly worth noting that the economic valuation of human-avian interactions can easily overwhelm all other valuations. If humans see birds *only* as an exchangeable commodity, then human-avian interaction serves only to solidify the "plane of equivalence" that reduces all value systems to the same field of exchange. From this perspective, human-red knot interactions might function as important aspects of capitalist subjectivity by showing that the birds have a quantifiable economic value. At the same time, these interactions could also serve to break up this "plane of equivalence" by focusing on other systems of value. To watch birds is certainly to watch more than an economic system at work. In addition to capitalist values, bird-watching connects to ecologic, aesthetic, spiritual, and intellectual values, among others. These values can easily be dismissed as insubstantial from within the dominant mode of capitalist subjectivity. But they can also be viewed as part of a worldview that can alter human understanding of, and interaction with, the world. Economic valuation can be seen not as an end in itself, but as a starting point for an alteration of human subjectivity. Birds such as the red knot do have economic value; the hope of those who champion their conservation is that this economic value might lead to other forms of valuation as well.

In conclusion, the human experiment on red knot populations—that is, the whole series of interactions between humans and red knots, which starts with the act of looking at the bird—can help to create different ways of seeing and valuing the world. A specific, dated encounter, such as the one narrated in the opening paragraph of this chapter, can lead from an act of identification to an exploration of the interplay between capitalism and conservation on the Delaware Bayshore. As the case of the red knot shows, valuations are not just of theoretical importance. They raise key questions for interspecies subjectivity: Are there ways of revaluing the red knot within a human system of understanding? Is twenty-first-century capitalist humanity capable of seeing and thus valuing another order of understanding? Does economic valuation exclude other ways of valuing? Does thinking of the red knot in a monetary system mean simply that losing monetary value equals extinction? As humans continue to experiment on red knots and other shorebirds, the results of the experiment will emerge. While the *rufa* red knot population is heading toward extinction, other birds thrive in the altered landscapes of twenty-first-century America. The next chapter examines how a growing population of a species—the resident Canada goose—raises many of the same questions of capitalist valuation as the decline of the knot does.

# 4

## Nuisance and Neighbor

.....................................................................................................................

### The Canada Goose

*The small signs in Greenfield Corporate Center Park say, "Do not feed the ducks, geese, or swans." Mostly the signs are ignored, usually by families with small children throwing bread to the mix of mallards, domestic ducks, Canada geese, and pair of mute swans. Today, and over the next few weeks, the reasons for the signs become clear, and the park pretty much empties out of families feeding the birds. The ducks are dying. Today I count six dead ones and at least that many more struggling.*

*This park seems to have been made for Canada geese. A walking path snakes around three ponds. Vast fields of green grass surround the area. Everything a Canada goose could need is here. The grass and the people with bread are food sources. The fields of grass provide long sight lines so any approaching danger can be seen. The ponds provide a refuge from danger. The small islands and piles of rocks in the ponds provide safe nesting areas. The corporation that runs the park has inadvertently created a waterfowl paradise. During fall migration, I've seen thousands of Canada geese on these ponds and the one across the street; in the spring, they are joined by hundreds of snow geese. But now, during the summer, the resident, nonmigratory geese number around one hundred. There are probably two hundred ducks. Goose poop is everywhere: visible on the walking paths and unseen at the bottom of the ponds.*

*The whole park smells rotten. The hot weather, stagnant water, sinking organic material (particularly bread and poop), and dead ducks have created a perfect environment for another form of life: avian botulism bacteria.*

On September 23, 2004, the front page of the *Lancaster Intelligencer Journal* reads: "Botulism Kills Dozens of Ducks at Greenfield Corp. Center." The subheadline reads: "High Ltd. Asks People to Stop Feeding the Fowls." By this point, not many people were feeding them anyway. Hot weather and dead ducks had kept most people out of the park. Over the next couple of weeks dozens of ducks died. Many went uncollected by maintenance crews for days.

The hot weather broke, and a few weeks later the headline, this time relegated to the afternoon paper's local section, read "Botulism Die-Off of Ducks Here Ends." Two days later, the sports section noted that, despite the botulism outbreak, the Game Commission had assured local hunters that they "should not be concerned about waterfowl taken in the area."[1] The story seems to end here, with the local duck population diminished, and the resident Canada goose population unchanged. There is no botulism outbreak in 2005. But then, in July 2006, Lancaster's mayor announces that the two hundred resident geese and forty resident ducks at Long's Park, a few miles up the road from Greenfield Corporate Center, will be "relocat[ed]" because of the threat of another avian botulism outbreak. The exact meaning of "relocation" is not provided by the mayor or by anyone else, but the meaning is clear nonetheless. Many municipalities have taken to killing Canada geese whose populations are overgrown. People get upset because they like feeding ducks, and because babies are cute. A seven-year-old girl quoted in the news article said, "When the geese have babies, that's cute." Her nine-year-old brother likes "when they come up and take the food out of your hand."[2] In large sections of suburban America, especially in but not limited to the mid-Atlantic states, such human-goose interactions are incredibly common. Resident Canada geese, unlike their migratory cohort, show little fear of humans, and they quickly acclimate to being fed.

In central Pennsylvania, in the middle of the summer, nearly every Canada goose is nonmigratory. But, depending on place and time of year, a bird-watcher might see one of seven geographically diverse subspecies. In fact, the possibility exists that the bird in question might be a cackling goose, one of four subspecies recently split from the Canada goose into their own distinct species. More than five million Canada geese reside in the continental United States and Canada.[3] Many of these geese migrate between breeding grounds in northern Canada and Alaska to more temperate winter climates along the Atlantic or Pacific coast, or throughout the Mississippi Valley, depending on the subspecies. A close observer can readily distinguish among these subspecies based on size, shape, and coloration. But a large population of Canada geese, *B.c. maxima*, or "common" subspecies, inhabit parks, lawns, and ponds throughout the United States and Canada. These birds do not migrate, largely because humans have created ideal year-round habitat. Abundant grass and the bread offered by humans ensure adequate food. Open fields of short grass provide long sight lines so approaching danger can be seen. Landscaped ponds provide refuges from danger, and small islands provide safe nesting areas. Suburban America has inadvertently created a Canada goose paradise, and populations have exploded.

Canada goose populations have been increasing since the mid-1930s, when the use of live decoys meant to draw migrating birds for hunters was banned.[4] At least 15,000 geese that had been used as decoys were released because of this regulation. Starting in the 1950s and continuing through the 1980s, states in the East and Midwest worked to restore populations of Canada geese. These efforts were so successful that Canada goose populations are increasing an "average of 2 percent per year since 1995."[5] Many of these birds have stopped migrating. Migratory behavior is learned in geese, and if one generation decides to not leave a wintering area, the behavior can be adopted by a whole flock. With abundant food and safe breeding areas, populations of resident Canada geese have increased immensely. In fact, as the *Birds of North America Online* (BNA) notes, "The rapid increase of local breeding populations in many areas and subsequent mixing of resident birds with migrants during winter has resulted in uncertainty of origin and racial identity that has created a multitude of management problems and may threaten the diversity of the species across its entire range."[6] Resident Canada geese have mixed with formerly geographically discrete subpopulations so that, in many cases, only a very careful observer can identify a given goose's subspecies. Canada geese have bred so successfully that reintroduction and conservation programs have been replaced by "programs designed to limit further population growth and distribution as nuisance and damage complaints associated with growing populations come into conflict with agricultural and suburban landowner interests."[7] In other words, with human help, Canada geese have thrived in America to the point that they have been deemed a nuisance species. The human experiment on Canada geese is an odd one. Human actions have directly led to a change in behavior and population in Canada geese; that is, many Canada geese no longer migrate, and their population has increased immensely. At the same time, the number of Canada geese deemed as "nuisance" has led to large numbers of geese being killed by humans. As a result of this population explosion, the resident Canada goose has become subject to an astounding level of government regulation.

## WHAT IS A "NUISANCE SPECIES"?

The concept of "nuisance species" has a long history in America. Spencer Schaffner, in *Binocular Vision*, shows that the concept has its roots in nineteenth-century definitions of "bad birds," such as the bald eagle and other birds of prey.[8] Nineteenth-century writers condemned many birds in moral terms. John James Audubon, in his *Ornithological Biography*, was perhaps the most well-known of these moral critics. After all, he called the bald eagle "a rank coward."[9] On its own, such moralizing might not have had much of an effect on these so-called nuisance birds. But, as Schaffner argues, when combined with a perceived economic threat to farming, it became much easier to place bounties on "birds of prey," a broad category that included hawks, eagles, and owls. He writes, "Old antipathies toward birds helped reinforce the bounties and vice versa, creating a belief that killing bounty birds meant performing legal and ethical forms of justice."[10] Likewise, in his discussion of the Alaskan bounty placed on bald eagles in the early twentieth century, Schaffner argues, "the character of the Bald Eagle had long been assailed, and this negative view combined with strong forms of economic protectionism to allow lawmakers to institute the Alaskan bounty."[11] The fact that birds such as eagles, hawks, and owls were once considered nuisance species shows that the concept itself is rooted in specific historical and social circumstances. The bald eagle, of course, later became perhaps the most protected bird species in the United States, and it seems nearly unthinkable today that the killing of owls and hawks would be subsidized by the federal government.

While nationwide bounties are no longer placed on birds, the U.S. government still classifies certain animals as nuisance species. And through Wildlife Services (ws), a unit of the U.S. Department of Agriculture's (usda) "Animal and Plant Health Inspection Service" (aphis), millions of animals are killed every year. ws defines its mission as "to provide Federal leadership and expertise to resolve wildlife conflicts to allow people and wildlife to coexist."[12] While ws strives to use nonlethal means to resolve human-animal conflicts because "wildlife is an important public resource greatly valued by the American people," they note that "by its very nature, however, wildlife is a highly dynamic and mobile resource that can damage agricultural and industrial resources, pose risks to human health and safety, and affect other natural resources."[13] Yet even as ws charts out a "goal to reduce damage caused by wildlife to the lowest possible levels while at the same time reducing wildlife mortality," it kills a lot of animals every year. In 2008, when a new computer program began to summarize kills and recorded a sharp increase in the eradication of invasive species, the total number of lethally removed wildlife increased by 106 percent compared to the previous year.[14] Since 2008 ws has "killed/euthanized" 4,120,291 animals in 2009; 5,008,928 in 2010; and 3,752,356 animals in 2011. The vast majority (more than 90 percent) of animals killed are European starlings (1,500,459 in 2011), red-winged blackbirds (657,134 in 2011), and brown-headed cowbirds (846,633 in 2011), primarily because these birds damage various grain and sunflower

crops and because they are "attracted to feedlots and defecate in cattle feed." The remaining 10 percent of kills in 2011 ranges from the
American alligator (1 killed) to lesser yellowlegs (31 killed), and even
includes endangered species such as the sandhill crane (23 killed) and
seemingly innocuous, tiny shorebirds such as the least sandpiper (125
killed). In recent years WS has noted that they have had to increase
management of resident Canada geese populations, which they estimate at 3.5 million as of 2008.[15] This large population can lead to
various problems. "Although most people find a few birds acceptable,
problems quickly develop as bird numbers increase. These problems
include overgrazing of grass and ornamental plants; accumulation of
droppings and feathers; attacks on humans by aggressive birds; and
the fouling of reservoirs, swimming areas, beaches, docks, lawns, and
golf courses. Flocks of geese and other waterfowl also feed on a variety
of crops, including corn, soybeans, rice, lettuce, winter wheat, barley,
and rye."[16] To mitigate these problems, WS killed 23,700 Canada
geese in 2011 and dispersed 682,007.[17] In 2010, 27,228 were killed,
and in 2009, 24,618 were killed.[18] My point here is not to condemn
the actions of WS. The killing and dispersion of Canada geese has not
been entered into in a haphazard manner.

In August 2006, after four years of study, Wildlife Services released
a "Final Rule" regarding "Migratory Bird Hunting and Permits; Regulations for Managing Resident Canada Goose Populations." This
final rule authorized "Alternative F," "which would authorize State
wildlife agencies, private landowners, and airports to conduct (or
allow) indirect and/or direct population control management activities,
including the take of birds, on resident Canada goose populations."[19]
This ruling depends on an underlying assumption that most of us
do not consider in our daily lives when we see a Canada goose or
any other bird for that matter: birds are "managed" by national laws
and international treaties. The Migratory Bird Treaty Act (MBTA) of
1918 gives umbrella protection to all birds that migrate in or through
North America. Federal law, though, manages populations of fifty-
eight species, including Canada geese, that may be hunted under the
MBTA. The August 2006 ruling applies only to a subset of Canada

geese, those deemed "resident," or nonmigratory, defined by the ruling as "Canada geese that nest within the lower 48 states in the months of March, April, May, or June, or reside within the lower 48 States and the District of Columbia in the months of April, May, June, July, or August."[20] In short, then, a "resident" Canada goose is one that breeds in the Lower 48 states in March, or appears in the continental United States between April and August. Resident Canada geese in America are now subject to three specific "program components": "control and depredation order Management," "expanded hunting methods and opportunities," and "a resident Canada goose population control program." In other words, a management decision was made to decrease resident goose populations in the continental United States.

Why did ws decide to do this? For several reasons: "conflicts between geese and people affect or damage several types of resources, including property, human health and safety, agriculture, and natural resources."[21] Excessive goose droppings can lead to the eutrophication of ponds, the closing of beaches due to high fecal chloroform levels, and degraded water quality. The aesthetic value and recreational use of public parks can decrease due to large populations of Canada geese, and people have been injured or threatened by Canada geese during breeding season. Canada geese have collided with airplanes and been sucked into airplane engines, resulting in costly damages and, in a few cases, crashes. Considering all this evidence, it seems reasonable to believe that there are too many resident Canada geese in highly populated human environments. The ws plan makes sense from the perspective of human safety, economics, and even aesthetics.

ws did not find broad public support of its claims. Of the 2,925 public comments regarding this ruling, "95% supported the use of nonlethal control and management alternatives," and "68% supported the use of lethal methods where nonlethal methods have failed or where 'true' human safety threats exist." In other words, 32 percent of respondents, or 936 people, do not support the use of lethal methods, even in the face of danger to humans. The report also includes specific questions and comments, which ws answers in detail. Two questions, in particular, seem to express the public concern. One commenter asks: "Isn't it archaic to allow the killing of a species simply because certain people find it to be a nuisance?" Another asks: "Isn't the real problem here humans and, therefore, it is people who are in need of 'management,' not resident Canada geese?" WS responds that their program would "allow killing of resident Canada geese only when they are associated with a specific problem, not because they are considered a pest or a nuisance." It is worth noting that WS never overtly defines Canada geese as a "nuisance species." In addition, WS points out the complexity of each individual Canada goose problem. "Certainly, among the broad range of stakeholders, there is a need to promote a better understanding of the biological and sociological complexities associated with resident Canada goose management."[22] Understanding these "complexities" can lead to a better understanding of both why Canada geese have come to be seen as a nuisance species and why some want to resist putting this label on the birds.

## MANAGING THE CANADA GOOSE

In its "Final Environmental Impact Statement: Resident Canada Goose Management," the U.S. Fish and Wildlife Service discusses the "challenging responsibility" of managing goose populations in a way that is "both sustainable and appropriate for environmental and sociological conditions." Part of the challenge comes from the fact that WS manages "19 management populations and 11 subspecies" of Canada geese.[23] As I discuss above, there is wide variance and overlap within and between these populations and subspecies. Some of these populations and subspecies are either stable or declining, but "resident" Canada geese are increasing at a regular rate. Just as the measurement of declining populations of *rufa* red knots and of horseshoe crabs plays an important role in conservation plans, a specific measurement of resident Canada geese populations underlies every management action that is taken.

Likewise, economic valuations play a key role in management decisions. Unlike economic valuations of endangered and rare species that seek to show the positive economic value created by birds, valuations of resident Canada goose populations strive to establish the economic cost of these birds. One case study conducted in 2010 by Wildlife Services in Union County, New Jersey, set a range of the "annual damage estimate" per resident Canada goose as between $20.08 and $61.77 (in 2010 dollars). These damage costs come mainly from "vegetation and turf maintenance, fecal removal, and reduced recreation and park user fees." Through instituting an "Integrated Wildlife Damage Management Program (IWDMP)" that employed both dispersion and removal, WS found that Union County could save $1.31 to $5.56 for every dollar spent on Canada goose control. In other words, spending money on an IWDMP, which would seek to curb goose populations, would lead to a "net savings" in the county budget. With no action, the goose population could triple and cost the county between $80,320 and $741,240. When this study was conducted, Union County had a resident Canada goose population of approximately four thousand.[24] Simply extrapolating from the Union County data means that the economic damage done by the 3.5 million resident geese in America potentially could be in the hundreds of millions or even billions of dollars.

Through measuring populations and establishing the economic, aesthetic, and public health risks associated with resident Canada geese, WS builds a strong case that goose populations should be subject to human control. All of this study would be pointless, though, if WS did not have the authority to take action based on its findings. WS gained its authority to manage wildlife populations through the Animal Damage Control Act of 1931. At the time WS was called the Division of Predatory Animal and Rodent Control, and its primary purpose was to protect livestock from predators.[25] Its mandate has expanded since then. Thanks to "increasingly diverse request for assistance," WS's responsibilities "now include threatened and endangered species conservation, the protection of public health and safety, wildlife disease surveillance and monitoring, a nationally coordinated research effort, [and playing] a vital role in our Nation's efforts to eliminate the negative effects of invasive species on the environment." In fiscal year 2010 WS had an operating budget of $110,558,653 and employed 1,700 "scientists, wildlife biologists, field specialists, and support specialists across the country."[26]

What force, exactly, does WS exercise over resident Canada geese? The usual first suggestion is to use nonlethal methods of dispersion, which WS groups under the broad categories "Resource Management" and "Physical Exclusions and Deterrents." The former includes such actions as altering landscape to make it less attractive to geese; modifying human behavior, including not feeding geese; and removing domestic waterfowl that might draw more birds to a specific place. The latter includes such things as barrier fencing, wire mesh, hazing, pyrotechnics, lasers, distress calls, and dogs. When these methods fail or are unfeasible, WS might then recommend "Population Control," which means egg destruction and killing.[27] It is worth noting that WS has recently stated that lethal methods are used only after careful consideration of other methods. In a publicity pamphlet called "Partnerships and Progress," WS note "the great care and diligence with which the program operates" through its commitment "to the principle that wildlife is a publicly-owned resource held in trust and carefully managed by State and Federal agencies."[28] Once "population control" has been deemed necessary, WS either uses lethal means itself or issues a permit to a state wildlife agency or to a landowner. WS will only issue a permit "when it will contribute to human health and safety, protect personal property, or allow resolution or prevention of injury to people or property."[29]

Before any eggs can be destroyed, permit holders must register with WS and provide a list of "each employee or agent working on their behalf."[30] Egg destruction may only be conducted between March 1 and June 30, and the method used must be from among the following: egg oiling "using 100 percent corn oil," freezing or puncturing eggs, or removing nests and/or eggs. Permit holders must also report the "date, numbers, and location of nests and eggs taken" by October 31, after which they can reapply for the next year.[31] A WS "factsheet" called "Management of Canada Goose Nesting" notes that, because geese are fiercely protective of their nests, egg destruction should be done by a two-person team. "One should work the eggs, while the other wards off goose attacks using a shield, such as a trash can lid or broom." At the same time, permit holders should "never strike the bird; merely hold the shield between yourself and the bird to prevent physical contact," as the geese themselves are still legally protected.[32]

Egg and nest destruction is expensive and labor intensive. Five eggs must be destroyed to equal the removal of one adult goose, and the cost of destroying five eggs has been estimated as forty dollars more than the cost of removing one adult goose. If egg destruction is done too early, geese may re-nest the same year. Egg destruction must also be repeated for multiple years to affect long-term populations. When nonlethal means and egg destruction are not enough, WS will then allow lethal means of control.[33]

WS dictates the following methods, to be used at the permit holder's "discretion": shotguns; lethal and live traps; nets; registered animal drugs, pesticides and repellants; cervical dislocation, and $CO_2$ asphyxiation.[34] WS provides descriptions of how these methods should be used. Noting that both cervical dislocation and $CO_2$ asphyxiation are euthanization methods approved by the American Veterinary Medical Association, WS offers the following details:

> Cervical dislocation: Cervical dislocation is sometimes used to euthanize birds which are captured by hand or in live traps and when relocation is not a feasible option. The bird is stretched and the neck is hyper-extended and dorsally twisted to separate the first cervical vertebrae from the skull.

> $CO_2$ asphyxiation: $CO_2$ is sometimes used to euthanize birds which are captured by hand or in live traps and when relocation is not a feasible option. Live birds are placed in a container such as a plastic 5-gallon bucket or chamber and sealed shut. $CO_2$ gas is released into the bucket or chamber and birds quickly die after inhaling the gas.[35]

WS also regulates the bodies of Canada geese that have been euthanized. Records must be kept and states must report the following: what individuals killed the geese; how many days the program took; the total number of geese killed. In addition, states that issue permits to kill resident Canada geese must monitor breeding populations.[36] Neither dead geese nor their feathers may be sold, but if they are killed without the use of poisons, they "may be processed for human consumption and donated to charitable organizations," although the cost for each goose so processed is eighteen to twenty-five dollars.[37]

ws's management of resident Canada geese in twenty-first-century America, then, is an extensive, detailed material practice, governed by federal and state power and enacted on the bodies of birds. If, as Timothy Luke argues, and as I discuss in chapter 3, "birding has changed into a type of govermentalizing biopolitics," then the role played by actual government bodies—that is, state and federal workers acting under the power of law—is a large one.[38] This form of contemporary avian governmentality has its roots, as Luke and others have shown, in early twentieth-century legislation that sought to conserve American wildlife. Such laws as the Migratory Bird Treaty Act of 1918 and the Federal Aid in Wildlife Restoration Act of 1937 protected species from hunting, as "federal legislation and many state houses both set up fish and wildlife services, bureaus of land management or natural resource departments to protect beleaguered species." As these services and departments came to study wildlife populations and habitats, they came to "represent a rearticulation of state sovereignty in more productive and less juridical modes of expression. . . . another marker of contemporary governmentality."[39] In other words, the early twentieth-century conservation movement depended on a regulatory system to manage wildlife. Agencies had to determine what a given species' population and habitat were, as a necessary first step in conservation. It is important to note, though, that the burgeoning conservation movement embodied by these government agencies also included the Division of Predatory Animal and Rodent Control, the forerunner of ws. Conservation was not just the preservation of populations and habitats; animals that were deemed harmful to human practices, such as birds of prey, were efficiently killed. The twentieth-century form of governmentality that came to manage wildlife was not inherently conservationist; it was primarily regulatory. Populations in danger of extinction, such as great egrets, for example, were afforded protections that were denied to, say, bald eagles. Luke argues that all of this led ornithology in a new direction, away from the collection of individual specimens for museums and toward "thinking about the range, migration, and life cycle of birds in the wild. Birdwatching remediated the workings of power into articulations of panoptic power. Binoculars replaced shotguns."[40] Watching birds became much more than a hobby, although it remained that, too. In the twentieth century bird-watching became a systematic study, of among other things, bird populations, habitats, movements, and behaviors.

In short, then, the human experiment on birds in twentieth-century America was one in which birds were brought into the realm of what Michel Foucault calls "biopolitics," meaning that their populations were subjected to specific forms of bodily management. Foucault defines biopolitics as "the endeavor, begun in the 18th century, to rationalize the problems presented to governmental practice by the phenomena characteristic of a group of living human beings constituted as a population: health, sanitation, birthrate, longevity, race."[41] The population becomes a locus of power through which political and economic forces operate. In the twenty-first century, biopolitical forces, or biopower, according to Majia Nadesan, serves "the interests of capitalist accumulation and market forces" even as it strives to create individual well-being.[42] Biopower works, as both Nadesan and Jeff Nealon note, on the level of mundane, everyday life, be it the social and technological space of daily interactions, the disciplinary space of school or the workplace, or the space of what Nealon calls "the subject's very relation to itself."[43] Foucault writes of "technologies of the self" that ask: "What should one do with oneself? What work should be carried out on the self?[44] Through this lens, humans are seen as self-normalizing beings. Biopolitics, through biopower, regulates historically specific ways of being in the world, so that, for example, contemporary subjects who have marketability and value within a capitalist framework are able to thrive.

While Foucault was explicitly writing of human populations, I want to extend his analysis to the avian world. Ornithologists, birdwatchers, governmental organizations, and nongovernmental nature and conservation groups have measured the population, habitat, and habits of every bird species that lives in America; they have established a monetary value for specific species (whether this value is positive in the case of birds and ecotourism or negative in the case of nuisance species is beside the point) and for birds in general. In short, humans have brought birds into the realm of biopolitics. Birds are managed in ways that focus on the health and economic value of individual species. Whether through experiments on blue jays or through an establishment of the monetary value of endangered *rufa* red knots, humans have profoundly altered the daily life of birds in multiple ways. Wildlife Services' intensive management of resident Canada geese exemplifies the force of biopolitical power acting on a population, but so do conservation efforts that protect endangered species. The Endangered Species Act and Wildlife Services can be seen as two sides of the same coin, both working to ensure that no population gets too small and that none gets too large, within the framework of twenty-first-century capitalism that insists on fixing an economic value on bird populations. *Rufa* red knots get protected; resident Canada geese get killed, and the balance sheet gets worked out.

Or does it? The *rufa* red knot is still endangered, and resident Canada goose populations have not diminished. In short, the biopolitical management of the avian world may never be able to reach the kind of economic, social, and biological balance that it seeks. Birds, of course, do not practice technologies of the self in the same ways that humans do. Humans attempt to manage birds; birds do not consciously resist per se, but the material fact of their existence shows that human attempts at population control do not always work. In a way, then, resident Canada goose populations are a form of resistance to human-created management plans.

In a biopolitical context, resident Canada geese have come to occupy the space of what Nadesan calls "bad subjects" who are "incapable of self-government."[45] Resident Canada geese, with their out-of-control populations and their negative contributions to (human) public health and safety, certainly do seem to be "bad" for humans. Canada geese, of course, cannot be said to be capable of self-regulation in any human sense of the word. That is, no evidence exists that nonmigratory Canada geese are making a "rational" choice to stay in park-like settings that provide abundant food and safe habitat. Nonetheless, the very fact that resident Canada geese have become subject to human governmentality shows that their behavior has been successful from a species perspective, as their reproductive rates have climbed. The question of any kind of goose motivation is irrelevant to the fact that humans have clearly brought these birds into the realm of contemporary biopolitics. Nadesan writes that "bad" subjects "are subject to more repressive authorities and/or interventions" precisely because they have failed at self-government.[46] Biopolitical humans must do what the geese themselves have not—decrease the surplus population.

For Nadesan, the ways that "bad" subjects become normalized is revealing. For her, contemporary governmentalities offer happiness and liberty to subjects, "but offer limited vocabularies and technologies of government for addressing people, events, and phenomena rupturing liberal fantasies." Further, Nadesan notes that "the matter remains as to whether they are flexible and responsive enough to represent and address threatened, marginalized, exploited, or alienated forms of life."[47] Nadesan's focuses here on the human realm and ways that "racialized" identities can lead to exploitation and alienation, but her argument, I hold, can be applied to the world of birds (and other nonhuman beings). In a sense, then, a "bad" subject can be compared to a "nuisance" species. Subjects who pose a threat to a certain market-based liberal order face disciplinary forms of normalization such as surveillance and incarceration that "normal" citizens tend to feel exempt from. Nadesan worries, though, about "liberal governmentalities' capacities to obviate totalitarian impulses and movements."[48] I wonder, in a different register, if the governmental disciplinary force brought to bear on nuisance species might point to a lesser, but still important, "rupturing" of fantasies.

In his discussion of nuisance species, Spencer Schaffner argues that "darker sentiments" are at work in "aggressive forms of avian management" that privilege "number of species," or populations, over "absolute numbers of birds," or individuals. Schaffner warns that nuisance species management strongly relies on "a belief that nuisance birds can be empirically determined."[49] While this claim might seem to have little significance to the management of resident Canada geese—numerous studies have measured their population and the problems it causes—it is worth noting that a twenty-first-century ornithologist would not even try to justify the early twentieth-century claim that "birds of prey" were ever a nuisance in any economic framework. Birds of prey have never killed livestock in numbers that would make extermination a smart economic decision. Perhaps more importantly, Schaffner argues that determinations of what bird qualifies as a nuisance often ignore historical specificity, the fact that "birds do not exist apart from their immediate habitats, just as they do not exist apart from cultural beliefs and environmental laws."[50] The decision to allow "lethal control" of resident Canada geese may seem, and indeed may be, a rational, economic decision, but it cannot help but make clear the violence that underlies human management of bird populations in the twenty-first century. Humans kill a lot of birds in the service of life. Lethal control of resident Canada geese echoes the killing of egrets that kicked the conservation movement into gear at the beginning of the twenty-first century.

In 1962's *Silent Spring*, Rachel Carson foresaw the death of birds as a seeming conservation measure. She wrote, "As the habit of killing grows—the resort to 'eradicating' any creature that may annoy or inconvenience us—birds are more and more finding themselves a direct target of poisons rather than an incidental one."[51] Carson goes on to question, "Who has made the decision that sets in motion these chains of poisonings, this ever-widening wave of death that spreads out, like ripples when a pebble is dropped into a still pond?" Carson's answer—"the decision is that of the authoritarian temporarily entrusted with power; he has made it during a moment of inattention by millions to whom beauty and the ordered world of nature still have a meaning that is deep and imperative"—seems dated, though.[52] The plan to allow lethal control of resident Canada geese was neither made by an authoritarian government nor was it made in secret, "during a moment of inattention." As I discuss above, nearly three thousand public comments were heard before the decision was made. Public documents regarding every aspect of the decision are readily available, and, indeed, ws prides itself on "delivering programs with transparency and accountability" in multiple ways, including using advisory committees made up of "individuals from a broad spectrum of agricultural, environmental, conservation, academic, animal welfare, and related interest groups who meet annually in an open public forum to discuss the direction of the ws program"; adhering to the National Environmental Policy Act, which mandates a consideration of not only scientific viewpoints, but also such things as "aesthetics and religious views"; abiding by the Freedom of Information Act; and publishing "commonly requested program information."[53] With a bit of research, anyone with a computer and Internet access can find out what ws does. And indeed, even as Wildlife Services acts with transparency, they have met with resistance.

Public Employees for Environmental Responsibility (PEER) is a nonprofit "national alliance of local state and federal resource professionals" who "speak out about issues concerning natural resource management and environmental protection." As a self-described "'watch dog' for the public interest," PEER publicizes environmental decisions that might be unknown to the general public; it also works to protect whistleblowers within government who speak out about environmental policy. PEER has ongoing campaigns related to "wildlife protection, public lands, public health, whistleblowers/integrity, [and] land use and sprawl."[54]

PEER has spoken out against Wildlife Services, arguing that its actions are dangerous and unnecessary. Ninety percent of all ws exterminations employ poisons; PEER notes that "non-target" species are often killed in the process. When poison is used to control starlings in cattle feedlots, it often kills owls, hawks, raccoons, and cats as well.[55] In addition, PEER has sought to publicize what it views as a national security issue in how ws uses and keeps tracks of toxins. "One big concern is the bio-terror threat from lethal chemical agents, such as sodium cyanide and aluminum phosphate, deployed across the country by ws as bait, in fumigants, sprays, and gases. Audits of ws operations have repeatedly found violations of the Bioterrorism Preparedness and Response Act for failing to secure "dangerous biological agents and toxins" and not keeping "accurate inventories to detect theft, unauthorized sale or other losses."[56] PEER also argue that WS provides "an unjustified subsidy" to the livestock industry because "government figures show that wildlife plays an insignificant role in livestock losses." For all of these reasons, PEER has campaigned to eliminate WS, asking concerned citizens to ask Congress to "zero out" WS's budget.[57]

While PEER advocates the elimination of WS itself, other groups have focused their protests specifically on the "lethal control" of resident Canada geese. Both the Humane Society of the United States and GeesePeace have worked to find nonlethal alternatives to reduce goose populations. GeesePeace is a community-training organization that seeks to "resolve conflicts with Canada geese, economically, humanely and without controversy." The GeesePeace program is quite similar to WS's recommendations, except that GeesePeace does not advocate killing resident Canada geese. Rather, they advocate for community or regional practices of egg and nest destruction, habitat alteration, site aversion, and "no-feeding" rules. Within three years, GeesePeace argues, these practices will result in a dramatically reduced population of resident geese that "will be a positive addition to the natural areas" they live in.[58] GeesePeace's current "60 Mile Tri-State Regional Canada Geese Populations Stabilization Project" seeks to nonlethally manage resident Canada geese in a section of Connecticut, New York, and New Jersey where populations are high.[59]

Like GeesePeace, the Humane Society of the United States (HSUS) advocates the same methods of population stabilization as WS, except for "lethal control." In "Canada Geese: Living with our Wild Neighbors in Urban and Suburban Communities," HSUS "objects to killing wild animals simply because they are regarded as nuisances."[60] David Feld, the national program director of GeesePeace, notes that conflict over the ethics of killing nuisance animals is at the root of his organization. When asked why he started GeesePeace, he said, "My community had a problem with Canada geese. Some people wanted to kill the geese, others did not."[61] HSUS and GP, then, function as what Nadesan calls "biopolitical authorities" who "are often called upon to shepherd risky subjects by teaching them preferred technologies of self-government."[62]

Instead of killing resident geese, GeesePeace seeks an alternative kind of self-government, attempting to teach resident geese new ways of life. Resident Canada geese who are subject to GP's practices for a few years "will have learned that the area where they were born is not a good place to nest or molt."[63] From GP's perspective, resident Canada geese should not be killed precisely because they can learn to live within a human framework; they can be taught to escape the position of bad subject or nuisance species.

It is widely agreed that resident Canada geese cause economic, safety, and aesthetic problems for humans. All management practices short of "lethal control" seem to be noncontroversial. The efficacy of these management practices remains in question, as resident Canada goose populations do not seem to shrinking. Instead of asking which management plan is most effective, and whether extermination is an ethical choice, I want to pose a different, perhaps broader, definitely Foucauldian question: What does it cost to live in a world that produces, and kills, large populations of resident Canada geese?

## THE COST OF RESIDENT CANADA GEESE

When I ask that question I want to emphasize that "cost" does not just mean monetary value. The negative monetary value of resident Canada geese is relatively easy to determine, as I discuss above. And their positive monetary value seems negligible at best. No one will travel to see resident Canada geese; such birds have no ecotourism value. "Cost," instead, following Nealon's reading of Foucault, can be defined more broadly as a measurement of the social effects of all the practices that have led to the production of resident Canada goose populations. At the beginning of *Foucault beyond Foucault*, Nealon establishes his focus "on a question that Foucault consistently asks about any given practice or theory: What does it cost?"[64] For Nealon this question is a diagnostic one because of Foucault's "consistent emphasis on social effects," on the way that subjects and practices work together to produce specific ways of life.[65] For example, Foucault analyzed how one might become an object of knowledge "as a madman, a patient, or a delinquent, through practices such as those of psychiatry, clinical medicine, and penalty."[66] Foucault's analysis of what he calls the "rather privileged case" of sex and sexuality in the nineteenth century is a prime example of how he probes the cost of subjectivity.[67] Foucault writes about how, through Christianity, "individuals were all called on to recognize themselves as subjects of pleasure, of desire, of lust, of temptation and were urged to deploy, by various means (self-examination, spiritual exercises, admission, confession), the game of true and false in regard to themselves and what constitutes the most secret, the most individual part of their subjectivity."[68] The self became its own object of knowledge, and sex and sexuality became ways of delineating a range of normative subjectivities that accounted for a wide variety of sexual practices.

The question of cost, then, asks how the range of subjectivities—nuisance species, administrator charged with killing resident geese, GeesePeace member, for example—produced by a set of practices enacts specific ways of life. For Foucault figuring out these costs is an extensive project, as one must understand the condition of possibilities for subject positions within a specific political economy. "The problem is to determine what the subject must be, to what condition he is subject, what status he must have, what position he must occupy in reality or in the imaginary, in order to become a legitimate subject of this or that type of knowledge."[69] Nealon writes, "Cost enacts or dramatizes the effects of social compulsion and their imbrication with individual desires."[70] Answering "what does it cost?" is a means of analyzing the interplay between individual motivations and social formations, even as the very definition of what can count as an individual or as a social formation is in play. Nealon writes that cost "is necessarily decided by a hazardous and discontinuous set of practices, a series of interactions with something or someone else."[71] Analyzing cost becomes useful for my purposes as it provides a way of thinking about the "series of interactions" between humans and Canada geese that has led to the present "problem" of overabundant resident Canada geese.

Understanding why the goose population is so high today requires what Foucault calls a "general history within which one could describe the singularity of practices, the play of their relations, the form of their dependencies."[72] That is, it is important to note that goose populations are not just natural facts. They are the product of a specific set of historical practices, even as these practices did not foresee the population explosion. The roots of the current "problem," then, are firmly ground in the conservation "success" of programs begun in the middle of the twentieth century to increase Canada goose populations. Early in the twentieth century, many naturalists thought the Canada goose was on the verge of extinction due to overhunting. A 2000 study of goose populations prepared by the Central Flyway Council, "Large Canada Geese in the Central Flyway: Management of Depredation, Nuisance, and Human Health and Safety Issues," cites a 1927 report that predicted the extinction of Canada geese within twenty to twenty-five years.[73] The Flyway report notes that Canada geese were worth $8.86 a piece (in 1998 dollars) "on the Eastern game markets" in the first decades of the twentieth century. But, as I discuss above, conservation measures in the middle decades of the twentieth century were incredibly successful, and goose populations were restored. The Flyway Council report notes that "Canada geese and their restoration were important topics across North America" starting in the 1960s, suggesting that goose restoration was part of the burgeoning environmental movement of the times. So how did this conservation success turn into the current problem of overabundance?[74]

According to U.S. Fish and Wildlife Service, a "number of factors" are involved. "Key among them is that most resident Canada geese live in temperate climates with relatively stable breeding habitat conditions. They tolerate human and other disturbances, have a relative abundance of habitat such as mowed grass and waterways, and fly short distances for winter compared with migratory Canada goose populations. The absence of waterfowl hunting and natural predators in urban areas has also contributed to perpetuating overabundance."[75] While this explanation is no doubt true, it does exclude one key historical fact: nonresident Canada geese are a direct result of the conservation measures that led to the recovery of goose populations. In other words, goose conservation led directly to goose overabundance. While Fish and Wildlife gloss over this connection, both HSUS and GP emphasize the human-created aspect of the overpopulation problem, perhaps to show that humans are responsible for finding a humane solution.

David Feld calls the events leading to the current resident goose population "one of the greatest cases of mismanagement by wildlife agencies (federal and state) in America." He argues that the reintroduction programs of the 1960s failed to consider that these geese would not learn to migrate, and that they would thrive because of the temperate climate and ideal habitat. He says, "It's not the geese's fault. By nature they return to the place where they were born to build their own nests."[76] By obvious implication, "fault" lies not with the geese, but with the wildlife managers who did not anticipate the results of their reintroduction programs. HSUS notes that as resident, reintroduced geese flocks expanded, "conflicts reached a point where the same state and federal agencies that had propagated Canada geese called for killing them."[77] A focus on this specific history—that is, on the fact that geese populations expanded well beyond what was anticipated by wildlife managers—emphasizes the idea that even strict regulation cannot control fluctuations in bird populations. C. Davison Ankney, in his 1996 article, "An Embarrassment of Riches: Too Many Geese," states that the population growth is not "well understood" by hunters, biologists, and managers, precisely because "most training in waterfowl ecology and management in North America is formulated from the (implicit) premise that waterfowl abundance and large 'harvestable surpluses' are the ultimate goals."[78] Ankney notes the historical rationale for this premise, namely that wildlife biologists worked through the twentieth century to counteract a steady decline in populations due to overhunting. He then argues that it is time to change this policy. "Overall, this approach has served us well in the 20th century as we have dug ourselves out of the hole created by gross overharvests in the 19th century. North American goose populations truly are one of the natural wonders of the world. Equally true, however, is that some of these populations are biologically and/or esthetically and/or economically, overpopulations."[79] Even as he writes that the overpopulation problem is "human-caused, albeit unintentional and indirect," Ankney realizes that his proposed solution of increased harvests might seem "heretical to many," especially as he advocates for hunting techniques such as the use of live decoys that led to population crashes in the first place. Ankney argues that these practices were not originally banned as a matter of ethics, but simply because they were too effective, "and that effectiveness is certainly in order now."[80]

While Ankney's proposed solutions differ quite a bit from those of GeesePeace and HSUS, they all call attention to the historical specificity of the overpopulation problem. In showing that public policy—or governmentality, to use the more Foucauldian term—led to both a crash and a surplus in population, this sort of history makes it clear that there is nothing natural about fluctuating goose numbers in nineteenth-, twentieth-, and twenty-first-century America. Canada geese have long been subject to human management on a scale that directly affects their overall population and distribution. Whether further management can stabilize populations is an open question, but this is not to imply that management is unnecessary or fruitless. In fact, it seems impossible to even imagine an unregulated population of birds. It does seem clear, though, that as long as there are urban and suburban parks that produce ideal habitat, there will be an abundance of resident Canada geese. Likewise, determining the "right" amount of geese, and then reaching that number, seems quite difficult. The naming and managing of "nuisance" species is always in flux. Just as perceptions of the bald eagle could change from nuisance to national symbol, perceptions of the Canada goose have changed from the nineteenth to the twenty-first century. Behaviors championed by nineteenth-century naturalists have become symptoms of nuisance behavior for goose managers.

For John James Audubon, the Canada goose was a paragon of domesticity and romantic love. Audubon observed that Canada geese form long-term pair bonds as he described the "love and mutual affection" that he saw in mated pairs. Watching a mated pair after the male fought off a rival, Audubon wrote of their courtship ritual: "Now he is close to her who in his eyes is all loveliness; his neck bending gracefully in all directions, passes all round her, and occasionally touches her body; and as she congratulates him on his victory, and acknowledges his affection, they move their necks in a hundred curious ways."[81] Audubon saw males as bravely fighting off rivals "with all the energy of rage"; once nesting has occurred, the male becomes a vigilant guard, chasing off all threats. "Should he spy a raccoon making its way among the grass, he walks up to him undauntedly, hurls a vigorous blow at him, and drives him instantly away." If the male suspects a more serious threat, "he urges his mate to fly off, and resolutely remains near the nest until he is assured of her safety."[82] Like I note in my discussion of Audubon in chapter 1, his nineteenth-century romantic terms often obscured keen scientific observations. For all Audubon's talk of rage, joy, bravery, and love, he aptly described the courtship behavior, pair bonding, and family formations of Canada geese. In fact, the ritual I cite above is now called the "Triumph Ceremony" and understood as "a central behavior in Canada Goose social organization, as it secures family and pair bonds, the dominant units in a complex social organization"; the *Birds of North America Online* entry for Canada geese further notes that the ceremony was "described as courtship by Audubon." Audubon's assertions about the strength of pair and family bonds have ample scientific backing.[83]

These bonding behaviors championed by Audubon play a key role in the Canada goose's designation as a nuisance species today. Geese that find a suitable nesting site will teach their young fidelity to the same site. If parent geese do not migrate from an ideal site, neither will their offspring. Likewise, egg treatment (oiling, puncturing, or addling) is seen as an effective means of population reduction precisely because resident Canada geese will protect their eggs and nests throughout the breeding season; if eggs are removed, most geese will simply re-nest. But the nest defense that Audubon portrays as heroic—"Nay I doubt if man himself, if unarmed, would come off unscathed in such an encounter"—becomes something different when viewed from the perspective of those attempting to treat eggs.[84] Wildlife Services recommends that egg addling always be done by teams of two, because geese "often attack viciously" when approached at their nest. WS goes on to note that "some individuals experienced in treating goose nests use a life jacket, boat paddle, or trash can lid to deflect goose attacks at nest sites."[85] In short, goose behavior, at least in terms of familial bonding and nest defense, has not changed since Audubon's time. Human reactions to goose behavior have changed, as humans have manipulated both habitat and goose populations over the past two hundred years.

One can find the seeds of the early twentieth-century population decline of Canada geese in writers like Audubon and Thoreau, even as there were no scientific measurements of geese at the time. In 1852 Thoreau wrote of the migratory flocks that he observed: "How many there must be, that one or more flocks are seen to go over almost every farm in New England in the spring!"[86] Audubon writes of the "immense flocks" he saw every winter in Kentucky, even as he postulates from anecdotal evidence gathered from "many old and respectable citizens of our country" that a population decline has already begun by the 1830s. Even as he observes the large winter populations of Canada geese along the Missouri and Mississippi Rivers, he notes that the bird's breeding grounds have shrunk. "It seems to me more than probable, that the species bred abundantly in the temperate parts of North America before the white population extended over them." While Audubon was never familiar with the concept of overhunting, he did write of a group of geese getting ready "to fly away from their greatest enemy[:] man."[87]

Likewise, Thoreau wrote of geese traveling north, that "each flock runs the gauntlet of a thousand gunners. . . . The echo of one gun hardly dies away before they see another pointed at them."[88] Audubon writes of a man who killed dozens of geese at a time "by means of a small cannon heavily charged with rifle bullets"; he describes shooting geese with a friend over the course of a day "until the number of geese obtained would seem to you so very large that I shall not specify it."[89] But, as Audubon notes, these episodes barely compare to the goose hunting on the East Coast, where geese were shot "with the prospect of pecuniary gain" using "wooden geese" and "actual birds" as decoys. Such a method led hunters to "destroy an immense number of them, by using extremely long guns."[90] Hunting with live decoys was banned in the 1930s because it was seen as a direct cause of population decline; this ban, in turn, led to other management decisions that then helped create the overpopulation of contemporary resident Canada geese. In short, then, Canada geese have been subject to human management—through capitalism, biopower, and governmentality—on a scale large enough to substantially alter their populations, since at least the nineteenth century.

This is not to say that nineteenth-century governmentality is even remotely similar to today's practices. The Central Flyway Council, which "placed a high priority on Canada Goose management," was not formed until 1948.[91] And while some population measurements from the 1950s are available, accurate and detailed assessments were not taken until the early 1970s.[92] Harold C. Hanson, in his *The Giant Canada Goose*, published in 1965, claimed that "only in the past two years has our knowledge of the taxonomy and distribution of Canada geese begun to coincide with reality."[93] Yet even before the intensive management practices of our contemporary world were instituted, humans were continually experimenting with Canada geese. Audubon himself details one such "experiment" that he performed on a group of Canada geese. Audubon, of course, often conducted experiments on bird populations that today seem unscientific and perhaps even barbaric, such as his attempt to introduce twenty-five blue jays from the American South to Great Britain (see chapter 1) that resulted in the death of all but one bird. Regarding Canada geese, Audubon writes of a particularly brave gander, who violently attacked Audubon numerous times when Audubon approached the bird's nest, mate, and gosling. After one attack Audubon thought that his arm might be broken. In response to this "defiance," Audubon decided to capture the bird, as he explained, "always intent on making experiments, I thought of endeavouring to conciliate this bold son of the waters."[94] At first Audubon only attempts to get closer to the birds by feeding them corn. After a week or so, the geese got used to his attention, allowing him to approach to within a few feet, but no closer. Audubon then baited a trap and captured, in turn, the male, the goslings, and the female.

He pinioned each bird so they could not fly away, and then "turned them loose in my garden, where I had a small but convenient artificial pond." He kept the birds and grew fond of them. "I found them useful in clearing the garden of slugs and snails; and although they now and then nipped the vegetables, I liked their company."[95] Audubon draws no wider conclusion from this "experiment," and he unceremoniously gave the geese away three years later. In a brief discussion on the possibilities of domesticating the Canada goose, Audubon wrote of another bird who was raised by humans, describing how "this goose was so gentle that she would suffer any person to caress her, and would readily feed from the hand." Clearly, Audubon was aware of how Canada geese living in proximity to humans could become tame. He even noted that the human-raised goose "at the period of migration . . . shewed by her movements less desire to fly off than any other I have known." (Audubon does not, of course, foresee how losing both the fear of humans and the inclination to migrate would lead to our contemporary overpopulation problem. Instead, he notes that domestication of birds such as Canada geese might "prove useful to mankind."[96]) The Canada goose had multiple uses for Audubon. Domesticated, they served the role of a companion; they demonstrated bravery and fidelity. Perhaps most importantly, they made for good game birds. Even as he found admirable traits in the birds, Audubon did not hesitate to claim that their primary importance was in their use for humans. He concludes his chapter on Canada geese with just such a thought. "Every portion of it is useful to man, for besides the value of the flesh as an article of food, the feathers, the quills, and the fat, are held in request. The eggs also afford very good eating."[97] For Audubon, then, it does not cost humans anything to use Canada geese in this way. While he notes the possibility of a slight population decline, conservation is simply not an issue at this time. Canada geese are one more resource to be used by man for his own purposes. The period of overhunting from the middle of the nineteenth century into the early twentieth century shows that conservation, followed by worries about overpopulation, would not be concerns for a long time.

Another experiment, conducted by the biologist Bernd Heinrich at the beginning of the twenty-first century, can help to show how management of goose populations, combined with more recent scientific and conservationist values, has led to a different understanding of the

Canada goose. Heinrich spent the summer of 1998, and some time over the next three years, observing and interacting with a group of Canada geese. His experiment was much less invasive then Audubon's; Heinrich neither trapped nor pinioned any birds. Instead, he took an ethological approach, as he attempted to understand goose behavior within their environment. Heinrich notes that his "experiment" is not "hard science" as it is purely made up of his own "very specific, often singular, observations."[98] In places, Heinrich's observations differ little from Audubon's. He watches geese form pair bonds, protect nests, and raise young. He writes about how it took time and patience before he could approach a nest, just as it did for Audubon.[99] Once the geese acclimated to him, though, Heinrich's experiment departs from Audubon's.

Heinrich forms an emotional connection to the geese he is observing, even as he writes, "I did not suspect I could have felt much emotion for a goose."[100] He grounds his emotional connection in the notion of individuality. He names the geese he observes, "not only in order to make it easier to remember them as individuals, but also because they reacted to each other as individuals themselves."[101] As the story continues, it becomes clear that Heinrich sees the geese reacting as individuals to him. That is, he views his strong bond with "Peep," the goose he writes most about, as reciprocal, as a form of mutual recognition. After calling her name one day, he notes that Peep walked toward him so that "as she got closer I heard the barely audible, throaty sound that she always made when she was at ease and comfortable and 'in contact.'"[102] Heinrich places this bond in a biological context, noting that "so-called biological rules are the sum of individual cases, and an observer of individual cases can be treated to surprising, anomalous observations." Thus, for Heinrich, naming the geese and interacting with them on an individual level serve to demonstrate the genetic uniqueness and behavior variability of every member of a species.[103]

In exploring his bond with Peep and the other geese, Heinrich focuses on the behavioral and emotional similarity between geese and humans. As both "have evolved similar social systems for long-term bonding to mates and young," Heinrich suggests that "we may therefore have similar standards of behavior."[104] Likewise, he emphasizes that geese may be driven by emotions quite similar to human emotions. He writes, "The behaviors that drive nutritional balance, reproductive success, and so on are probably driven by emotions in geese that are not alien to us and vice versa." While noting that consciousness "differs greatly" between humans and geese, Heinrich dwells more on the emotional similarities between humans and geese.[105] In fact, the emotional bond that he forms with geese becomes perhaps the most valuable aspect of his experiment, because it allows him to forge a strong connection with a hitherto unknown species. Watching flocks of geese fly over, he realizes that his interaction with Peep and others "was as if I had been to a foreign land and had made a link through it to one of its inhabitants. I could now experience through them what previously I could not perceive."[106] This emotional connection, rooted for Heinrich in evolutionary continuity, allows him to conclude that the relationship he shared with Peep should be called "friendship."[107]

Heinrich's main text ends on that very word, and he pays very little attention to our current overpopulation of resident Canada geese. In an appendix called "Canada Goose Populations," though, he provides a capsule history of the events that have led to the current population levels. Heinrich does not outright reject "lethal control" of these populations, but he does, like GeesePeace and HSUS, acknowledge that the resident goose populations "exist largely because of recent human agency."[108] Likewise, Heinrich emphasizes that wide-scale extermination comes with its own costs. For him, if geese are seen simply as an expendable commodity, a strong human connection to the natural world might be lost. He writes that the Canada goose, precisely because of its proximity to humans, is "an ideal representative through which people of all ages can experience a close relationship with wildlife, and perhaps reestablish their psychological and physical roots in nature."[109] He continues, "The more ways we have and the more different kinds of interests and needs we can engage, the more we will try to maintain vigorous animal populations, and thus the beaver bogs that support them."[110] In other words, Canada geese can become a means of understanding the value of populations within ecosystems. Such an understanding might in turn lead to conservation of habitat. Thriving wild populations of Canada geese might then help humans to form a strong bond with the natural world. Highlighting the similarities between humans and geese, such as the propensity to form long-term familial bonds, might lead to an understanding of how evolutionary biology shapes the behavior of all species. Humans and geese might then be seen as reflecting each other's behaviors in a mutual relationship that one might indeed call "friendship."

While not embracing this notion of interspecies friendship, Diane P. Michelfelder, in her "Valuing Wildlife Populations within Urban Environments," argues that a sense of community should form the basis of human relations with resident Canada geese and other urban wildlife. Michelfelder questions a court ruling that allowed lethal control of a flock of Canada geese in downtown Seattle: "On what basis could it be determined that this is or is not an ethical management solution? How can human population-wildlife population be resolved in a moral manner when they do arise?"[111] The short answer, for Michelfelder, is that ethics depends on community. That is, Michelfelder argues that humans and nonhumans sharing a "space, time, and a place" make up a community of living beings whose needs should all be accommodated as they interact.[112] She writes, "Wildlife that inhabit and have found a home in urban settings are our nonhuman neighbors. As a result we have a moral obligation to respond to them accordingly and treat them as the neighbors they are."[113] This obligation involves welcoming bio-diversity within cities and managing habitat so that both humans and geese can interact without conflict. Michelfelder's essay uses Canada geese as one example of urban wildlife among others including foxes and moose. But, like others who call for nonlethal means of control of resident geese, Michelfelder asserts that we must "accept that we have created the environment in which geese find their home." This, in turn, makes "us participants in a larger community with them, [so that] we ought not to translocate them, deceive them, or eliminate them from public view and the place they have made their home."[114] In creating the mutual spaces of habitation that are city parks and golf courses, humans should accept that geese will use these areas.

The key for Michelfelder is embracing this notion of community by creating "social spaces" of interaction.[115] The cost of lethal control, from this perspective, is nothing less than the loss of interspecies community in a specific time (the present) and place (wherever geese and humans interact).

## HUMANS, GEESE, AND GOVERNMENTALITY

The possibility of friendship and community between humans and Canada geese is a compelling argument against the use of lethal control. At the same time, I think that too strong of a focus on interspecies friendship and community can obscure the biopolitical and governmental connections that must exist before these things can become possible. Both friendship and community rely on a certain sense of welcoming the other, of embracing those who are different. I want to emphasize, instead, that biopolitical management of Canada geese has already accounted for any sort of radical difference geese might have from humans. Both humans and Canada geese are subjects of/ to governmentality; that is, both species are already quite similar in this regard.

Michelfelder's vision of a "multispecies society" of humans and nonhumans occupying urban spaces and Heinrich's notion that he had befriended an "inhabitant" of a foreign land both speak to a welcoming of otherness in which humans reach out across the species border to form a new community. My claim is that such a reaching out is only possible from within the realm of biopolitical governmentality. Nadesan writes that biopower works by "eliciting and optimizing the life forces of a state's population, maximizing their capacity as human resources and their utility for market capitalization."[116] One of the ways that this "eliciting and optimizing" might work is through the formation of friendship and community. That is, the human work of befriending geese can be seen as a means of rescuing geese from the realm of "bad subject" or "nuisance species." Such a rehabilitation can only happen if resident Canada geese become knowable in an intimate way. The governing of Canada geese of course entails all of the regulations and management practices that I have been discussing in this chapter, but more is involved. In his essay "Governmentality," Foucault writes that "the finality of government resides in the things it manages, and in the pursuit of the perfection and intensification of the processes which it directs; and the instruments of government, instead of being laws, now come to be a range of multiform tactics."[117] To be truly effective, governmentality must be internalized by all involved. Laws are a necessity—Canada geese and those who interact with them are subject to such things as the Migratory Bird Treaty Act and the rules of Wildlife Services. But resistance to those laws is also a key component of governmentality. That is, those who seek to protect resident Canada geese from lethal control, those who say geese should be left alone, and those who seek to befriend geese are all aspects of the "multiform tactics" of biopolitical power. Every living being involved in the resident Canada goose "problem" exists within the field of governmentality. Living within the realm of biopolitical power unites humans and geese.

What purpose might this biopolitical community serve? Whose interests are served by regulating resident Canada geese? These questions are difficult to answer. While the management of resident Canada geese seeks to regulate a "safe" population of geese, no larger motives seem to be at work. The kind of power at work here has no distinct ultimate goal precisely because biopolitical power is decentralized. Nealon writes that power for Foucault is "a series of local, sometimes crazy (but still rational, all-too-rational) schemas, deployed almost blindly, certainly experimentally, with no central organized principle."[118] No one person or government organization rules over Canada geese. Likewise, power does not flow in the same way through the human and nonhuman world. Most human understandings of resident Canada geese have their basis in a straightforward rationality, be it the mitigation of risk that underlies the argument for lethal control, or the multispecies ethics that champions living peacefully with resident geese. But it would be difficult to claim that resident geese themselves proceed from the same kind of rationality. Their biological desires—to inhabit "safe" park-like areas, to reproduce and live in those same areas—drive them toward certain behaviors. Resident Canada geese are subject to a whole set of laws and ways of being that they have no say in.

Resident Canada geese do not make a choice to become a nuisance species. Instead, they become subject to what Foucault calls "a whole series of governmental apparatuses" that regulate their behavior, and thus their population. But resident geese also get placed within what Foucault calls "a whole complex of *savoirs*" or knowledges.[119] Resident Canada geese exist, in part, because of the intensive management practices put into place by federal and state agencies starting in the 1930s. The study of goose biology and behavior and the scientific measurement of goose populations are among the conditions of possibility for the "bad" subject position that resident Canada geese occupy. But the intensive management of Canada geese is just one example of biopower's grasp on avian and human life. Birds and humans have value within the realm of twenty-first-century governmentality, whether that value is as bad subject defining the norm, as government agent reducing risks for citizens, or as ethical person working to protect geese. Humans and Canada geese, then, are both subject to a centuries-long experiment whose results are not yet clear. What is clear is that both species are entangled in our late capitalist framework of governmentality.

If the previous chapter shows how conservation management must rely on the framework of economic value to protect a diminishing population, I hope to have shown in this chapter that the management of overpopulation relies on a similar framework. In the next chapter I will look more closely at just how the desire to classify birds underlies human-avian interactions.

# 5 Confusion and Classification

·····························································································

## The Black-Crested Titmouse or Tufted Titmouse

OCTOBER 24, 2003: HORNSBY BEND, TEXAS

*Peter-peter-peter. A titmouse is calling. But which species? Tufted? Black-crested? A year ago, before the split, the question would have been: which subspecies? But now, black-crested has been granted species status, and I am in its range in central Texas. But I can't see the bird. I hear it, but it keeps eluding the sight lines of my binoculars. I've seen plenty of tufteds on the East Coast, so I want this one to have the telltale black crest. But I can't see the bird. I keep looking and looking but eventually I give up. I have a good list of new species—crested caracara, black-bellied whistling duck, eared grebe, American avocet, great-tailed grackle, scissor-tailed flycatcher—but I just can't be sure which titmouse I heard.*

FEBRUARY 5, 2013: DES MOINES, IOWA

*Which titmouse was that ten years ago? The map on eBird shows black-crested titmice near Hornsby Bend. Can I use this information to identify my bird from ten years ago as a black-crested? Maybe I should do a bit more research. "The Birds of Hornsby Bend" checklist online only lists tufted titmouse, but the checklist hasn't been updated since July 2000, before the split. What about the "recent sightings"? Click on that link. There are a bunch of recent sightings. On a long list from January 22, 2013, I find this: "Tufted/ Black-crested Titmouse 6." Scanning the past couple of years of*

*lists, that's what they all say: "tufted/black-crested." Hornsby Bend*
*must be in the hybridization zone. Just to be safe, I do an image*
*search for "Hornsby Bend titmouse." I find someone's photoblog,*
*with a close-up of an intergrade titmouse, with a "slightly darker*
*crest"[1] that is clearly neither the pure black of the black-crested or*
*the gray of the tufted. The titmouse I heard was probably a hybrid,*
*and thus, uncountable on my species life list, which doesn't make*
*room for a bird that fits between two species.*

## SPLITTING AND LUMPING

Among other changes, the thirty-third supplement to the American Ornithologists' Union's (AOU) checklist announced "*Parus atricristatus* is considered conspecific with *Parus bicolor* .... The English name for the combined species becomes Tufted Titmouse, with 'Black-crested Titmouse' remaining available for the *atricristatus* group."[2] In other words, as of 1976, tufted titmouse and black-crested titmouse were "lumped," as new evidence led to the conclusion that what had previously been thought to be two species was in fact one. Keith L. Dixon, the preeminent black-crested titmouse expert, explained that "despite their conspicuous morphologic differences, black-crested and tufted titmice interbreed freely in those restricted areas of central Texas where populations are in contact." Because of this interbreeding, Dixon concluded that the birds were conspecific—that is, one species; his claim was "upheld by the American Ornithologists' Union Checklist Committee."[3]

But, as I note above, in 2002 the AOU checklist committee reversed the earlier lumping, so that *atricristatus* was again given species status in the forty-third checklist supplement. While noting that the (once-again) two species hybridize in a narrow contact zone, the checklist committee cited "a reevaluation of the nature of the hybrid zone, genetics, and vocal differences" as the grounds for their decision.[4] The checklist committee refers to numerous molecular studies of titmouse DNA in support of its conclusion. Avise and Zink used "the powerful molecular approaches of allozymes and mtDNA analysis" to illustrate the genetic distance between tufted and black-crested titmice was "of a magnitude frequently observed between some avian taxa whose status as species has not been subject to debate."[5] Likewise, Braun et al. used "electrophoretic techniques to make a preliminary estimate of molecular differentiation," and concluded that "*bicolor* and *atricristatus* have achieved differentiation more in line with species than subspecies."[6] In short, then, the molecular evidence of differentiation outweighed the fact that the two species hybridize in a limited area. In addition, genetic difference seems to have been more convincing than morphological difference, since the obvious visible differences, of which crest color is the most prominent, did not lead the checklist committee to split the species. Genotype trumps phenotype, at least in this case.

For the AOU, splitting has recently been a lot more popular than lumping, partially because of advances in molecular genetic studies. Peter Pyle has noted that the AOU has split 148 species and lumped only 9 since 1983. While acknowledging the importance of recent "molecular and audio-analytical techniques," Pyle also argues that "human opportunism" has influenced this change, as "splitting is more 'exciting' than lumping." While Pyle argues against what he calls "species-splitting mania," it is worth noting that determining exactly what counts as a species has never been easy.[7] Charles Darwin himself, in *On the Origin of Species*, wrote about this very problem, even as he saw the importance of making such distinctions. In the last pages of his book, Darwin looks toward the future of taxonomy and argues that his theory of natural selection will radically alter human's understanding of the order of life, especially when considered on the species level. He writes:

> When the views entertained in this volume on the origin of species, or when analogous views are generally admitted, we can dimly foresee that there will be a considerable revolution in natural history. Systematists will be able to pursue their labours as at present; but they will not be incessantly haunted by the shadowy doubt whether this or that form be in essence a species. This I feel sure, and I speak after experience, will be no slight relief. . . . Systematists

will have only to decide (not that this will be easy) whether any form be sufficiently constant and distinct from other forms, to be capable of definition; and if definable, whether the differences be sufficiently important to deserve a specific name.[8]

For Darwin the key point here is that species will no longer be considered immutable as special creation has it. The systematists' goal will no longer be to locate the God-given essence of a species. If species are seen as what Darwin calls "artificial combinations made for convenience," their ordering power is revealed as a scientific construct. Without an essence to worry about, the mutability of the species is paralleled by the mutability of the species concept itself. No longer is its definition a given; rather, the systematist must now decide whether these closely observed differences, rendered visible by the observer, mark a form as different enough to be labeled a species. This shift, from searching for God's plan in nature to judging the degree of difference in closely related forms, breaks up the ordered surface of nineteenth-century thought regarding life. The abandonment of the search for an essence that would reveal God's hand in the creation of a species undermined the ground that special creationists placed under all life. If God's intent no longer defines speciation, the taxonomic grid that replaces it is not much easier to render, not because it's invisible but because the grid itself is in constant flux, a surface constantly altering and mutating, changing, one might even say evolving, with new languages, thoughts, and technologies.

Darwin's parenthetical remark "(not that this will be easy)" points to this unending change. At the time of writing this sentence, Darwin could not have been aware of what an understatement he was making. With the twentieth-century synthesis of genetics and evolution, means of determining what is and what is not a species became immensely more complicated.

If one considers the multiple "species concepts" in existence today, along with the multiple methods of determining what is a species—from traditional morphology studies to the myriad ways that DNA can be analyzed (mitochondrial versus nuclear DNA, DNA barcoding, DNA-DNA hybridization), not to mention the complications that result from studying asexually reproducing microscopic life—one might reach the conclusion that no universal species concept will ever work for all of the estimated three to one hundred million species in existence. As Rohini Balakrishnan writes in "Species Concepts, Species Boundaries and Species Identification: A View from the Tropics," the philosophical debate on the validity of different species concepts is unlikely to be resolved in the near future.[9] While emphasizing the importance of the species concept for biology and conservation, Balakrishnan notes that the ways species "are delimited and identified receive scant attention."[10] He offers a history of the species concept and discusses multiple ways that "species" has been defined, from the biological species concept to more recent DNA-based analyses. While much of Balakrishnan's essay focuses on the practical and methodological problems of how to define species, I find his discussion of what he calls the "philosophical" problem equally compelling.

## THE PHILOSOPHICAL PROBLEM OF THE SPECIES CONCEPT

For Balakrishnan, the "philosophical" problem seems to be a conceptual one. That is, he wonders if any one way of defining species can delimit and identify every living thing. In looking at the problem of species identification, Balakrishnan makes a practical conclusion: a pluralistic approach should be used to define species, because of the key role that species identification plays in biodiversity conservation.[11] Yet, even as he makes this practical methodological argument, he writes that "one may even dispute the wisdom of imposing a universal species concept on philosophical or conceptual grounds alone."[12] In other words, Balakrishnan argues, it may be impossible to define a species concept that can account for all living things.

Balakrishnan seems to be using "philosophical" in the colloquial sense, to mean something to be deeply thought about but never actually resolved; from this perspective, a "philosophical debate" about the species concept would never come up with a definition of "species." Balakrishnan's comment also makes sense, though, from within the field of continental philosophy. Writers like Nietzsche, Derrida, and Deleuze and Guattari all call into question the very idea of a "universal species concept"; their reasoning, though, is certainly worth investigating.

In *What Is Philosophy?*, Deleuze and Guattari answer their titular question as follows: "Philosophy is the art of forming, inventing, and fabricating concepts."[13] A philosophical concept differs from a scientific concept in that it does not seek to delimit and order the world. They write that there "is neither constant nor variable in the concept and we no more pick out a variable species for a constant genus than we do a constant species for variable individuals."[14] In other words, a philosophical concept would not help one to form a taxonomy of life. This sort of concept would not seek to universalize from the particular, whether that particular is similarity in DNA or in morphology. Likewise, Deleuze and Guattari question the notion of identifying a species from a group of individuated beings. Instead, what they emphasize are "pure and simple *variations*" themselves. These variations are "processual, modular"; they constantly change. For these reasons, Deleuze and Guattari argue that concepts "speak" an event; a concept is a temporary grouping of parts, so that "the concept of a bird is found not in its genus or species but in the composition of its postures, colors, and songs."[15] Even as a concept, a bird is in flux, or as Deleuze and Guattari put it, "it is like the bird as event."[16] Anyone who has looked at the wide variations within a group of herring gulls, which are well-known for multiple plumage variations and for an inclination for hybridity, would be hard-pressed to disagree with this idea.

In writing about the concept, Deleuze and Guattari are indebted to Nietzsche's critique of taxonomy as thoroughly anthropomorphic. Nietzsche's critique of the species concept seems simplistic, and even unscientific, at first. He writes, "Nature knows neither forms nor concepts and hence no species, but only an 'X' which is inaccessible to us and indefinable by us."[17] For Nietzsche, denoting species is an anthropomorphic act that tells one little about the natural world. "If I create the definition of a mammal and then, having inspected a camel, declare 'Behold, a mammal,' then a truth has certainly been brought to light, but it is of limited value, by which I mean that it is anthropomorphic through and through."[18] Defining and naming species produces knowledge that only makes sense within a human-centered system of representation based in language. Such a conception, then, refers only to the ones who have created it. Taxonomy is an all-too-human way of ordering the world that, from Nietzsche's perspective, has no connection at all with "nature."

Instead, a taxonomic ordering of the world, with species as its basic unit, is one symptom of what Nietzsche sees as the fundamental human drive to create order out of sensuous experience. The primary motor of this drive is language and its reliance on metaphor, which serves to render the world as an abstraction. And it is abstraction itself that is Nietzsche's ultimate target. His critique of the species concept works as one example among others; Nietzsche attacks the notion of conceptualization itself as a problem of anthropomorphic abstraction that leads to a rational ordering of the world in man's image. Humans form concepts "within the territory of reason"; these concepts, though, do not explain the world, they obscure things through "the construction of a pyramidical order based on castes and degrees, the creation of a new world of laws, privileges, subordinations, definitions of borders [that are] . . . something firmer, more general, more familiar, more human, and hence as something regulatory and imperative."[19] Concepts such as "species" serve only to produce a world organized according to human thought. Taxonomy, then, would work in a "regulatory and imperative" way that seems to produce knowledge of the natural world. But this knowledge would really be only a reflection of a limited human perspective disguised as objective knowledge. From the regulatory perspective of the taxonomist and the bird-watcher, one could look at a small gray bird somewhere in Texas and say "that is a tufted titmouse" or "that is a black-crested titmouse," or even "that is a hybrid titmouse." From this point of view, defining the bird by its species serves multiple purposes, from understanding the phenology, or evolutionary history, of the various species of titmice, to being able to add a specific species to one's life list. From a Nietzschean perspective, though, naming the bird's species would only produce knowledge of the "purposeless and arbitrary" nature of the human intellect.[20]

Defining a bird's species, from this point of view, could be considered an act of assimilation, a means of reasserting the centrality of human thought in nature. The differences between a tufted and black-crested titmouse could be said to reside not in the birds, but within the human mind. From this perspective, the differences of plumage and body shape between the two birds become an end in themselves. It is no doubt true that the species difference between these birds points to actual biological difference as the two species fill different niches, behave differently, vocalize differently, and have genetic differences. The birds themselves, of course, "know" this difference in some way, as evidenced by the limited ways in which they hybridize. But the human bird-watcher or taxonomist has no means of experiencing this difference as the titmice experience it. As Nietzsche writes, "If each of us still had a different kind of sensuous perception, if we ourselves could only perceive things as, variously, *a bird*, a worm, or a plant does . . . none of us would ever speak of nature as something conforming to laws; rather they would take it be nothing other than a highly subjective formation."[21] Simply, and perhaps obviously, put, the human act of differentiating species does not necessarily produce any objective knowledge. It brings birds into the realm of human intellect that is limited and partial, even as it seeks to regulate and order. In *The Genealogy of Morals* Nietzsche writes, "Let us beware of the tentacles of such contradictory notions as 'pure reason,' 'absolute knowledge,' 'absolute intelligence.' All these concepts presuppose an eye such as no living being can imagine, an eye required to have no direction, to abrogate its active and interpretative powers, precisely those powers that alone make of seeing a seeing of *something*. All seeing is essentially perspective, and so is all knowing."[22] No single act of human vision can be viewed as transcendent. All seeing is a local seeing; all formulations of knowledge and values begin from specific perspectives. There is no outside, overarching perspective from which to order the natural world according to species. Thus, no "universal species concept" is possible.

Such a claim is not to imply that taxonomy is a pointless or useless endeavor. Rather, philosophy can help to show that the delimiting nature of taxonomy can cover over the variability, or difference, that underlies any species concept whatsoever. When Darwin wrote that systematists would be freed from "the shadowy doubt whether this or that form be in essence a species," he rejected the special creationist notion of immutable species. His claim, instead, that a species can be defined if it is "sufficiently constant and distinct from other forms" completely shifted the definition of what a species is.[23] Instead of being thought of as an unchanging entity, a species becomes something defined through its variability. The word "sufficiently" is key here, as it implies a changeable difference. As Tim Gough writes in his "Non-origin of Species," "We would say that in place of the thing or essence 'species' we have the phenomena of 'differences between' species."[24] Difference itself is at the origin of species. Darwinian evolution is primarily about mapping differences. Determining whether those differences are "sufficiently" different to denote a species is secondary; in this way, the danger of the species concept is that it might cover over the central role of mutable difference itself—individual variation could get erased, along with the fact that living things are constantly, if infinitesimally, changing on the molecular and morphological level. In short, from the "philosophical" perspective, the "species concept" does not describe nature at all; it delimits and categorizes at the expense of unending mutability.

All of this is not to say that taxonomy is then "false" in some way. Rejecting the species concept as natural and universal shows that, in Gough's words, that the concept has "com[e] to exist . . . by means of and within a history/temporality which at each moment has been affected (acted upon)."[25] That is, just as every living species has a history, so does the concept of species itself. Difference is at the base of life and at the base of our conceptual understanding of life. Life constantly differentiates itself, and taxonomy strives to account for this differentiation; taxonomy, though, can never define all life forms. At the same time, and obviously, taxonomy does important work. Gough notes that the species concept works as "matter for thought"; more concretely, perhaps, as I note above, Balakrishnan highlights the role of species identification in biodiversity conservation.[26] The management of both the *rufa* subspecies of the red knot and the resident Canada goose, as

I discuss in chapters 3 and 4, depends in large part on governmental practices that strongly rely on the very species concept that philosophy questions. Even more fundamentally, ornithology itself finds its roots in classification.

## FROM CLASSIFICATION TO GOVERNMENTALITY

Paul Lawrence Farber's *Discovering Birds: The Emergence of Ornithology as a Scientific Discipline, 1760–1850* shows the central role that classification played in the codification of ornithology as a biological science. Farber discusses multiple reasons why classification played such a key role in what would become nineteenth-century ornithology, but he highlights what he calls a "simple and straightforward explanation . . . the quantity of material and the quality of examination suggested, empirically, an order."[27] What naturalists did with these materials is another question. Farber argues that early nineteenth-century classification was a wide-ranging, decentralized endeavor practiced in multiple European countries using multiple methods; nonetheless, for Farber, these practitioners "shared a common rigor in method and common interest in a natural classification of birds."[28] In other words, the work being done to classify birds was anything but systematic. Farber also notes "the lack of any agreed upon philosophical foundation for a biological classification."[29] Despite the variance in ornithological classification during this time period, Farber finds many commonalities that together make a strong argument for classification as the ground of the science of ornithology.

In part because of the sheer number of specimens available to researchers and in part due to a contemporary ideology that viewed "natural history as an edifying activity revealing God's plan," early nineteenth-century naturalists believed that they could discover a natural order in nature, and specifically in birds. Through work like Georges Cuvier's systematic ordering of bird specimens, and the comparative anatomists who followed him, there emerged "the confidence that a natural system would be forthcoming."[30] Indeed, with the empirically-focused work of classification based on morphology, many naturalists of the time thought that only the "finer detail" of a classification system needed to be worked out. Farber notes that "Parisian professors" created "the serious expectation that a natural system could be attained." But just as Darwin would later warn that deciding what is and is not a species is difficult work, Farber notes that many early nineteenth-century classificationists admitted that a natural system was not "necessarily close to attainment."[31] Farber cites a nineteenth-century French naturalist who argued that a natural system was impossible "as long as one does not know all the species of birds which are distributed over the globe. Only then would one have one which left nothing to be desired, and this will be the natural system."[32] In short, a lack of knowledge of every living thing would prevent the completion of a natural order, just as a jigsaw puzzle cannot be completed if pieces are missing.

In *The Order of Things*, Michel Foucault makes a similar point about the drive to produce a systematic natural history of plants, in that every natural entity would have to be compared to every other. "Such an endless task would push the advent of natural history back into an inaccessible never-never land, unless there existed techniques that would avoid this difficulty and limit the labour of making so many comparisons."[33] A certain arbitrariness, then, would have to be a fundamental component of any ordering system. Certain attributes would have to be seen as more important than others. Foucault's analysis of Jorge Luis Borges's "The Analytical Language of John Wilkins" at the beginning of *The Order of Things* can help make this point. Foucault reads the story as a work that breaks up "all the ordered surfaces and all the planes with which we are accustomed to tame the wild profusion of existing things, and continuing long afterwards to disturb and threaten with collapse our age-old distinction between the Same and the Other."[34] The specific taxonomy through which Foucault sees this dissolution comes from, according to Borges, "a certain Chinese encyclopedia called *The Celestial Emporium of Benevolent Knowledge*" that classifies animals according to fourteen lettered criteria, including animals "a. belonging to the Emperor . . . c. included in this classification . . . j. innumerable . . . l. et cetera . . . n. from a distance look like flies."[35] According to Robert Wicks, this classification had different meanings for Borges and Foucault. "For Borges, the Chinese Encyclopedia excerpt represents, in recognition of a universe experienced by him as inscrutable, the arbitrariness of every classificatory scheme, no matter how coincident with appearances that scheme might be."[36] Foucault's understanding, again according to Wicks, has been read in two ways. "There are those who read the passage as expressing Foucault's advocacy of epistemological relativism, and there are those who interpret it more radically as an expression of Foucault's skepticism regarding the adequacy of any conceptual arrangement which aims to reflect the positive truth of things."[37] I understand Foucault's interest in the classification not so much as skepticism toward an expression of positive truth (which one can take for granted) but rather as a means of making visible what he calls the "grid" of ordering that invisibly underlies any system and situates that system within the language of a specific historical moment. Foucault asks, "According to what grid of identities, similitudes, analogies, have we become accustomed to sort out so many different and similar things?"[38] Borges's list threatens any specific way of ordering the world as it makes visible the difference between the means of ordering and "the wild profusion of existing things." For Foucault, Borges fable, as it illustrates "the exotic charm of another system of thought," brings to light "the limitation of our own, the stark impossibility of thinking that."[39] The true power of Borges's fable, then, lies not in its creation of a wholly other system of thought. Rather, the fable gives Foucault a glimpse of "the modes of being of order," the ways that societies impose order alongside the idea of order as a thing itself, "the fact, in short, that order *exists*."[40] That is, a natural order of living things, for instance, can never be natural; any order is expressed only "according to the culture and the age in question."[41] In other words, the ordering of things is context bound in a radical way; it determines what knowledge can be produced by a given culture, even as the production of knowledge shapes how things are ordered.

To bring this back to birds, Foucault's study of the classical age roughly overlaps with the early nineteenth-century period analyzed by Farber when classification led to the discipline of ornithology. While

Farber focuses on what naturalists wanted to do through classification (find a natural order), Foucault focuses on how visibility itself became a ground of knowledge formation during this time period. Writing of "the general grid of differences" that classification sought to order, Foucault argues that taxonomists created new ways of seeing and of describing what was seen.[42] In collections, such as those curated by Cuvier, Foucault writes that "creatures present themselves one beside another, their surfaces visible, grouped according to their common features, and thus already virtually analyzed, and bearers of nothing but their own individual names." From these collections, the catalogues and taxonomies created became "a new way of connecting things both to the eye and to discourse."[43] That is, natural history of the late eighteenth and early nineteenth century created knowledge of living things through putting them on a Foucauldian "grid" that itself became invisible as comparative anatomy produced visual knowledge of species difference.

On this grid, then, Foucault locates the ultimate goal of classification: "a description acceptable to everyone: confronted with the same individual entity, everyone will be able to give the same description; and inversely, given such a description everyone will be able to recognize the individual entities that correspond to it."[44] The taxonomist creates a space where differences are rendered visible; the visible can be described, dependent on agreed-upon criteria: color, feather structure, beak size, et cetera. This et cetera, of course is a problem, for two reasons. First, one would need an agreed-upon "continuous, ordered, and universal tabulation of all possible differences" among species that have been collected and thus observed.[45] Second, as Darwin and many others point out, "the number of existing species is so great that it would be impossible to deal with them all."[46] In short, a universal or natural order is by definition impossible to produce. No system can account for all difference. Nonetheless, just as Farber notes, Foucault writes that "to establish the great, unflawed table of the species, genera, and classes, natural history had to employ, criticize, and finally reconstitute at new expense a language whose condition of possibility resided precisely in this continuum."[47] Early nineteenth-century natural history, through classification, attempted to render species visible through the creation of a systematic taxonomy.

Even with the Darwinian abandonment of a search for a natural, God-given order, in the late nineteenth century a complete taxonomy remained elusive. But early nineteenth-century classification is responsible for more than just an incomplete taxonomy of birds. Foucault writes of how late nineteenth-century knowledge formation focused on questions such as "the synthesis of the diverse" and "the possibility of linking representations together, from the right name to the basis for attribution."[48] These are the kinds of questions that the emergent science of ornithology began to ask in the late nineteenth century as it examined how and why the speciation that underlies classification, but is only made visible through classification, works.

Farber shows that the work of natural scientists and comparative anatomists in the early nineteenth century laid the groundwork for the discipline of ornithology. "The tendencies noticeable between 1800 and 1820 more fully demonstrated their potential and one can legitimately speak of the discipline of ornithology."[49] Classification by definition divided the world of living beings, which led to the emergence of all zoological disciplines. In short, according to Farber, classification "defined the emergence of ornithology for the simple reason that it divided nature into large groups, and one of the largest, most interesting, and most natural is the birds."[50] The rigor of the early classificationists led directly, if slowly, to the field of contemporary ornithology. This disciplinarity, in turn, sets the stage for birds as subjects of biopower as discussed throughout this book. The long line from avian classification to governmentality is neither negative nor positive in and of itself, as I hope I have demonstrated in the previous two chapters on red knots and Canada geese. The continuing—and I want to argue, intensifying—management of birds is a kind of experiment that has material consequences for birds and biodiversity. In the next parts of this chapter, I want to look at two contemporary ways of ordering birds that would have seemed inconceivable to nineteenth-century taxonomists: DNA barcoding, and eBird.

AN ENCYCLOPEDIA OF (BIRD) LIFE?

A complete taxonomy of life seems just as impossible today as it was in the nineteenth century. Taxonomists do not even know how many species of life exist. Nonetheless, the drive to catalogue everything remains. Many scientists argue that such a key of all life would be an invaluable conservation tool. E. O. Wilson, a strong advocate for such a list, writes, "In order to render the conservation effort exact and cost-effective, complete the mapping of the world's biological diversity. Scientists have estimated that 10 percent or more of flowering plants, a majority of animals, and a huge majority of microorganisms remain undiscovered and unnamed, hence of unknown conservation status. As the map is filled in, it will evolve into a biological encyclopedia of value not only in conservation practice but also in science, industry, agriculture, and medicine. The expanded global biodiversity map will be the instrument that unites biology."[51] For Wilson, this "biological encyclopedia of value" would place all of life on Foucault's grid of visibility. Every living thing could be compared to every other living thing. The differences between every form of life would become visible, and thus available to conservation and capitalism. As I argue in chapter 3, twenty-first century conservation can be understood as a part of global capitalism, so, in a sense, Wilson's uniting instrument could be seen as the ultimate tool for the governmental management of all life. "Science, industry, agriculture, and medicine" would have a key that makes everything comparable, and thus exchangeable. At the same time, Wilson seems right that a complete mapping would be of enormous benefit to conservation.

Lynn Margulis, in 2005, noted that most forms of life have not been named: "Estimates vary from 3 million to 100 million for the number of extant species, yet fewer than 2 million species of plants, fungi, animals, protoctists and bacteria enjoy Latin binomial descriptions: *Genus* and *specie*."[52] Margulis calls for a consortium that would "unite the plethora of field biologists and genomic/computer experts to conform practices that name and document all of Nature's prodigality" so that unnamed species may be scientifically described. In their 2011 study "How Many Species Are There on Earth and in the Ocean?," Mora et al. estimate that 1.2 million species have been catalogued, but that "some 86% of existing species on Earth and 91% of species in the ocean still await description."[53] They estimate approximately 8.7 million total species populate the earth. Like Wilson, Mora et al. view this lack of description as a conservation issue. "Our results also suggest that this slow advance in the description of species will lead to species becoming extinct before we know they even existed. High rates of biodiversity loss provide an urgent incentive to increase our knowledge of Earth's remaining species."[54] Mora et al. end with a call for "a renewed interest in exploration and taxonomy by both researchers and funding agencies, and a continuing effort to catalogue existing biodiversity data in publicly available databases."[55] Multiple organizations have focused on these issues. For my purposes, I will focus on two that are strongly related to the cataloguing of birds: the Consortium for the Barcode of Life (CBOL) and the eBird database.

I have noted a few twenty-first-century calls (by Wilson, Margulis, and Mora) for a renewed interest in taxonomy. The same sorts of calls were being made in the 1990s. A *Scientific American* essay from 2005 looks back with a dire warning. "By the close of the 20th century, taxonomy had reached a crossroads. Funds were declining and academic interest dwindling, even as biologists and conservationists raced to identify and quantify species."[56] Likewise, a group of scientists, led by Paul Hebert, declared, "Although much biological research depends upon species diagnoses, taxonomic expertise is collapsing."[57] Hebert and others proposed that DNA "barcoding" as the solution to this problem. On their website, the Consortium for the Barcode of Life describes the technique. "Barcoding uses a very short genetic sequence from a standard part of the genome the way a supermarket scanner distinguishes products using the black stripes of the Universal Product Code (UPC)."[58] Beardsley, looking back from 2005, writes, "These so-called DNA bar codes instantly won public favor, heralding a day when researchers could run simple DNA tests in the field, perhaps even with a Star Trek-ian 'tricorder' device."[59] In short, DNA barcoding seemed to offer the promise of a simple means of defining every living thing through a brief analysis of a small section of DNA, "a 648 base-pair region in the mitochondrial cytochrome c oxidase 1 gene ("COI")."[60] Only "tiny amounts of tissue" are needed to do this analysis, so the method is easy to use in the field and on collections that may have deteriorated. Hebert et al. saw the term "barcode" as more than just a metaphor. "In a very real sense, these [COI] sequences can be viewed as genetic 'barcodes' that are embedded in every cell." They note that the information contained in a Universal Product Code can "generate 100 billion unique identifiers," more than "the number that would be required to discriminate life if each taxon was uniquely branded."[61] DNA barcoding, then, offered the promise of a short, unique, readily identifiable code that could be "read" in every living thing. Hebert et al. state just such a goal. "If advanced comprehensively, a COI database could serve as the basis for a global bioidentification system (GBS) for animals." After arguing that such a GBS is financially and practically feasible, they note, "Its assembly promises both a revolution in access to basic biological information and a newly detailed view of the origins of biological diversity."[62] In short, DNA barcoding offers the promise of a complete ordering, as all of life might become readable as part of a total biological encyclopedia.

The DNA barcoding of birds has yielded some interesting results. A 2003 study, "Identification of Birds through DNA Barcodes," examined "COI barcodes for 260 species of North American birds and found that distinguishing species was generally straightforward."[63] That is, barcoding was able to delimit the differences between most of the 260 established species. Four species, though—the eastern meadowlark, marsh wren, warbling vireo, and solitary sandpiper—showed more divergence within their respective species than expected. As the authors note, all four of these species, for various reasons, had been the "subject of prior scrutiny" for splitting into two species, mostly because of the birds' wide geographic range.[64] A more comprehensive 2007 follow-up study examined 643 species of North American birds and found that 94 percent of "species possess distinct barcode clusters"; the remaining 6 percent, birds that did not show wide genetic divergence, were closely related species like the mallard and American black duck, and the northwestern and American crow.[65] Fifteen species, though, including the four from the earlier study, showed enough genetic divergence to be labeled as possible "cryptic species" by the authors, who noted that "nine of our 15 cases have been previously cited" for possible splitting.[66] In short, then, the authors concluded that their study was a success. "This study confirms that DNA barcoding can be effectively applied across the geographical and taxonomic expanse of North American birds."[67]

This success, though, was interpreted in widely varying ways. The authors of the earlier study saw the close correlation between identified bird species and DNA barcoded species as a possible "first step toward a DNA barcode system for all animal and plant life, an initiative with potentially widespread scientific and practical benefits."[68] The 2007 study extolled the benefits of barcoding by arguing, "The tight clustering of mtDNA sequences within species observed in our study not only bolsters the view that species are fundamental biological units, but also reveals that their identification is usually uncomplicated."[69] In short, a barcode of life seemed possible. But over the last few years many challenges have arisen to the validity of an encyclopedia of life based on DNA barcoding. Will et al. argue that "now is the time to invest in the fertile option of integrative taxonomy, not the noisome weed of DNA barcoding." By advocating for "integrative taxonomy," while by no means rejecting the utility of DNA-based species identification, the authors claim that "taxonomic research, broadly comparative and historical, is a necessary intellectual counterbalance to general experimental biology.[70] The authors voice concern that a simple reliance on DNA barcoding can erase the rigor that taxonomy has recently gained "with 'descriptive' alpha taxonomy driven by critical species hypothesis testing, predictive phylogenetic classifications, and increasingly informative Linnaean names."[71] In short, integrative taxonomy says that barcoding is much too simple and reductionist.

Many other critiques have been leveled against DNA barcoding as the source of an encyclopedia of life. Most critics note that barcoding has a role to play in species identification, but that much more is needed to build such an encyclopedia. A 2012 study argues that DNA barcoding is quickly becoming irrelevant as new methods of genetic analysis, such as next-generation sequencing (NGS), produce better and more detailed information. "The ground has shifted, and it is now DNA barcoding, rather than traditional taxonomy, which runs the risk of becoming irrelevant if it refuses to embrace change." Other challenges to the simplicity of DNA barcoding emerge from such methods as "ecologic genetics," whose proponents argue against the use of any one gene for species identification.[72] "Iterative taxonomy," a term proposed by Yeates et al., even suggests that "that a repeatable, quantifiable method of truly 'integrative taxonomy' is not available yet."[73] There is little agreement on whether an encyclopedia of life is even possible. And just as Jorge Luis Borges proved useful to Foucault in illustrating how a certain system of though underlies any system of ordering, Borges's short fiction might have something to say about this drive for an encyclopedia of life. Borges's story, "The Library of Babel," posits a library that contains all possible books. "Everything: the minutely detailed history of the future, the archangels' autobiographies, the faithful catalogues of the Library, thousands and thousands of false catalogues, the demonstration of the fallacy of those catalogues, the demonstration of the fallacy of the true catalogue, the Gnostic gospel of Basilides, the commentary on that gospel, the commentary on the commentary on that gospel, the true story of your death, the translation of every book in all languages, the interpolations of every book in all books."[74] Borges's narrator notes the feeling of "extravagant happiness" that overcame humankind when this discovery was made. After the thrilling idea that any and all information could be found in the library came a period of "excessive depression" when people realized that there was no key to the library, and thus no possibility of finding any specific information in its nearly limitless spaces. Borges writes of the mythical "Man of the Book," a librarian who had catalogued everything in "a book which is the formula and perfect compendium of all the rest."[75] Of course, this book itself would be nearly impossible to find and its usefulness would be questionable, as it would seem to reduce all difference to one key. Borges's story offers a fictional means of thinking about the impossibility of an encyclopedia of life.

Life itself is too varied to be completely catalogued, especially if one remembers that there is not even widespread agreement on exactly what a "species" is: sometimes a black-crested titmouse is a species, sometimes it is a subspecies, and now it is a species again. If one bird species cannot be permanently delimited, the possibility that all life can seems beyond our grasp.

A MAP OF BIRD LIFE?

Creating an encyclopedia of life entails many difficulties that I have only touched on here. Lynn Margulis writes about how difficult classification becomes outside the realm of animals. "The bacterial nomenclature code can contradict both the botanical and the zoological codes. The mycologists, fungi experts, have virtually seceded from the plant kingdom and made their own rules."[76] Likewise, E. O. Wilson notes that if one defines a species as a group of sexually reproducing organisms "that are capable of freely interbreeding under natural conditions," it becomes problematic to classify plants that hybridize and populations that do not sexually reproduce.[77] Birds, then, in many ways, are easier to classify than other species. They sexually reproduce, and with some exceptions, inhabit known ranges, and exhibit obvious morphological differences. As I discuss above, DNA barcoding confirmed the species status of 94 percent of 643 North American bird species, while suggesting that a few others should be lumped or split. In short, all of the bird species of North America, and especially of the United States and Canada, have been catalogued. Species might be created or collapsed by splitting or lumping, but the possibility of finding a previously undescribed bird species in the United States is exceedingly slight.

While keeping the slipperiness of the species concept in mind, I turn now to a project that is more map-like than encyclopedic (although, as I will discuss, it does have encyclopedic potential): eBird. eBird is an online database of bird sightings started in 2002 and run jointly by the Cornell Lab of Ornithology and the National Audubon Society. eBird is a "citizen science" project; that is, anyone can enter bird sightings into its database. These "observations provide an open data resource containing the most current and comprehensive information on bird distribution, migratory pathways, population trends, and landscape use."[78] Bird identification can be tricky, especially when one tries to differentiate between similar species, so eBird has created a protocol that evaluates the data's quality using emergent filters and regional editors. By analyzing "the frequency in which a particular bird species was reported during a particular period of time" in the database, the filter is able to estimate the likelihood of that same species being seen in a specific place on a specific date. Because the database has over one hundred million observations entered, the historical data "can be used to filter unusual observations that require review, but allow entry of expected species within the expected times when species should occur."[79] If an observation gets flagged for review, the person entering the record is immediately notified that the record is unusual. If the record is still entered, the user will then be contacted by a regional editor via email. A typical inquiry will begin,

> Dear [name of eBird user]
>
> I am a regional data reviewer for eBird. My goal is to keep up with data submissions and try to ensure the accuracy of reports of rare and unusual species, as well as unusually high counts of common species.
>
> Can you please provide additional details on the following observation? It is unusual either because it is a species that does not normally occur in this region on this date, or the count you've reported is above expected levels of occurrence.[80]

For a specific example, I once received a query from a regional editor in Pennsylvania for the following sighting.

> Dear Jeff,
>
> Any details at all? Light or dark morph? Location? Seen by other observers?
> Species: Rough-legged Hawk
> Count: 1
> Observation date: Apr 13, 2005

> Location: Middle Creek WMA (IBA) (Lancaster Co.),
> Lancaster, US-PA
> Submission ID: S11533561

I responded with the following:

> I remember this one pretty well because I was surprised to see it
> so late. It was a light morph, and it was hovering. I haven't been
> to Middle Creek in 10 years, but I remember I was driving the
> loop and the bird was over the fields about half way through the
> driving loop, near where a lot of short-eared owls were observed
> at a different time. No other observers.[81]

The editor replied "Thanks, Jeff." This is just one example of the more
than 3.5 million records reviewed by eBird's regional editors.[82] It is also
worth noting that "all records, their flags, and their review history are
retained in the eBird database.[83] In short, eBird review protocol ensures
accurate records through statistical modeling and a review process.

When eBird began in 2002, participation was low, partially because
"initial incentives focused on helping scientists study birds." The
interface was redesigned to focus more on the interests of the birding
community. Four features were added to allow participants to "(1) keep
track of their bird records; (2) sort their personal bird lists by date and
region; (3) share their lists with others; and (4) visualize their observations on maps and graphs." These four tools have led to an exponential
increase in entries so that more entries were made "in May 2012 than
during the first three years of the project."[84] As eBird has managed to
increase participation, it has also worked to improve the quality of the
data that users input by "changing behavior through tools and visualization."[85] For instance, to encourage birders to submit full checklists
of every bird seen during a day, and not just a few "highlight" birds,
eBird produces automated bar charts of species frequencies that work
best when observers submit "complete lists of all species recorded."
eBird also provides "Top 100" lists to allow "our community to engage
with each other in competitions to submit more complete checklists
or see more species."[86] In short, eBird has trained citizen scientists to

enter more and better data into the database. Or, as Sullivan et al. put it: "You can 'teach old birders new tricks.'"[87]

Kelling et al. have called eBird a "human computer learning network" (HCLN) that uses "both human and mechanical computation to solve complex problems through active learning and feedback processes." Such networks "can leverage the contributions of broad recruitment of human observers and process their contributed data with AI algorithms for a resulting total computational power far exceeding the sum of their individual parts."[88] In the case of eBird, well-trained observers and regional managers input data that can be put to a multitude of uses. Before discussing the uses of eBird's enormous data set, though, I want to suggest that this particular HCLN should include birds as part of its system, so that it becomes a human bird computer learning network, or HBCLN. Compared to other methods of studying bird populations, eBird is radically different in one simple way: it does not kill birds. DNA barcoding and other genetic analysis depend on extraction from tissue samples from "collected" birds. Early ornithologists like Frank Chapman provided detailed instructions for killing and preparing specimens, and Audubon, of course, killed thousands of birds. eBird, though, relies only on observation and data entry to produce an incredibly detailed map of bird movement and population in the United States.

I can log into eBird and produce a range map that shows all sightings of tufted titmice at my home address. More interestingly, I can compare range maps of tufted, black-crested, and hybrid titmice in southeastern Texas, and Hornsby Bend in particular, to visualize the range of each particular bird. While a Borgesian encyclopedia of life may never be possible, the mapping application of eBird bears comparison to another Borges short story. In "On Exactitude in Science," Borges tells of cartographers who "struck a map of the empire whose size was that of the Empire, and which coincided point for point with it." Borges writes that following generations lost interest in geography, so that "tattered ruins of the map, inhabited by animals and beggars," are all that remain of the map and of the "Disciplines of Geography" itself.[89] Borges's 1:1 map, the crowning achievement of geography, in some unexplained way (the story is only one short paragraph) marks the field of study's decline and eventual disappearance. My point here is not that this is the fate of eBird, taxonomy, or population studies of birds. Rather, I want to note that eBird, in letting users zoom in to almost street level, offers the promise of a more detailed study of bird populations, movements, and migrations than has ever been possible before. While these maps are fun to look at, and while they also work to encourage data entry on the part of bird observers, more importantly, the HBCLN that is eBird holds great potential for the scientific study and management of birds.

### BIRDS AS DATA

Because eBird is a "globally accessible unified database" that grows every day, it has the potential to become a new kind of resource and to change the ways that humans relate to birds. Sullivan et al. write, "Birders, scientists, and conservationists are using eBird data worldwide to better understand avian biological patterns and the environmental and anthropogenic factors that influence them" precisely because "eBird has created a near real-time avian data resource producing millions of observations per year."[90] Users can even watch a real-time map of checklist submissions at http://ebird.org/ebird/livesubs; this map places a dot in the place a checklist has been submitted and keeps a running daily tally. On April 17, 2013, as I am writing this, 1,834 checklists have been submitted as of 9:33 a.m.

Sullivan et al. note that "the ability to create, manage, and manipulate vast, real-time data resources is influencing the ways in which we study biology and conduct conservation research and planning."[91] Munson et al. determined that eBird's data is an effective means of species monitoring, especially when combined with other data such as breeding bird atlases that can be used in conservation assessment.[92] As such, eBird data has been used to determine "which threatened or endangered birds occur on which federal agency's land at which time of year—knowledge the agencies use to determine budget priorities (SA)." In addition, Fink et al. have shown that eBird data can be used to build a "spatiotemporal exploratory model (STEM)" that can be used "to create a nearly nonparametric dynamic species distribution model for broad-scale intra-annual migrations."[93] This model takes into account how a specific bird species, in this case the tree swallow, responds to its environment as it migrates.[94] This STEM model can be adjusted for local, regional, and perhaps global parameters, which could in turn prove "useful for determining the 'scale' for designing interconnected reserves systems to support migratory species or species experiencing distributional dynamics due to other causes."[95] eBird data thus becomes a strong conservationist tool.

eBird data has been used to create the Avian Knowledge Network (AKN), whose goal is "to understand the patterns and dynamics of bird populations across the Western Hemisphere."[96] The Avian Knowledge Network is based on the eBird Reference Dataset (ERD). ERD 3.0 has 41.7 million records that link "locations from eBird checklists to remotely-sensed data on landscape variables, human population, climate, and other information to site-specific checklists on bird occurrence."[97] The ERD is freely available to researchers, educators, and conservationists. The AKN is currently researching how its data is being used by scientists, and the organization has listed some of the uses to which the data has been put. The AKN's data has been used in conservation mapping, predictive modeling, and bird life historical analysis. Perhaps most importantly, the AKN "federates data from disparate sources into a common format,"[98] so that it can be used widely in the study of the complex systems of bird populations.

eBird data has also been used to create BirdCast, a forecast model that answers the question: "When, where and how far will birds migrate?"[99] During spring and fall migration seasons, BirdCast provides weekly forecasts, complete with radar maps, of bird migration. In addition to allowing "birding by radar" for the first time in human history, BirdCast shows scientists how environmental change affects bird migratory behavior. Along with their potential contribution to science, there is the hope that these forecasts might "prompt cities to turn off their downtown lights or wind farms to shut off their turbines on nights when thousands of birds are passing overhead" in order to save the lives of migrating birds.[100]

"The State of the Birds 2011: Report on Public Lands and Waters, United States of America," described as "the most important bird conservation report in the United States," relied on eBird data for the first time.[101] Thus, the 2011 report claims to be the most detailed report ever produced, thanks in large part to eBird's data. "This year's report provides the nation's first assessment of the distribution of birds on public lands and helps public agencies identify which species have significant potential for conservation in each habitat. This assessment used high-performance computing techniques to analyze a massive data set on bird distribution from citizen-science participants across the U.S. (eBird), along with the first comprehensive database of public land ownership."[102] Clearly, eBird, and the management of the massive data that it produces, has the potential to alter human-bird interactions. Real-time data, large-scale models, and continual input combine to provide an incredible amount of information about bird populations. How this information will be used is still unclear.

"State of the Birds 2011" reads as an optimistic report. It focuses on "the tremendous promise of public lands and waters for conserving America's wildlife and habitats," and notes that "the United States has a long history of conservation on public lands."[103] The report groups public lands by habitat: aridlands, grasslands, wetlands, arctic and alpine, forests, islands, coasts, oceans, game birds. For each habitat, the report is divided into three sections: "[specific habitat, for example] Grassland Birds on Public Land"; Conservation Successes"; "Conservation Challenges." Habitat destruction and disturbance, along with climate change, are the primary "challenges" listed throughout the report. While the report does not downplay these challenges in each section, a comparison to the tone and organization of the 2009 State of the Birds report reveals a few striking differences in voice. The 2009 report, within each habitat grouping, has the following sections: "The State of [specific habitat such as] Grassland Birds," "Birds in Trouble," Major Threats," "Solutions," and "Beyond Our Borders." The 2009 report also includes a section on "Endangered Species" and one on "Challenges" that provide more information than the 2011 report on the problems facing birds.

Likewise, the forewords to each report show dissimilar tones. The 2011 report recognizes the need for increased conservation. "The state of our birds is a measurable indicator of how well we are doing as stewards of our environment. The signal is clear. Greater conservation efforts on public lands and waters are needed to realize the vision of a nation sustained economically and spiritually by abundant natural resources and spectacular wildlife." But the bulk of its foreword discusses the importance of public lands and civic duty, "which empowers all Americans to share in the responsibility to conserve, restore, and provide better access to our lands and waters in order to leave a healthy, vibrant outdoor legacy for generations yet to come."[104] In contrast the 2009 report notes that the United States' population has "skyrocketed" to 300 million, as it notes that four American bird species have gone extinct "since the birth of our nation," and that at least ten more are threatened with extinction.[105] Like the 2011 report, the 2009 one makes a call to action, but, again, the tone is radically different. "It is imperative that we redouble our efforts now, before habitat loss and degradation become even more widespread, intractable, and expensive to solve. Together, we can ensure that future generations will look back at this first State of the Birds report with disbelief that their common birds could ever have been so troubled."[106] There is no empowering vision of a nation here; instead, there is an urgent need to act before it is too late. How might one account for these differing persuasive techniques? Overall bird populations did not change so radically between the writing of the two reports to account for the change. That is, nothing actually happened to birds to reflect the more recent report's optimistic attitude. No major legislative changes happened between 2009 and 2011 either. No data suggests that human attitudes toward birds changed all that significantly during this time period. In fact, the major difference between the two reports seems to be in the amount and quality of data they use.

As I note above, the 2011 report made use of eBird's "massive data set." The 2011 report also used "a national spatial database," "the Protected Areas Database of the United States (PAD-US version 1.1), to determine land ownership and biodiversity protection status of all public lands for the continental U.S., Alaska, Hawai'i, Puerto Rico, and the U.S. Virgin Islands." Using this database gave the report's writers access to "the most detailed, consistent map of vegetation associations available for the United States." Combining these two resources, the report was able to analyze more than 600,000 eBird checklists from 107,000 different locations. Seventy thousand hours of computer time were used to analyze all of this data in order to produce detailed habitat distribution maps for American birds. In short, the report used "used the best data available for the United States."[107]

Of course, the 2009 report surely used the best data available at the time. But, as the authors describe the data used, it becomes clear that the 2009 report has less quality data than the 2011 report. The 2009 report used data from the North American Breeding Bird Survey (BBS), the National Audubon Society's Christmas Bird Count, and waterfowl breeding and population reports "conducted by trained pilots and wildlife biologists across the northern U.S. and Canada."[108] While this data is reliable, it is a much smaller set than that used in 2011. For instance, the BBS collects data from 4,000 sites. The 2009 report also notes that reliable data is missing for some birds and habitats. "New monitoring efforts for these species and habitats are essential for future State of the Birds reports."[109]

Even the statistical analysis of the available data differs between the two reports. The 2009 report notes: "Analysis for this State of the Birds report represents the first integration of long-term results across these three important surveys, using new statistical techniques developed by scientists at the USGS and National Audubon Society."[110] The 2011 report takes this a step further. "With support from the National Science Foundation and Leon Levy Foundation, collaborators at Oak Ridge National Laboratory, DataONE, TeraGrid, the Institute for Computational Sustainability, and the Cornell Lab of Ornithology used statistical models to account for gaps and biases in volunteer-collected data and to associate bird distributions with important environmental factors, including land cover, elevation, local climate, and human housing density for 139 species with sufficient eBird data."[111] My point here is not to say that the 2009 report is invalid or statistically inaccurate.

I do, though, want to highlight both the increase in data and in data analysis in the 2011 report. I suggest that the more sophisticated and more accurate data analysis of the 2011 report may account for some of its optimism. The 2011 report notes that it "provides the nation's first assessment of the distribution of birds on public lands and the opportunities for public agencies in each habitat."[112] In other words, the 2011 report champions the management responsibility of government agencies. Governmentality of birds seems to breed optimism for conservation.

Hand in hand with the role of "public agencies," the report also heralds "citizen support and involvement" through engaging and supporting conservationist organizations, both public and private.[113] In addition, the 2011 report seems greatly enthusiastic about the potential impact of citizen scientists who report sightings through eBird. In a sidebar titled, "Thank You to eBird Volunteers," the report acknowledges, "Our understanding of bird distributions has greatly improved thanks to the thousands of birdwatchers who have contributed observations to www.eBird.org. This effort is especially important for tracking seasonal and fine-scale changes in bird distributions, which is not possible with other bird-monitoring programs."[114] In short, then, the 2011 State of the Birds report sees great hope in large-scale data analysis performed by public (governmental) and private (citizens, corporations, and NGOs) organizations. The logos of twenty-eight governmental, nongovernmental, and corporate entities appear on the last page of the report, while only twelve are at the end of the 2009 report. In conclusion the 2011 State of the Birds report had more data, more groups, and more people involved. We know more about bird populations and distribution than has ever been known.

If the roots of ornithology are in the taxonomic discovering and defining of bird species, the future may be in mapping and understanding the complexity of population and distribution. The species distinction between a tufted titmouse and a black-crested titmouse may never be clear, since what is split might once again be lumped. Despite this mutable species line, the tufted titmouse and the black-crested titmouse can serve as markers of the exponentially increasing information about birds in the twenty-first century, as real-time range maps are practically at my fingertips. As I write this sentence, yet more information is being gathered. However, as I will discuss in my conclusion, more information does not necessarily mean better conservation decisions. It simply means that bird management will intensify as the human experiment on birds continues. And, for reasons I will discuss in my conclusion, this experiment will still be scarlet.

# *Conclusion*
## The Future of Birds

The future of birds in America is unclear. Intensive management, in and of itself, is neither a good nor a bad thing. That is, the fact that birds are subject to governmentality does not determine what their future will be. A series of practices, or experiments, will continue to affect birds in multiple ways. Foucault defines "practices" as "the ensemble of more or less regulated, more or less deliberate, more or less finalized ways of doing things, through which can be seen both what was constituted as real for those who sought to think it and manage it and the way in which the latter constituted themselves as subjects capable of knowing, analyzing, and ultimately altering reality." Foucault is writing of the past here, as a given set of actions is always easier to see as a grouped practice in retrospect. For instance, the conservation movement at the turn of the nineteenth century can be viewed today as a linked set of practices that brought governmentality into the natural world. Predicting how practices will work in the future is never easy, and something else that Foucault writes in this passage shows how prediction might be exceedingly difficult. He couches his discussions of regulation, deliberateness, and finality with the phrase "more or less."[1] Practices are always contingent; they are not driven by one overriding ideology. In short, a Foucauldian analysis of biopower, governmentality, and birds can only say of the future: it will be driven by contingent practices that will demand vigilance from those who seek a certain way of life for humans and birds. The future is limited by past and present practices, but its emergence can never be wholly determined.

In other words, we cannot know the future until it happens. But I think more is at stake than that simple claim would suggest. By looking at past and present practices, one might map out several possible futures for birds in North America. In terms of the intensive management of birds, the roles of four interest groups seem especially important: citizens, government, corporations, and nongovernmental organizations.

## CITIZENS

Citizen science has become the engine of much of the data collected about birds in the twenty-first century, through the eBird database. But citizen action is not limited simply to data collection. In chapter 3, I discuss how citizen scientists have played a role in the conservation of the *rufa* red knot. I also discuss Larry Niles's argument that one key to conservation efforts is getting more people passionately involved by making conservation an interesting and inspiring recreational activity. As Niles and others have noted, citizen science goes back to the beginnings of ornithology. Coues's nineteenth-century guide was written for the dedicated amateur, and birders have always collected data. The ease of entering data that the Internet has enabled combined with scientists' abilities to measure the accuracy of citizen input (as I discuss in chapter 5) means that citizens can make larger, more important contributions to science than ever before. In her essay about eBird and citizen science, "Data on Wings," Hillary Rosner notes that "citizen science solves a problem of scale" as it facilitates the collection of data "points on a map where we have almost no historical data on phenomena such as weather events or biodiversity. Expanding the number of people observing the world, whether flowers or stars or toxins, improves our capacity to understand it."[2] As a practice, then, citizen science can contribute to a broader understanding of the natural world as more and more data is collected by more and more observers. In a study of citizen science's role in scientific research, Wiggins and Crowston write, "This domain of practice is rapidly expanding with the availability of enabling technologies and mounting evidence in favor of the efficacy of the research strategy."[3] Citizen science's scope, then, is intensifying as more people take part and more projects are created.

In addition to direct citizen science projects, there are other ways that residents of the United States will affect the future of birds. The State of the Birds 2011 report offers the patriotic reminder that "throughout our nation's history, conservation actions have been grounded in the premise that our natural heritage belongs to the people, and that its protection is shared by all Americans."[4] The report also encourages public input on and advocacy of strong conservation policies.[5] In a similar vein, Chris Cokinos writes of the "work" that must be done to realize any hope for the future of birds. He writes of the mundane conservation meetings that go hand in hand with moments of "delight" watching birds as he celebrates the "elegance of individual decisions coupled with communal actions . . . especially as they accumulate, one by one."[6] For Cokinos, much of this action seems to be emotion-driven; the "delight" of watching pelicans fly is balanced by the "sadness at loss" of extinct birds. Hope, even when it becomes work, returns to the human soul for Cokinos, as he asks: "Of course, sometimes right action—civic activism—seems to drain away not only hours of the day but part of the spirit. Where does attention turn, after a lost battle, after another small wounding we failed to heal?"[7] For me, this conflict sums up the possibility and the danger of the role individual humans play in human-bird interactions. Citizen science and collective action can obviously be positive forces for conservation. But I am wary of a reliance on the human soul or spirit engaging in care for birds. This seems to create a formation of subjectivity where the human becomes the caregiver and the bird becomes the cared for; the human does conservation work and the bird provides solace for the soul. In short, this version of the human-bird relationship costs too much. It relies on an outmoded model of disciplinary subjectivity: I will watch out for you as long as it does me good, as long as your bird otherness feeds my sense of human interiority.

As a final note, here, it is also worth noting that, even as large numbers of individuals enter data into eBird and practice bird-watching, the vast majority of Americans pay little to no attention to birds in everyday life.

## GOVERNMENT

The 2011 State of the Birds report makes a strong argument for the role of the federal and state governments in bird protection, as it argues, "Effective Management is Key to Healthy Bird Populations." Such management is presented as a series of negotiated needs. "All agencies are faced with the challenge of balancing needs for resource extraction, energy development, recreation, and other uses with the growing urgency to conserve birds and other wildlife." As the 2011 report is subtitled "Report on Public Lands and Waters," it focuses on governmental land holdings across multiple departments, including the Bureau of Land Management, the Department of Defense, the National Oceanic and Atmospheric Administration, the National Park Service, the United States Forest Service, and the United States Fish and Wildlife Service. Taken together, these departments manage birds on well more than 850 million acres of public land in multiple habitats, "from the arctic tundra to southwestern aridlands."[8] Because of these vast land holdings, vast numbers of birds rely on public land, and "public agencies therefore have a major influence on the success of conservation efforts to restore declining species and keep common birds."[9]

The federal government's legislative role in conservation dates back to the Lacey Act and Migratory Bird Treaty Act of the early twentieth century. Of course, the Endangered Species Act, signed into law by Richard Nixon in 1973, declares that the federal government must "provide a means whereby the ecosystems upon which endangered species and threatened species depend may be conserved, to provide a program for the conservation of such endangered species and threatened species, and to take such steps as may be appropriate to achieve the purposes of the treaties and conventions" listed in the act.[10] The 2011 report also mentions the importance of "Executive Order 13186 (Responsibilities of Federal Agencies to Protect Migratory Birds)" from

2001, "which directs federal agencies that have or are likely to have measurable negative effects on migratory bird populations to develop and implement a Memorandum of Understanding (MOU) with the USFWS regarding bird conservation on their lands."[11] The combined force of legislation and land holdings makes the federal government the key component to the future of birds.

Of course, the role the federal government plays in bird conservation is always contingent on the ideological, political, and economic conditions of its time. The 2011 State of the Birds report itself calls for "additional resources" that might not be forthcoming during a recession.[12] Even the Weeks-McLean bill of 1913, which sought protection for migratory birds, only passed through legislative trickery. According to Gibbons and Strom, the act was attached at the last minute to the Department of Agriculture's appropriation bill, and was signed by President Taft even as "he later admitted that he signed it without noticing what it was, though on more considered subsequent review he judged it unconstitutional and said he should have vetoed it."[13] And to speak just a bit more of political contingency, during the third presidential debate between Barack Obama and Mitt Romney on October 16, 2012, Romney spoke contemptuously of the Migratory Bird Treaty Act of 1918 as he defended oil production in North Dakota. Romney argued that the Obama administration "brought a criminal action against the people drilling up there for oil. . . . And what was the cost? 20 or 25 birds were killed and brought out a migratory bird act to go after them on a criminal basis."[14] In a few short words, Romney dismissed perhaps the most important piece of bird conservation legislation ever passed.

## CORPORATIONS AND NONGOVERNMENTAL ORGANIZATIONS

Even as the federal government plays an important role in bird conservation, the roles of corporations and nongovernmental organizations should not be downplayed. In fact, the 2011 State of the Birds report references "the U.S. North American Bird Conservation Initiative (NABCI)," which "fosters collaboration" between "government agencies, private organizations, and bird initiatives helping federal, state, and nongovernmental organizations . . . to meet their common bird conservation objectives."[15] In chapter 3 I discuss how corporations and NGOs can be seen as complicit in creating a neoliberal worldview that views nature and biodiversity only through its exchange value. Brockington and Duffy write of "an aggressive faith in market solutions to environmental problems" that characterizes such alliances. Although these formations have been around for a long time, the authors find that they have increased in "intensity and variety" of late.[16] In "The Birth of Biopolitics" Foucault writes that "American neoliberalism seeks rather to extend the rationality of the market, the schemes of analysis it proposes, and the decision making criteria it suggests to areas that are not exclusively or not primarily economic."[17] In its management of birds, the United States, through government, citizens, corporations, and NGOs, has done just that. As I hope to have shown, birds in twenty-first-century America are subject to intensive management practices. The governmentality of North American birds is the continuation of the scarlet experiment that started in the nineteenth century. This experiment cannot be reversed. I can think of no reason why bird management would cease to intensify as habitat destruction and global warming create more and more risk for bird populations.

## DOUBT OR HOPE?

Human-bird interactions, to follow this train of thought, are a series of practices that are good for some birds (starlings and blue jays, for instance) and dangerous for others (*rufa* red knots and resident Canada geese, for instance). So what does this say about the future of birds? As an avid birder, I do care about birds. I do have hope for their future, but I am also a doubting Thomas. So I seek out optimistic outlooks that do not rely on what I see as outmoded forms of human subjectivity. Such optimism, I think, can be found in a few places.

The last paragraph of Hardt and Negri's *Empire* strangely ends with a brief discussion of Saint Francis of Assisi. They posit Assisi in opposition to nascent capitalism, and say that "he posed a joyous life, including all of being and nature, the animals, sister moon, brother son, *the birds of the field*, the poor and exploited humans, together against the will of power and corruption."[18] Combined with their earlier discussion of the fact that capitalism is not a natural state, a different future can be imagined. Toward the end of their *Declaration*, Hardt and Negri write that "we should remember that throughout history unexpected and unforeseeable events arrive that completely reshuffle the decks of political powers and possibilities."[19] I cite these lines because I hope to have shown that birds are part of the political economy, in however small of a way, in the twenty-first century. "We can't know when the event will come," they write, or even what it will be.[20] But in championing the development of "new subjectivities that desire and are capable of democratic relations," Hardt and Negri look toward the possibility of a future that includes "equality, freedom, sustainability."[21] Hardt and Negri are by no means "environmentalists," yet their hopeful look toward the possibility of new forms of subjectivity can certainly be stretched to include the nonhuman and the human.

The second moment of optimism I wish to highlight is from Felix Guattari's *Chaosmosis: An Ethico-aesthetic Paradigm*. Toward the end of this short book, Guattari writes, "I hold my hand out to the future . . . that the world can be rebuilt from other Universes of value and that other existential Territories should be constructed towards this end. The immense ordeals which the planet is going through—such as the suffocation of its atmosphere—involve changes in production, ways of living and axes of value."[22] I discuss these other universes of value in chapter 3, but I want to reiterate that the human experiment on birds has produced multiple avenues through which these other values might be constructed. Birds actively live in the world with humans. While humans continually experiment on birds, Guattari's thought allows for the idea that birds are experimenting on humans as well. Mozart's starling (see chapter 2) can stand in for all of the real human-bird friendships that I document in this book. The dedication to saving the red knot and the protections sought for resident Canada geese also suggest other ways of valuing the world. Many bird species have adapted and thrived in human-altered environments.

In his *The Human Nature of Birds*, Theodore Xenophon Barber argues that a human awareness of avian intelligence will lead toward a radically altered "relationship to nature and the universe." He writes, "Humanity's philosophy of life will turn around along with human cultural institutions. Science, religion, and philosophy will be fundamentally different."[23] I am not sure that I can agree with Barber, but I can briefly imagine what his imagined future might look like. In this future humans might come to understand that we are much closer to birds and other living beings than we had thought. We might see the world as full of many more minds, intelligences, and lives than we had previously believed.

And finally, to end on a more concrete note, Foucault's notion of practice, which I rely on for much of my argument, is all about the production and use of knowledge. To hope that such knowledge production might be used to help birds is perhaps not overly optimistic.

# NOTES

INTRODUCTION

1.  Cokinos, *Hope Is the Thing*, 2.
2.  Cokinos, *Hope Is the Thing*, 2.
3.  Dickinson, *Poems*, 140.
4.  Cokinos, *Hope Is the Thing*, 335, 336.
5.  Cokinos, *Hope Is the Thing*, 335.
6.  Cokinos, *Hope Is the Thing*, 334.
7.  Koeppel, *To See Every Bird*, xv.
8.  Kaufman, *Kingbird Highway*, 312.
9.  Cokinos, *Hope Is the Thing*, 2.
10. Dickinson, *Poems*, 391.
11. Loss, Will, and Parra, "Direct Human-Caused Mortality," 357.
12. Loss, Will, and Parra, "Direct Human-Caused Mortality," 361.
13. Loss, Will, and Parra, "Direct Human-Caused Mortality," 357.
14. American Bird Conservancy, "Strategic Bird Conservation Framework."
15. Loss, Will, and Parra, "Impact of Free-Ranging."
16. Manville, "Towers, Turbines, Power Lines, and Buildings," 263
17. USDA, "Animals Taken—FY 2011" 2.
18. NABCI, "State 2010," 2.
19. NABCI, "State 2010," 4.
20. Butcher, "Wake Up Call."
21. United States Fish and Wildlife Service, "Species Reports."
22. Gibbons and Strom, *Neighbor to the Birds*, 155
23. Barrow, *Passion for Birds*, 127.

24. Derrida, *Animal That Therefore I Am*, 23.

25. Derrida, *Animal That Therefore I Am*, 25.

26. Derrida, *Animal That Therefore I Am*, 25.

27. "Experiment," *Oxford English Dictionary*, http://www.oed.com
    .cowles-proxy.drake.edu/search?searchType=dictionary&q=experiment
    &_searchBtn=Search.

28. "Experiment," *Oxford English Dictionary*, http://www.oed.com
    .cowles-proxy.drake.edu/search?searchType=dictionary&q=experiment
    &_searchBtn=Search.

29. American Birding Association, "Listing Central."

30. Foucault, "Governmentality," 102.

31. Foucault, "Governmentality," 102.

32. Hardt and Negri, *Empire*, 277.

## 1. EMOTION AND INTELLIGENCE

1. Dickinson, *Poems*, 418.

2. Dickinson, *Poems*, 418.

3. Dickinson, *Poems*, 421, 372.

4. Tarvin and Woolfenden, "Blue Jay."

5. Tarvin and Woolfenden, "Blue Jay"; Catesby, *Catesby's Birds*, 95.

6. Sibley, *Sibley Guide to Birds*, 418.

7. Dickinson, *Poems*, 586.

8. Wilson, *American Ornithology*, 253.

9. Thoreau, *On Birds*, 256.

10. Audubon, *Writings and Drawings*, 291.

11. Dickinson, *Poems*, 586; Thoreau, *On Birds*, 259; Audubon, *Writings and Drawings*, 288.

12. Savage, *Bird Brains*, 30.

13. Griffin, *Animal Minds*, v.

14. Griffin, *Animal Minds*, ix.

15. Dickinson, *Poems*, 421, 586.

16. Dickinson, *Poems*, 421.

17. Dickinson, *Poems*, 421.

18. Dickinson, *Poems*, 603.

19. Dickinson, *Poems*, 586, 421, 586.

20. Dickinson, *Poems*, 586.

21. Dickinson, *Poems*, 849.

22. Thoreau, *Walden*, 56.

23. Thoreau, *On Birds*, 256.

24. Thoreau, *On Birds*, 253.

25. Thoreau, *On Birds*, 253.

26. Thoreau, *On Birds*, 256.

27. Thoreau, *On Birds*, 255.

28. Thoreau, *Walden*, 182.

29. Thoreau, *Walden*, 182–83.

30. Thoreau, *Walden*, 156.

31. Thoreau, *Walden*, 157.

32. Thoreau, *Walden*, 183.

33. Audubon, *Ornithological Biography*, 289.

34. Audubon, *Ornithological Biography*, 289.

35. Audubon, *Ornithological Biography*, 292.

36. Acampora, *Nietzschean Bestiary*, 2–3.

37. Cited in Acampora, *Nietzschean Bestiary*, 4.

38. Nietzsche, *Genealogy of Morals*, 178.

39. Nietzsche, *Genealogy of Morals*, 179.

40. Nietzsche, *Genealogy of Morals*, 179.

41. Audubon, *Ornithological Biography*, 292.

42. Savage, *Bird Brains*, 92.

43. Bekoff, *Minding Animals*, 74.

44. Bekoff, Allen, and Grant, "Feeding Decisions," 393.

45. Audubon, *Ornithological Biography*, 289.

46. Audubon, *Ornithological Biography*, 290.

47. Audubon, *Ornithological Biography*, 290.

48. Audubon, *Ornithological Biography*, 289.

49. Audubon, *Ornithological Biography*, 290.

50. Audubon, *Ornithological Biography*, 289 (emphasis added).

51. Audubon, *Ornithological Biography*, 289.

52. Tarvin and Woolfenden, "Blue Jay."

53. Tarvin and Woolfenden, "Blue Jay."

54. Audubon, *Ornithological Biography*, 293.

55. Griffin, *Animal Minds*, 213.

56. Audubon, *Ornithological Biography*, 293.

57. Audubon, *Ornithological Biography*, 290.

58. Jones and Kamil, "Tool-Making and Tool-Using," 1076.

59. Jones and Kamil, "Tool-Making and Tool-Using," 1077.

60. Reiner et al., "Avian Brain Nomenclature Forum," E3.

61. Sandra Blakeslee, "Minds of Their Own: Birds Gain Respect," *New York Times*, February 1, 2005, F1, 4.

62. Bekoff, *Minding Animals*, 96.

63. Bekoff, *Minding Animals*, 13.

64. DeLillo, *Body Artist*, 54.
65. DeLillo, *Body Artist*, 54, 8, 20, 15, 17, 21.
66. DeLillo, *Body Artist*, 80, 67.
67. DeLillo, *Body Artist*, 32.
68. DeLillo, *Body Artist*, 8.
69. DeLillo, *Body Artist*, 12.
70. DeLillo, *Body Artist*, 17, 12–13.
71. DeLillo, *Body Artist*, 21.
72. Nel, "Don DeLillo's Return," 742.
73. Nel, "Don DeLillo's Return," 743.
74. DeLillo, *Body Artist*, 22.
75. DeLillo, *Body Artist*, 21.
76. DeLillo, *Body Artist*, 21.
77. DeLillo, *Body Artist*, 22.
78. Nel, "Don DeLillo's Return," 743.
79. DeLillo, *Body Artist*, 23.
80. Haraway, *Simians, Cyborgs, and Women*, 191.
81. Haraway, *Simians, Cyborgs, and Women*, 198.
82. DeLillo, *Body Artist*, 20.
83. DeLillo, *Body Artist*, 22.
84. DeLillo, *Body Artist*, 54.
85. Sibley, *Birding Basics*, 33.
86. DeLillo, *Body Artist*, 53.
87. Clark, "Form and Function," 4–46.
88. DeLillo, *Body Artist*, 54.
89. DeLillo, *Body Artist*, 69.
90. Deleuze and Guattari, *What Is Philosophy?*, 85.
91. Deleuze and Guattari, *What Is Philosophy?*, 130.
92. DeLillo, *Body Artist*, 22.
93. DeLillo, *Body Artist*, 22–23.
94. DeLillo, *Body Artist*, 78.
95. Bugnyar, Stöwe, and Heinrich, "Ravens, *Corvus corax*, Follow Gaze Direction," 1331.
96. Carter et al., "Subtle Cues," 1709.
97. Bugnyar, Stöwe, and Heinrich, "Ravens, *Corvus corax*, Follow Gaze Direction," 1335.
98. Haraway, *When Species Meet*, 151–52.
99. Bekoff, *Minding Animals*, 96.
100. Berry, *Life Is a Miracle*, 3.
101. Berry, *Life Is a Miracle*, 13.

102. Berry, *Life Is a Miracle*, 11.
103. Formato, *Jayson*, vii.
104. Formato, *Jayson*, 28–29.
105. Formato, *Jayson*, 129, 103.
106. Formato, *Jayson*, 112.
107. Formato, *Jayson*, 104.
108. Formato, *Jayson*, 113.
109. Formato, *Jayson*, 125.
110. Formato, *Jayson*, 125–26.
111. Bekoff, Allen, and Grant, "Feeding Decisions," 394.
112. Tarvin and Woolfenden, "Patterns of Dominance," 434.
113. Formato, *Jayson*, 68, 151.
114. Formato, *Jayson*, 90–91.
115. Formato, *Jayson*, 229.
116. Formato, *Jayson*, 148.
117. Formato, *Jayson*, 149.
118. Bekoff, *Minding Animals*, 33.
119. Bekoff, *Minding Animals*, 13.
120. Zinsser, "Watching the Birds," 7.
121. Zinsser, "Watching the Birds," 25.
122. Zinsser, "Watching the Birds," 7.
123. Peterson, *All Things Reconsidered*, 309.
124. Zinsser, "Watching the Birds," 7.
125. Zinsser, "Watching the Birds," 19.
126. Bekoff, *Minding Animals*, 48.
127. Bekoff, *Minding Animals*, 85.
128. Allen and Bekoff, *Species of Mind*, 180.
129. Griffin, *Animal Minds*, 285.
130. Berry, "Is Life a Miracle?," 185.
131. Berry, "Is Life a Miracle?," 185.
132. Conley, *Ecopolitics*, 150.
133. Conley, *Ecopolitics*, 150.

## 2. INTERPELLATION AND INTERIORITY

1. Gannon, *Skylark Meets Meadowlark*, 316.
2. Whitman, *Specimen Days*, 113; Thoreau, *Walden*, 58.
3. Forkner, "Writing the American Woods," xiii.
4. Audubon, *Ornithological Biography*, 160, 163.
5. Audubon, *Ornithological Biography*, 36.
6. Althusser, *Lenin and Philosophy*, 173, 176.

7. Althusser, *Lenin and Philosophy*, 176.

8. Althusser, *Lenin and Philosophy*, 176.

9. Althusser, *Lenin and Philosophy*, 177.

10. Gannon, *Skylark Meets Meadowlark*, 316.

11. Gannon, *Skylark Meets Meadowlark*, 313.

12. Gannon, *Skylark Meets Meadowlark*, 301.

13. Gannon, *Skylark Meets Meadowlark*, 299.

14. Alexie, "Avian Nights," 23.

15. Gannon, *Skylark Meets Meadowlark*, 301.

16. Alexie, "Avian Nights," 22.

17. Gannon, *Skylark Meets Meadowlark*, 301.

18. Guattari, *Three Ecologies*, 27.

19. Armstrong, "Audubon's *Ornithological Biography*," 115.

20. Armstrong, "Audubon's *Ornithological Biography*," 112.

21. Audubon, *Ornithological Biography*, 2.

22. Audubon, *Ornithological Biography*, 14.

23. Audubon, *Ornithological Biography*, 15.

24. Stanger, *That Quail*, 14.

25. Stanger, *That Quail*, 25.

26. Stanger, *That Quail*, 23.

27. Stanger, *That Quail*, 20.

28. Stanger, *That Quail*, 104.

29. Stanger, *That Quail*, 16.

30. Stanger, *That Quail*, 68.

31. USDA, "Table G," 33.

32. West and King, "Mozart's Starling," 107.

33. Izumi Kyle, "Kuro," Starling Talk: Care and Rehabilitation of Injured and Orphaned Starlings, 1999, http://www.starlingtalk.com/kuro.htm.

34. Corbo and Barras, *Arnie*, 2.

35. Corbo and Barras, *Arnie*, 14, 21.

36. Corbo and Barras, *Arnie*, 47, 126–27.

37. Corbo and Barras, *Arnie*, 52.

38. Corbo and Barras, *Arnie*, 231.

39. Haraway, *Companion Species Manifesto*, 3.

40. Haraway, *When Species Meet*, 213.

41. Wolfe, "Human, All Too Human," 570.

42. Wolfe, "Human, All Too Human," 572.

43. Derrida, *Animal That Therefore I Am*, 25.

44. Derrida, *Animal That Therefore I Am*, 79.

45. Wolfe, "Human, All Too Human," 572.

46. Derrida, *Animal That Therefore I Am*, 23.

47. Derrida, *Animal That Therefore I Am*, 32.

48. Derrida, *Animal That Therefore I Am*, 25.

49. Derrida, *Animal That Therefore I Am*, 25.

50. Derrida, *Animal That Therefore I Am*, 43.

51. Derrida, *Animal That Therefore I Am*, 47.

52. Derrida, *Animal That Therefore I Am*, 48.

53. Derrida, *Animal That Therefore I Am*, 29.

54. Haraway, *When Species Meet*, 20.

55. Haraway, *When Species Meet*, 296.

56. Haraway, *When Species Meet*, 279.

57. Haraway, *When Species Meet*, 278.

58. Haraway, *When Species Meet*, 280.

59. Haraway, *When Species Meet*, 279.

60. Haraway, *When Species Meet*, 280.

61. Haraway, *When Species Meet*, 280–81.

62. Haraway, *When Species Meet*, 280.

63. Forgotten Felines of Sonoma County, http://www.forgottenfelines.com.

64. TNR Reality Check, "TNR Reality Check: Basic Info," http://www.tnr realitycheck.com.

65. Haraway, *When Species Meet*, 295.

66. Haraway, *When Species Meet*, 280.

67. Haraway, *When Species Meet*, 280.

68. Haraway, *When Species Meet*, 278.

69. Haraway, *When Species Meet*, 277.

70. Haraway, *When Species Meet*, 280.

71. Haraway, *When Species Meet*, 280.

72. Haraway, *When Species Meet*, 21.

73. Rotman, "Going Parallel," 56–57.

74. Rotman, "Going Parallel," 57.

75. Rotman, "Going Parallel," 56.

76. USDA, "Fact Sheet—Controlling Starling Damage."

77. Vantassel, Hygnstrom, and Ferraro, "Urban Pest Birds."

78. Carter et al., "Subtle Cues," 1709.

79. Carter et al., "Subtle Cues," 1709.

80. Corbo and Barras, *Arnie*, 2.

81. Corbo and Barras, *Arnie*, 231.

82. West and King, "Mozart's Starling," 113.

83. Carter et al., "Subtle Cues," 1713.

84. Carter et al., "Subtle Cues," 1714.

85. Gannon, *Skylark Meets Meadowlark*, 316.

86. Guattari, *Chaosmosis*, 120.

87. Guattari, *Chaosmosis*, 121.

88. West and King, "Mozart's Starling," 110.

89. Deleuze and Guattari, *Thousand Plateaus*, 238–39.

90. West and King, "Mozart's Starling," 110.

91. West and King, "Mozart's Starling," 113.

92. Deleuze and Guattari, *Thousand Plateaus*, 331.

93. Guattari, *Three Ecologies*, 46.

94. Quoted in Armstrong, "Audubon's *Ornithological Biography*," 113.

95. Armstrong, "Audubon's *Ornithological Biography*," 113.

96. Armstrong, "Audubon's *Ornithological Biography*," 114.

97. McHugh, "Literary Animal Agents," 488.

98. McHugh, "Literary Animal Agents," 487.

99. Derrida, *Animal That Therefore I Am*, 94.

100. Derrida, *Animal That Therefore I Am*, 95

101. Derrida, *Animal That Therefore I Am*, 95.

102. Haraway, *When Species Meet*, 21.

103. Bekoff, *Minding Animals*, 141.

104. Bekoff, *Minding Animals*, 45.

105. Bekoff, *Minding Animals*, 47.

106. Bekoff, *Minding Animals*, 48.

107. Bekoff, *Minding Animals*, 97.

108. Birke, "Naming Names," 1.

109. Birke, "Naming Names," 5.

110. Birke, "Naming Names," 7.

111. Braidotti, "Animals, Anomalies, and Inorganic Others," 529.

112. Braidotti, "Animals, Anomalies, and Inorganic Others," 528.

113. Braidotti, "Animals, Anomalies, and Inorganic Others," 526.

114. Braidotti, "Animals, Anomalies, and Inorganic Others," 530.

115. Braidotti, "Animals, Anomalies, and Inorganic Others," 531.

116. Braidotti, "Animals, Anomalies, and Inorganic Others," 530.

117. Haraway, *When Species Meet*, 301.

118. Haraway, *When Species Meet*, 300.

119. Knudsen and Gentner, "Mechanisms of Song Perception," 65.

120. Prather and Mooney, "Neural Correlates," 496.

121. Knudsen, Thompson, and Gentner, "Distributed Recognition of Natural Songs," 288.

122. Chaiken, Gentner, and Hulse, "Effects of Social Interaction," 379.

123. Gentner et al., "Recursive Syntactic Pattern," 1204.

124. Gentner et al., "Recursive Syntactic Pattern," 1204.
125. Prather and Mooney, "Neural Correlates," 496.
126. Prather and Mooney, "Neural Correlates," 496.
127. Knudsen and Gentner, "Mechanisms of Song Perception," 65.
128. Prather and Mooney, "Neural Correlates," 496.
129. Gentner et al., "Recursive Syntactic Pattern," 1206.
130. Mieville, *Perdido*, 300 (emphasis added).

### 3. CAPITAL AND CONSERVATION

1. Cordell and Herbert, "Popularity of Birding," 3.
2. Carver, "Birding in the United States," 4–5.
3. Cordell and Herbert, "Popularity of Birding," 7.
4. Carver, "Birding in the United States," 4.
5. Carver, "Birding in the United States," 14.
6. NJDEP, "Imperiled Shorebirds," pamphlet.
7. Sutton, "Ecological Tragedy," 32.
8. Niles et al., "Status of the Red Knot," i.
9. Niles et al., "Effects of Horseshoe Crab Harvest,"153.
10. Niles et al., "Status of the Red Knot," 89.
11. Sutton, "Ecological Tragedy," 33.
12. Myers, Parsons, and Edwards, "Measuring the Recreational Use Value," 248.
13. Sutton, "Ecological Tragedy," 34.
14. Sutton, "Ecological Tragedy," 33.
15. Carver, "Birding in the United States," 4–5.
16. Carver, "Birding in the United States," 3.
17. Schaffner, *Binocular Vision*, 4.
18. Schaffner, *Binocular Vision*, 3.
19. Sibley, *Birding Basics*, 4.
20. Sibley, *Field Guide*, 14.
21. Peterson, *Peterson Field Guide*, copyright page.
22. Schaffner, *Binocular Vision*, 3.
23. Lawrence Niles, *A Rube with a View* (blog), http://arubewithaview.com.
24. Niles et al., "Effects of Horseshoe Crab Harvest," 162.
25. Niles, *Rube with a View*.
26. Niles, *Rube with a View*.
27. Schaffner, *Binocular Vision*, 17.
28. Schaffner, *Binocular Vision*, 17.
29. Schaffner, *Binocular Vision*, 29.
30. Schaffner, *Binocular Vision*, 44.

31. Schaffner, *Binocular Vision*, 48.
32. Gelber, quoted in Schaffner, *Binocular Vision*, 19
33. Schaffner, *Binocular Vision*, 19.
34. Schaffner, *Binocular Vision*, 19.
35. Schaffner, *Binocular Vision*, 19.
36. Schaffner, *Binocular Vision*, 18.
37. Schaffner, *Binocular Vision*, 28.
38. Schaffner, *Binocular Vision*, 18.
39. Coues, *Key to North American Birds*, xliii.
40. Coues, *Key to North American Birds*, 1.
41. Coues, *Key to North American Birds*, 22.
42. Coues, *Key to North American Birds*, 15.
43. Coues, *Key to North American Birds*, 15.
44. Coues, *Key to North American Birds*, 13.
45. Coues, *Key to North American Birds*, 9.
46. Coues, *Key to North American Birds*, 9.
47. Luke, "Beyond Birds," 25.
48. Coues, *Key to North American Birds*, 14–15.
49. Luke, "Beyond Birds," 26.
50. Luke, "Beyond Birds," 25.
51. Luke, "Beyond Birds," 27.
52. Jay, *Downcast Eyes*, 6.
53. Jay, *Downcast Eyes*, 3.
54. Jay, *Downcast Eyes*, 59.
55. Hardt and Negri, *Empire*, 271.
56. Hardt and Negri, *Empire*, 272.
57. Luke, "Beyond Birds," 36.
58. Luke, "Beyond Birds," 37.
59. Myers, Parsons, and Edwards, "Measuring the Recreational Use Value," 247.
60. Edwards, Parsons, and Myers, "Economic Value of Viewing Migratory Shorebirds," 442.
61. Myers, Parsons, and Edwards, "Measuring the Recreational Use Value," 247.
62. Edwards, Parsons, and Myers, "Economic Value of Viewing Migratory Shorebirds," 435.
63. Stoll, "Platte River Birding," 252.
64. Stoll, "Platte River Birding," 253.
65. Stoll, "Platte River Birding," 252.
66. Hawken, *Ecology of Commerce*, 12.

67. Hawken, *Ecology of Commerce*, 14.
68. Hawken, *Ecology of Commerce*, 182.
69. Costanza et al., "Managing Our Environmental Portfolio," 156, 149.
70. Brockington and Duffy, "Capitalism," 470.
71. Carrier, "Protecting the Environment," 673.
72. Corson, "Shifting Environmental Governance," 578.
73. Igoe, Neves, and Brockington, "Spectacular Eco-tour around the Historic Bloc," 498.
74. "About," Manomet Center for Conservation Sciences (Manomet), https://www.manomet.org/about-us.
75. "The Shorebird Recovery Project: Restoring Shorebird Populations and Ecosystems across the Americas," Manomet, https://www.manomet.org/sites/default/files/publications_and_tools/Manomet's%20Shorebird%20Recovery%20Project%20Roadmap%2011%2010-24.pdf.
76. "Recovery of *rufa* Red Knots," Manomet, https://www.manomet.org/program/shorebird-recovery/recovery-rufa-red-knots.
77. "Celebrate Delaware Bay," Facebook, https://www.facebook.com/CelebrateDelawareBay/.
78. "Shorebird Recovery Project," Manomet.
79. "Friends of the Red Knot," Facebook, https://www.facebook.com/FriendsoftheRedKnot/.
80. "Delaware Bayshore Initiative Launched to Spur Conservation, Recreation and Eco-tourism in State's Coastal Communities," Department of Natural Resources and Environmental Control (DNREC), State of Delaware, The Official Website of the First State, http://www.dnrec.delaware.gov/News/Pages/Delaware-Bayshore-Initiative-given-national-launch-to-spur-conservation,-recreation-and-eco-tourism-within-state.aspx.
81. Niles, Burger, and Dey, *Life Along the Delaware Bay*, ix.
82. Hoose, *Moonbird*, 3.
83. Niles, *Rube with a View*.
84. Igoe, Neves, and Brockington, "Spectacular Eco-tour around the Historic Bloc," 489.
85. Luke, "Beyond Birds," 7.
86. Corson, "Shifting Environmental Governance," 596.
87. Igoe, Neves, and Brockington, "Spectacular Eco-tour around the Historic Bloc," 495.
88. Nealon, *Post-Postmodernism*, 95.
89. Nealon, *Post-Postmodernism*, 97.
90. Nealon, *Post-Postmodernism*, 97.

91.  Hardt and Negri, *Empire*, 386.

92.  Guattari, *Three Ecologies*, 27.

93.  Guattari, *Three Ecologies*, 47.

94.  Guattari, *Three Ecologies*, 50.

95.  Cordell and Herbert, "Popularity of Birding," 7.

96.  Guattari, *Three Ecologies*, 29.

97.  Guattari, *Three Ecologies*, 27.

98.  Guattari, *Three Ecologies*, 68.

99.  Nealon, *Post-Postmodernism*, 96.

100.  Nealon, *Post-Postmodernism*, 98, 96.

101.  Nealon, *Post-Postmodernism*, 96.

102.  Hardt and Negri, *Empire*, 386–87.

103.  Hardt and Negri, *Empire*, 387.

104.  Hardt and Negri, *Empire*, 388–89.

105.  Guattari, *Three Ecologies*, 68.

106.  Guattari, *Three Ecologies*, 52.

107.  Guattari, *Chaosmosis*, 120.

108.  Guattari, *Chaosmosis*, 31.

109.  Hawken, *Ecology of Commerce*, 21

110.  Niles, *Rube with a View*.

111.  Guattari, *Chaosmosis*, 128–29

112.  Niles, *Rube with a View*.

113.  Niles, *Rube with a View*.

114.  Niles, *Rube with a View*.

115.  Niles, *Rube with a View*.

116.  Coues, *Key to North American Birds*, 1.

117.  Niles, *Rube with a View*.

4. NUISANCE AND NEIGHBOR

1.  P. J. Reilly, "Good News for Duck Hunters; Game Commission Clears Waterfowl for Consumption," *Lancaster Intelligencer Journal*, October 14, 2004, C-3.

2.  John Kopp, "Park Patrons Want Fowl to Stay, Despite the Droppings: Many Visit Long's Park Just to Feed the Birds," *Lancaster Online*, July 13, 2006, http://lancasteronline.com/news/park-patrons-want-fowl -to-stay-despite-the-droppings/article_693a00e4-6bbb-5da5-af14- 49a076900144.html.

3.  Mowbray et al., "Canada Goose."

4.  "Migratory Bird Hunting and Permits."

5.  "Migratory Bird Hunting and Permits."

6.  Mowbray et al., "Canada Goose."
7.  Mowbray et al., "Canada Goose."
8.  Schaffner, *Binocular Vision*, 17.
9.  Audubon, *Ornithological Biography*, 163.
10. Schaffner, *Binocular Vision*, 63.
11. Schaffner, *Binocular Vision*, 61.
12. USDA, "Wildlife Damage Management."
13. USDA, "Wildlife Damage Management."
14. USDA, "Animals Taken—FY 2008."
15. USDA, "Animals Taken—FY 2010."
16. USDA, "2010 Managing Wildlife Damage."
17. USDA, "Animals Taken—FY 2011."
18. USDA, "Animals Taken—FY 2010, FY 2009."
19. "Migratory Bird Hunting and Permits."
20. "Migratory Bird Hunting and Permits."
21. "Migratory Bird Hunting and Permits."
22. "Migratory Bird Hunting and Permits."
23. "News Release: U.S. Fish and Wildlife Service Releases Final Environmental Impact Statement on Resident Canada Geese Management," USFWS, 2005, http://www.fws.gov/mountain-prairie/pressrel /DC%2018.htm.
24. USDA, "Estimating the Value."
25. USDA, "Partnerships and Progress," 3.
26. USDA, "2010 Managing Wildlife Damage."
27. USFWS, "Final Environmental Impact Statement."
28. USDA, "Partnerships and Progress," 6.
29. USFWS, "Final Environmental Impact Statement."
30. "Migratory Bird Hunting and Permits."
31. USFWS, "Final Environmental Impact Statement."
32. USDA, "Factsheet: Management of Canada Goose Nesting."
33. USFWS, "Final Environmental Impact Statement."
34. "Migratory Bird Hunting and Permits."
35. USDI, "Memorandum: Section 7 Consultation," 8.
36. "Migratory Bird Hunting and Permits."
37. USFWS, "Final Environmental Impact Statement."
38. Luke, "Beyond Birds," 36.
39. Luke, "Beyond Birds," 24.
40. Luke, "Beyond Birds," 27.
41. Foucault, "Birth of Biopolitics," 73.
42. Nadesan, *Governmentality, Biopower, and Everyday Life*, 3.

43. Nealon, *Foucault beyond Foucault*, 108.

44. Foucault, "Subjectivity and Truth," 87.

45. Nadesan, *Governmentality, Biopower, and Everyday Life*, 215.

46. Nadesan, *Governmentality, Biopower, and Everyday Life*, 213.

47. Nadesan, *Governmentality, Biopower, and Everyday Life*, 215.

48. Nadesan, *Governmentality, Biopower, and Everyday Life*, 215.

49. Schaffner, *Binocular Vision*, 81.

50. Schaffner, *Binocular Vision*, 81.

51. Carson, *Silent Spring*, 126.

52. Carson, *Silent Spring*, 127.

53. USDA, "Partnerships and Progress," 2.

54. "About Us," Public Employees for Environmental Responsibility (PEER), 2002, http://www.peer.org/about-us/.

55. "Animal Slaughter," PEER, 2005, http://www.peer.org/campaigns /wildlife-protection/animal-slaughter/.

56. "Suit to Uncover Human Hazards of Federal Wildlife Eradication," PEER, 2008, http://www.peer.org/news/news-releases/2008/07/16 /suit-to-uncover-human-hazards-of-federal-wildlife-eradication/.

57. "Animal Slaughter," PEER.

58. GeesePeace, 2004, http://www.geesepeace.com.

59. "David Feld, Director of GeesePeace, Answers Questions," *Grist: A Beacon in the Smog*, February 20, 2007, http://grist.org/article/feld/.

60. HSUS, "Canada Geese."

61. "David Feld, Director of GeesePeace," *Grist*.

62. Nadesan, *Governmentality, Biopower, and Everyday Life*, 212.

63. GeesePeace, 2004, http://www.geesepeace.com.

64. Nealon, *Foucault beyond Foucault*, 17.

65. Nealon, *Foucault beyond Foucault*, 20.

66. Foucault, "Foucault," 461.

67. Foucault, "Foucault," 460.

68. Foucault, "Foucault," 461.

69. Foucault, "Foucault," 460.

70. Nealon, *Foucault beyond Foucault*, 20.

71. Nealon, *Foucault beyond Foucault*, 20.

72. Foucault, "Politics," 64.

73. Gabing, "Large Canada Geese in the Central Flyway," 8.

74. Gabing, "Large Canada Geese in the Central Flyway," 8.

75. USFWS, "Final Environmental Impact Statement."

76. "David Feld, Director of GeesePeace," *Grist*.

77. HSUS, "Canada Geese."

78. Ankney, "Embarrassment of Riches," 217.

79. Ankney, "Embarrassment of Riches," 217–18.

80. Ankney, "Embarrassment of Riches," 222.

81. Audubon, *Writings and Drawings*, 2.

82. Audubon, *Writings and Drawings*, 4.

83. Mowbray et al., "Canada Goose."

84. Audubon, *Writings and Drawings*, 4.

85. USFWS, "Final Environmental Impact Statement."

86. Thoreau, *On Birds*, 52.

87. Audubon, *Writings and Drawings*, 6.

88. Thoreau, *On Birds*, 67–68.

89. Audubon, *Writings and Drawings*, 13.

90. Audubon, *Writings and Drawings*, 16.

91. Gabing, "Large Canada Geese in the Central Flyway," 8.

92. Gabing, "Large Canada Geese in the Central Flyway," 12.

93. Hanson, *Giant Canada Goose*, 4.

94. Audubon, *Writings and Drawings*, 8.

95. Audubon, *Writings and Drawings*, 9.

96. Audubon, *Writings and Drawings*, 10.

97. Audubon, *Writings and Drawings*, 18.

98. Heinrich, *Geese of Beaver Bog*, xiii.

99. Heinrich, *Geese of Beaver Bog*, 10.

100. Heinrich, *Geese of Beaver Bog*, 11.

101. Heinrich, *Geese of Beaver Bog*, xiii.

102. Heinrich, *Geese of Beaver Bog*, 11.

103. Heinrich, *Geese of Beaver Bog*, xiv.

104. Heinrich, *Geese of Beaver Bog*, 91.

105. Heinrich, *Geese of Beaver Bog*, 171.

106. Heinrich, *Geese of Beaver Bog*, 174.

107. Heinrich, *Geese of Beaver Bog*, 177.

108. Heinrich, *Geese of Beaver Bog*, 194.

109. Heinrich, *Geese of Beaver Bog*, 199.

110. Heinrich, *Geese of Beaver Bog*, 202.

111. Michelfelder, "Valuing Wildlife Populations," 83.

112. Michelfelder, "Valuing Wildlife Populations," 85.

113. Michelfelder, "Valuing Wildlife Populations," 86.

114. Michelfelder, "Valuing Wildlife Populations," 87.

115. Michelfelder, "Valuing Wildlife Populations," 88.

116. Nadesan, *Governmentality, Biopower, and Everyday Life*, 3.

117. Foucault, "Governmentality," 95.

118. Nealon, *Foucault beyond Foucault*, 99.
119. Foucault, "Governmentality," 102–3.

### 5. CONFUSION AND CLASSIFICATION

1. Mary Beth Stowe, "Austin Adventure: Day 4: Hornsby Bend to Bastrop State Park," *Mary Beth Stowe's Website*, 2013, http://miriameagle mon.com/Trip%20reports/Austin%20area/Hornsby%20Bend.html.
2. AOU, "Thirty-Third Supplement," 878.
3. Dixon, "Distributional History," 29.
4. Banks et al., "Forty-Third Supplement," 902.
5. Avise and Zink, "Molecular Genetic Divergence," 516, 525.
6. Braun, Kitto, and Braun, "Molecular Population Genetics," 170, 172.
7. Ted Floyd, "Peter Pyle and Michael Retter Discuss Checklist Changes," American Birding Association, *The ABA Blog*, November 28, 2012, http://blog.aba.org/2012/11/peter-pyle-and-michael-retter-discuss -checklist-changes.html.
8. Darwin, *Origin of Species*, 598.
9. Balakrishnan, "Species Concepts," 691.
10. Balakrishnan, "Species Concepts," 692.
11. Balakrishnan, "Species Concepts," 689, 692.
12. Balakrishnan, "Species Concepts," 691.
13. Deleuze and Guattari, *What Is Philosophy?*, 2.
14. Deleuze and Guattari, *What Is Philosophy?*, 21.
15. Deleuze and Guattari, *What Is Philosophy?*, 20.
16. Deleuze and Guattari, *What Is Philosophy?*, 21.
17. Nietzsche, "On Truth and Lying," 878.
18. Nietzsche, "On Truth and Lying," 878.
19. Nietzsche, "On Truth and Lying," 881, 878–79.
20. Nietzsche, "On Truth and Lying," 878.
21. Nietzsche, "On Truth and Lying," 881 (emphasis added).
22. Nietzsche, *Genealogy of Morals*, 225.
23. Darwin, *Origin of Species*, 596.
24. Gough, "Non-origin of Species," 333.
25. Gough, "Non-origin of Species," 332.
26. Gough, "Non-origin of Species," 332.
27. Farber, *Discovering Birds*, 81.
28. Farber, *Discovering Birds*, 79.
29. Farber, *Discovering Birds*, 80.
30. Farber, *Discovering Birds*, 81.
31. Farber, *Discovering Birds*, 83.

32. Farber, *Discovering Birds*, 84.
33. Foucault, *Order of Things*, 139.
34. Foucault, *Order of Things*, xv.
35. Borges, "Analytical Language of John Wilkins," 104.
36. Wicks, "Literary Truth," 82.
37. Wicks, "Literary Truth," 87.
38. Foucault, *Order of Things*, xix.
39. Foucault, *Order of Things*, xv.
40. Foucault, *Order of Things*, xx.
41. Foucault, *Order of Things*, xxxi.
42. Foucault, *Order of Things*, 145.
43. Foucault, *Order of Things*, 131.
44. Foucault, *Order of Things*, 134.
45. Foucault, *Order of Things*, 144.
46. Foucault, *Order of Things*, 142.
47. Foucault, *Order of Things*, 160.
48. Foucault, *Order of Things*, 192.
49. Farber, *Discovering Birds*, 91.
50. Farber, *Discovering Birds*, 89.
51. Wilson, *Future of Life*, 162.
52. Margulis, "From the President," 290.
53. Mora et al., "How Many," 1.
54. Mora et al., "How Many," 5.
55. Mora et al., "How Many," 6–7.
56. Beardsley, "Bending to Bar Codes," 26.
57. Hebert et al., "Biological Identifications," 313.
58. "What Is DNA Barcoding?," Consortium for the Barcode of Life (CBOL), Smithsonian Institute, 2008, http://www.barcodeoflife.org/content /about/what-dna-barcoding.
59. Beardsley, "Bending to Bar Codes," 27.
60. "What Is DNA Barcoding?," CBOL.
61. Hebert et al., "Biological Identifications," 313.
62. Hebert et al., "Biological Identifications," 320.
63. Hebert et al., "Identification of Birds through DNA Barcodes," 1661.
64. Hebert et al., "Identification of Birds through DNA Barcodes," 1661.
65. Kerr et al., "Comprehensive DNA Barcode Coverage," 536.
66. Kerr et al., "Comprehensive DNA Barcode Coverage," 539.
67. Kerr et al., "Comprehensive DNA Barcode Coverage," 535.
68. Hebert et al., "Identification of Birds through DNA Barcodes," 1663.
69. Kerr et al., "Comprehensive DNA Barcode Coverage," 541.

194 NOTES TO PAGES 156–164

70. Will, Mishler, and Wheeler, "Perils of DNA Barcoding," 851.

71. Will, Mishler, and Wheeler, "Perils of DNA Barcoding," 850.

72. Taylor and Harris, "Emergent Science," 386.

73. Yeates et al., "Integrative Taxonomy," 214

74. Borges, "Library of Babel," 112.

75. Borges, "Library of Babel," 113.

76. Margulis, "From the President," 290.

77. Wilson, "Encyclopedia of Life," 79.

78. Wood et al., "eBird: Engaging Birders," 1.

79. Kelling et al., "eBird: A Human/Computer Learning Network," 14.

80. Karnicky, Jeffrey. "Personal Email." January 11, 2013.

81. Karnicky, Jeffrey. "Personal Email." January 24, 2013

82. Wood et al., "eBird: Engaging Birders," 3.

83. Kelling et al., "eBird: A Human/Computer Learning Network," 12.

84. Kelling et al., "eBird: A Human/Computer Learning Network," 12.

85. Wood et al., "eBird: Engaging Birders," 2.

86. Wood et al., "eBird: Engaging Birders," 3.

87. Sullivan et al., "eBird: A Citizen-Based Bird Observation Network," 2290.

88. Kelling et al., "eBird: A Human/Computer Learning Network," 11.

89. Borges, "On Exactitude in Science," 325.

90. Sullivan et al., "eBird: A Citizen-Based Bird Observation Network," 2282.

91. Sullivan et al., "eBird: A Citizen-Based Bird Observation Network," 2290.

92. Munson et al., "Method for Measuring," 262.

93. Fink et al., "Spatiotemporal Exploratory Models," 2131, 2144.

94. Fink et al., "Spatiotemporal Exploratory Models," 2132.

95. Fink et al., "Spatiotemporal Exploratory Models," 2145.

96. "Home," *Avian Knowledge Network* (AKN), Cornell Lab of Ornithology, 2007, http://www.avianknowledge.net/.

97. "eBird Reference Dataset (3.0) Released!," AKN, 2007, http://www.avianknowledge.net/content/features/archive/ebird-reference-dataset-3-0-released (site discontinued).

98. "McAllen PowerPoints," AKN, 2007, http://www.avianknowledge.net/content/about/mcallenpowerpoints (site discontinued).

99. "Bird Migration Forecasts in Real Time," *BirdCast*, 2013, http://birdcast.info.

100. "Bird Migration Forecasts in Real Time," *BirdCast*.

101. "Latest News: 2011 State of the Birds Report Features eBird," *eBird*, Audubon and Cornell Lab of Ornithology, accessed May 3, 2013, http://ebird.org/content/ebird/news/2011-state-of-the-birds.

102. NABCI, "State 2011," 2.

103. NABCI, "State 2011," 3.

104. NABCI, "State 2011," 3.

105. NABCI, "State 2009," 2.

106. NABCI, "State 2009," 3.

107. NABCI, "State 2011," 44–45.

108. NABCI, "State 2009," 34.

109. NABCI, "State 2009," 39.

110. NABCI, "State 2009," 39.

111. NABCI, "State 2011," 45.

112. NABCI, "State 2011," 4.

113. NABCI, "State 2011," 29.

114. NABCI, "State 2011," 45.

CONCLUSION

1. Foucault, "Foucault," 463.

2. Rosner, "Data on Wings," 69.

3. Wiggins and Crowston, "Conservation to Crowdsourcing," 9.

4. NABCI, "State 2011," 9.

5. NABCI, "State 2011," 29.

6. Cokinos, *Hope Is the Thing*, 334–35.

7. Cokinos, *Hope Is the Thing*, 335.

8. NABCI, "State 2011," 5.

9. NABCI, "State 2011," 4.

10. USFWS, "Endangered Species Act."

11. NABCI, "State 2011," 8.

12. NABCI, "State 2011," 5.

13. Gibbons and Strom, *Neighbor to the Birds*, 157.

14. "Transcript: Presidential Debate, Oct. 22, 2012," *Politico*, October 22, 2012, http://www.politico.com/story/2012/10/third-debate-transcript-082712.

15. NABCI, "State 2011," 27.

16. Brockington and Duffy, "Capitalism and Conservation," 470.

17. Foucault, "Birth of Biopolitics," 79.

18. Hardt and Negri, *Empire*, 413 (emphasis added).

19. Hardt and Negri, *Empire*, 386–87; *Declaration*, 91.

20. Hardt and Negri, *Declaration*, 92.

21. Hardt and Negri, *Declaration*, 93.

22. Guattari, *Chaosmosis*, 134.

23. Barber, *Human Nature of Birds*, 148.

# BIBLIOGRAPHY

Acampora, Ralph. *A Nietzschean Bestiary*. Oxford: Rowan & Littlefield
Publishers, 2004.

Alexie, Sherman. "Avian Nights." *New Letters* 69, no. 4 (2003): 21–23.

Allen, Colin, and Marc Bekoff. *Species of Mind: The Philosophy and Biology of
Cognitive Ethology*. Cambridge MA: MIT Press, 1997.

Althusser, Louis. *Lenin and Philosophy and Other Essays*. Translated by Ben
Brewster. London: Monthly Review Press, 1971.

American Bird Conservancy. "The Strategic Bird Conservation Framework." 2010.
http://abcbirds.org/about/mission-and-strategy/conservation-framework/.

American Birding Association. "Listing Central." 2013. http://listing.aba.org.

American Ornithologists' Union (AOU). "Thirty-Third Supplement to the
American Ornithologists' Union Check-List of North American Birds."
*The Auk* 93, no. 4 (October 1976): 875–79.

Ankney, C. Davison. "An Embarrassment of Riches: Too Many Geese." *The
Journal of Wildlife Management* 60, no. 2 (April 1996): 217–23.

Armstrong, James W. "Audubon's *Ornithological Biography* and the Question
of 'Other Minds.'" In *Animal Acts: Configuring the Human in Western History*, edited by Jennifer Ham and Matthew Senior. New York:
Routledge, 1997.

Audubon, John James. *Ornithological Biography*. Philadelphia: E. L. Carey
and A. Hart, 1832. Print.

——. *Writings and Drawings*. New York: The Library of America, 1999
(1831–1839).

Avise, John C., and Robert M. Zink. "Molecular Genetic Divergence between Avian Sibling Species: King and Clapper Rails, Long-Billed and Short-Billed Dowitchers, Boat-Tailed and Great-Tailed Grackles, and Tufted and Black-Crested Titmice." *The Auk* 105, no. 3 (July 1988): 516–28.

Balakrishnan, Rohini. "Species Concepts, Species Boundaries and Species Identification: A View from the Tropics." *Systematic Biology* 54, no. 4 (August 2005): 689–93.

Banks, Richard C., C. Cicero, J. L. Dunn, A. W. Kratter, P. C. Rasmussen, J. V. Remsen Jr., J. D. Rising, and D. F. Stotz. "Forty-Third Supplement to the American Ornithologists' Union Check-List of North American Birds." *The Auk* 119, no. 3 (2002): 897–906.

Barber, Theodore Xenophon. *The Human Nature of Birds: A Scientific Discovery with Startling Implications.* New York: Penguin Books, 1993.

Barrow, Mark V., Jr. *A Passion for Birds: American Ornithology after Audubon.* Princeton NJ: Princeton University Press, 1998.

Beardsley, Sara. "Bending to Bar Codes." *Scientific American* 292, no. 5 (May 2005): 26–28.

Bekoff, Marc. *Minding Animals: Awareness, Emotions, and Heart.* New York: Oxford University Press, 2002.

Bekoff, Marc, Colin Allen, and Michael C. Grant. "Feeding Decisions by Steller's Jays (*Cyanocitta stelleri*): The Utility of a Logistic Regression Model for Analyses of Where, What, and With Whom to Eat." *Ethology* 105 (1996): 393–406.

Berry, Wendell. "Is Life a Miracle?" In *Citizenship Papers*, 181–89. Washington DC: Shoemaker and Hoard, 2003.

———. *Life Is a Miracle: An Essay against Modern Superstition.* Washington DC: Counterpoint, 2000.

Birke, Lynda. "Naming Names—Or, What's in It for the Animals?" *Humanimalia* 1, no. 1 (September 2009): 1–9. http://www.depauw.edu /humanimalia/issue01/pdfs/Lynda%20Birke.pdf.

Borges, Jorge Luis. "The Analytical Language of John Wilkins." In *Otras Inquisiciones*, translated by Ruth L. C. Simms, 104. Austin: University of Texas Press, 1964.

———. "The Library of Babel." In *Jorge Luis Borges, Collected Fictions*, translated by Andrew Hurley, 112–18. New York: Penguin, 1998.

———. "On Exactitude in Science." In *Jorge Luis Borges, Collected Fictions*, translated by Andrew Hurley, 325. New York: Penguin, 1998.

Braidotti, Rosi. "Animals, Anomalies, and Inorganic Others." *PMLA: Publications of the Modern Language Association of America* 124, no. 2 (March 2009): 526–32.

Braun, David, G. B. Kitto, and M. J. Braun. "Molecular Population Genetics of Tufted and Black-Crested Forms of *Parus bicolor*." *The Auk* 101, no. 1 (January 1984): 170–73.

Brockington, Dan, and Rosaleen Duffy. "Capitalism and Conservation: The Production and Reproduction of Biodiversity Conservation." *Antipode* 42, no. 3 (2010): 469–84.

Bugnyar, Thomas, Mareike Stöwe, and Bernd Heinrich. "Ravens, *Corvus corax*, Follow Gaze Direction of Humans around Obstacles." *Proceedings of the Royal Society: Biological Sciences* 1546 (2004): 1331–36.

Butcher, Greg. "Wake Up Call." *Audubon: Common Birds in Decline, A State of the Birds Report, Summer* 2007. http://www.audubon.org/sites /default/files/documents/sotb_cbid_magazine.pdf.

Carrier, James G. "Protecting the Environment the Natural Way: Ethical Consumption and Commodity Fetishism." *Antipode* 42, no. 3 (2010): 672–89.

Carson, Rachel. *Silent Spring.* Boston: Mariner Books, 2002. First published 1962.

Carter, J., N. J. Lyons, H. L. Cole, and A. R. Goldsmith. "Subtle Cues of Predation Risk: Starlings Respond to a Predator's Direction of Eye-Gaze. *Proceedings of the Royal Society: Biological Sciences* 1644 (2008): 1709–15.

Carver, Erin. "Birding in the United States: A Demographic and Economic Analysis: Addendum to the 2011 National Survey of Fishing, Hunting and Wildlife-Associated Recreation." Washington DC: Division of Federal Aid, U.S. Fish and Wildlife Service, 2011. http://www.fws.gov /southeast/economicImpact/pdf/2011-BirdingReport--FINAL.pdf.

Catesby, Mark. *Catesby's Birds of Colonial America.* Edited by Alan Feduccia. Chapel Hill: University of North Carolina Press, 1985.

Chaiken, MarthaLeah, Timothy Q. Gentner, and Stewart H. Hulse. "Effects of Social Interaction on the Development of Starling Song and the Perception of These Effects by Conspecifics." *Journal of Comparative Psychology* 3, no. 4 (1997): 379–92.

Clark, George A., Jr. "Chapter 3: Form and Function: The External Bird." In *Cornell Lab of Ornithology Home Study Course in Bird Biology.* 2nd ed.: 3.1–3.70. Ithaca NY: Cornell Lab of Ornithology, 2001.

Cokinos, Christopher. *Hope Is the Thing with Feathers: A Personal Chronicle of Vanished Birds.* New York: Warner Books, 2000.

Conley, Verena Andermatt. *Ecopolitics: The Environment in Poststructuralist Thought.* New York: Routledge, 1997.

Corbo, Margarete Sigl, and Diane Marie Barras. *Arnie, the Darling Starling.* Boston: Houghton Mifflin, 1983.

Cordell, Ken, and Nancy G. Herbert. "The Popularity of Birding Is Still Growing." *Birding* (February 2002).

Corson, Catherine. "Shifting Environmental Governance in a Neoliberal World: U.S. Aid for Conservation." *Antipode* 42, no. 3 (2010): 576–602.

Costanza, Robert, et al. "Managing Our Environmental Portfolio." *BioScience* 50, no. 2 (February 2000): 149–55.

Coues, Elliott. *Key to North American Birds*. Boston: The Page Company, 1872.

Darwin, Charles. *On the Origin of Species*. In *Darwin, the Indelible Stain*, edited by James D. Watson. Philadelphia: Running Press Book Publishers, 2005.

Deleuze, Gilles, and Felix Guattari. *A Thousand Plateaus: Capitalism and Schizophrenia*. Translated by Brian Massumi. Minneapolis: University of Minnesota Press, 1987.

———. *What Is Philosophy?* Translated by Hugh Tomlinson and Graham Burchell. New York: Columbia University Press, 1994.

DeLillo, Don. *The Body Artist*. New York: Scribner, 2001.

Derrida, Jacques. *The Animal That Therefore I Am*. Edited by Marie-Louise Mallet. Translated by David Wills. New York: Fordham University Press, 2008.

Dickinson, Emily. *The Poems of Emily Dickinson*. Edited by R. W. Franklin. Cambridge MA: The Belknap Press of Harvard University.

Dixon, Keith L. "A Distributional History of the Black-Crested Titmouse." *American Midland Naturalist* 100, no. 1 (July 1978): 29–42.

Edwards, Peter E. T., George R. Parsons, and Kelley H. Myers. "The Economic Value of Viewing Migratory Shorebirds on the Delaware Bay: An Application of the Single Site Travel Cost Model Using On-Site Data." *Human Dimensions of Wildlife* 16, no. 6 (2011): 435–44.

Farber, Paul Lawrence. *Discovering Birds: The Emergence of Ornithology as a Scientific Discipline, 1760–1850*. Baltimore MD: Johns Hopkins University Press, 1996.

Fink, Daniel, Wesley M. Hochachka, Benjamin Zucerberg, David W. Winkler, Ben Sahby, M. Arthur Munson, Giles Hooker, Mirek Riedewald, Daniel Sheldon, and Steve Kelling. "Spatiotemporal Exploratory Models for Broad-Scale Survey Data." *Ecological Applications* 20, no. 8 (2010): 2131–47.

Forkner, Ben. "Writing the American Woods: The Journals and Essays of John James Audubon." Introduction to *Selected Journals and Other Writings*, by John James Audubon. New York: Penguin, 1996.

Formato, Vicki. *Jayson: The True Story of a 20 Year Old Blue Jay.* Harwich MA: CEM Ventures, 2004.

Foucault, Michel. "The Birth of Biopolitics." In *Ethics: Subjectivity and Truth,* edited by Paul Rabinow, translated by Robert Hurley, 73–79. New York: The New Press, 1994.

———. "Foucault." In *Aesthetics, Method, and Epistemology,* edited by James D. Faubion, translated by Robert Hurley, 459–64. New York: The New Press, 1998.

———. "Governmentality." In *The Foucault Effect: Studies in Governmentality, with Two Lectures by and an Interview with Michel Foucault,* edited by Graham Burchell, Colin Gordon, and Peter Miller, 87–104. Chicago: University of Chicago Press, 1991.

———. *The Order of Things: An Archaeology of the Human Sciences.* New York: Vintage Books, 1994. First published 1966.

———. "Politics and the Study of Discourse." In *The Foucault Effect: Studies in Governmentality, with two Lectures by and an Interview with Michel Foucault,* edited by Graham Burchell, Colin Gordon, and Peter Miller, 53–72. Chicago: University of Chicago Press, 1991.

———. "Subjectivity and Truth." In *Ethics: Subjectivity and Truth,* edited by Paul Rabinow, translated by Robert Hurley, 87–92. New York: The New Press, 1994.

Gabing, Joseph P. "Large Canada Geese in the Central Flyway: Management of Depredation, Nuisance, and Human Health and Safety Issues." Prepared for the Central Flyway Council, 2000. http://central.flyways.us /large-canada-geese.

Gannon, Tom. *Skylark Meets Meadowlark: Reimagining the Bird in British Romantic and Contemporary Native American Literature.* Lincoln: University of Nebraska Press, 2009.

Gentner, Timothy Q., Kimberly M. Fenn, Daniel Margoliash, and Howard C. Nusbaum. "Recursive Syntactic Pattern Learning by Songbirds." *Nature* 440 (April 27, 2006): 1204–7.

Gibbons, Felton, and Deborah Strom. *Neighbor to the Birds: A History of Birdwatching in America.* New York: W. W. Norton and Company, 1998.

Gough, Tim. "Non-origin of Species." *Culture and Organization* 12, no. 4 (December 2006): 331–39.

Griffin, Donald R. *Animal Minds: Beyond Cognition to Consciousness.* Chicago: University of Chicago Press, 2001. First published 1992.

Guattari, Felix. *Chaosmosis: An Ethico-aesthetic Paradigm.* Translated by Paul Bains and Julian Pefanis. Bloomington: Indiana University Press, 1995.

———. *The Three Ecologies*. Translated by Ian Pindar and Paul Sutton. London and New Brunswick NJ: The Athlone Press, 2000. First published 1989.

Hanson, Harold C. *The Giant Canada Goose*. Rev. ed. Carbondale: Southern Illinois University Press, 1997.

Haraway, Donna. *The Companion Species Manifesto*. New York: Prickly Paradigm Press, 2003.

———. *Simians, Cyborgs, and Women: The Reinvention of Nature*. New York: Routledge, 1991.

———. *When Species Meet*. Minneapolis: University of Minnesota Press, 2007.

Hardt, Michael, and Antonio Negri. *Declaration*. N.p.: Argo-Navis Author Services, 2012.

———. *Empire*. Cambridge MA: Harvard University Press, 2000.

Hawken, Paul. *The Ecology of Commerce: A Declaration of Sustainability*. Rev. ed. New York: Harper Business Press, 2010.

Hebert, Paul D. N., Alina Cywinska, Shelley L. Ball, and Jeremy R. deWaard. "Biological Identifications through DNA Barcodes." *Proceedings of the Royal Society: Biological Sciences* (2003): 313–21.

Hebert, Paul D. N., Mark Y. Stoeckle, Tyler S. Zemlak, and Charles M. Francis. "Identification of Birds through DNA Barcodes." *PLOS Biology* 2, no. 10 (October 2004): 1657–63.

Heinrich, Bernd. *The Geese of Beaver Bog*. New York: HarperCollins, 2004.

Hoose, Phillip. *Moonbird: A Year on the Wind with the Great Survivor B95*. New York: Farrar, Straus and Giroux, 2012.

The Humane Society of the United States (HSUS). "Solving Problems with Canada Geese: A Management Plan and Information Guide." *The Humane Society of the United States* (2012): 1–12. http://www.humane society.org/assets/pdfs/wild_neighbors/canada_goose_guide.pdf.

Igoe, Jim, Katja Neves, and Dan Brockington. "A Spectacular Eco-tour around the Historic Bloc: Theorising the Convergence of Biodiversity Conservation and Capitalist Expansion." *Antipode* 42, no. 3 (2010): 486–512.

Jay, Martin. *Downcast Eyes: The Denigration of Vision in Twentieth-Century French Thought*. Berkeley: University of California Press, 1993.

Jones, Thony B., and Alan Kamil. "Tool-Making and Tool-Using in the Northern Blue Jay." *Science*, n.s., 180, no. 4090 (June 8, 1973): 1076–78.

Kaufman, Kenn. *Kingbird Highway: The Story of a Natural Obsession That Got a Little Out of Hand*. New York: Houghton Mifflin, 2000. First published 1997.

Kelling, Steve, Carl Lagoze, Weng-Keen Wong, Jun Yu, Theodoros Damou-las, Jeff Gerbracht, Daniel Fink, and Carla Gomes. "eBird: A Human/ Computer Learning Network to Improve Biodiversity Conservation and Research." *AI Magazine* 34, no. 1 (Spring 2013): 10–20.

Kerr, Kevin C. R., Mark Y. Stoeckle, Carla Dove, Lee Weigt, Charles Francis, and Paul D. N. Hebert. "Comprehensive DNA Barcode Coverage of North American Birds." *Molecular Ecology Notes* 7, no. 4 (July 2007): 535–43.

Knudsen, Daniel, and Timothy Q. Gentner. "Mechanisms of Song Perception in Oscine Birds." *Brain and Language* 115 (2010): 59–68.

Knudsen, Daniel, Jason V. Thompson, and Timothy Q. Gentner. "Distributed Recognition of Natural Songs by European Starlings." *Learning and Motivation* 41 (2010): 287–306.

Koeppel, Dan. *To See Every Bird on Earth: A Father, a Son, and a Lifelong Obsession.* New York: Plume, 2006.

Loss, Scott R., Tom Will, and Peter T. Parra. "Direct Human-Caused Mortal-ity of Birds: Improving Quantification of Magnitude and Assessment of Population Impact." *Frontiers in Ecology and the Environment* 10, no. 7 (September 2012): 357–64.

———. "The Impact of Free-Ranging Domestic Cats on Wildlife of the United States." *Nature Communications* 4, no. 1 (January 2013). http://www .nature.com/ncomms/journal/v4/n1/full/ncomms2380.html %3FWT.mc_id%3DFBK_NCOMMS?message-global=remove&WT .mc_id=FBK_NCOMMS.

Luke, Timothy W. "Beyond Birds: Biopower and Birdwatching in the World of Audubon." *Capitalism, Nature, Socialism* 11, no. 3 (September 2000): 7–37.

Manville, Albert M. "Towers, Turbines, Power Lines, and Buildings—Steps Being Taken by the U.S. Fish and Wildlife Service to Avoid or Minimize Take of Migratory Birds at These Structures." *Proceedings of the Fourth International Partners in Flight Conference: Tundra to Tropics,* 262–72. http://www.partnersinflight.org/pubs/mcallenproc/articles /pif09_anthropogenic%20impacts/manville_pif09.pdf.

Margulis, Lynn. "From the President: The Names of Life." *American Scientist* 93 (2005): 290

McHugh, Susan. "Literary Animal Agents." *PMLA: Publications of the Mod-ern Language Association of America* 124, no. 2 (March 2009): 487–95.

Michelfelder, Diane P. "Valuing Wildlife Populations within Urban Environ-ments." *Journal of Social Philosophy* 34, no. 1 (Spring 2003): 79–90.

Mieville, China. *Perdido Street Station.* New York: Del Ray, 2003.

"Migratory Bird Hunting and Permits; Regulations for Managing Resident Canada Goose Populations; Final Rule." *Federal Register* 71:154 (Thursday, August 10, 2006). https://www.federalregister.gov /articles/2006/08/10/06-6739/migratory-bird-hunting-and-permits -regulations-for-managing-resident-canada-goose-populations.

Mora, Camilo, Derek Tittensor, Sina Adl, Alastair Simpson, and Boris Worm. "How Many Species Are There on Earth and in the Ocean?" *PLOS Biology* 9, no. 8 (August 2011): 1–8.

Mowbray, Thomas B., Craig R. Ely, James S. Sedinger, and Robert E. Trost. "Canada Goose (*Branta canadensis*)." In *The Birds of North America Online*, edited by A. Poole. Ithaca NY: Cornell Lab of Ornithology, 2002. http://bna.birds.cornell.edu/bna/species/682/articles/introduction.

Munson, Arthur M., Rich Caruana, Daniel Fink, Wesley M. Hochachka, Marshall Iliff, Kenneth V. Rosenberg, Daniel Sheldon, Brian L. Sullivan, Christopher Wood, and Steve Kelling. "A Method for Measuring the Relative Information Content of Data from Different Monitoring Protocols." *Methods in Ecology and Evolution* 1 (2010): 263–73.

Myers, Kelley H., George R. Parsons, and Peter E. T. Edwards. "Measuring the Recreational Use Value of Migratory Shorebirds: A Stated Preference Study of Birdwatching on the Delaware Bay." *Marine Resource Economics* 25 (2010): 247–64.

Nadesan, Majia Holmer. *Governmentality, Biopower, and Everyday Life*. New York: Routledge, 2008.

Nealon, Jeffrey T. *Foucault beyond Foucault: Power and Its Intensifications since 1984*. Stanford CA: Stanford University Press, 2008.

———. *Post-Postmodernism: Or, The Cultural Logic of Just-in-Time Capitalism*. Stanford CA: Stanford University Press, 2012.

Nel, Philip. "Don DeLillo's Return to Form: The Modernist Poetics of *The Body Artist*." *Contemporary Literature* 43, no. 4 (2002): 736–59.

New Jersey Department of Environmental Protection (NJDEP). "Imperiled Shorebirds on the Delaware Bay: What You Can Do to Help Them." Pamphlet. 2005.

Nietzsche, Friedrich. *The Birth of Tragedy and the Genealogy of Morals*. Translated by Francis Golfing. New York: Doubleday and Company, 1956.

———. "On Truth and Lying in a Non-moral Sense." Translated by Ronald Speirs. In *The Norton Anthology of Literary Theory*, edited by Vincent Leitch, 874–84. New York: Norton, 2001.

Niles, Lawrence J., Joanna Burger, and Amanda Dey. *Life Along the Delaware Bay: Cape May, Gateway to a Million Shorebirds*. New Brunswick NJ: Rivergate Books, 2012.

Niles, Lawrence J., et al. "Status of the Red Knot (*Calidris canutus rufa*) in the Western Hemisphere." New Jersey Department of Environmental Protection Division of Fish and Wildlife, Endangered and Nongame Species Program. 2007. http://www.state.nj.us/dep/fgw/ensp/pdf /literature/status-assessment_red-knot.pdf.

Niles, Lawrence J., et al. "Effects of Horseshoe Crab Harvest in Delaware Bay on Red Knots: Are Harvest Restrictions Working?" *BioScience* 59, no. 2 (February 2009): 153–64.

North American Bird Conservation Initiative (NABCI), U.S. Committee. "The State of the Birds: United States of America, 2009." Washington DC: U.S. Department of the Interior, 2009. http://www.stateofthe birds.org/2009/pdf_files/State_of_the_Birds_2009.pdf.

———. "The State of the Birds: 2010 Report on Climate Change, United States of America." Washington DC: U.S. Department of the Interior, 2010. http://www.stateofthebirds.org/2010/pdf_files/State%20of%20 the%20Birds_FINAL.pdf.

———. "The State of the Birds 2011: Report on Public Lands and Waters, United States of America." Washington DC: U.S. Department of the Interior, 2011. http://www.stateofthebirds.org/2011/State%20of%20 the%20Birds%202011.pdf.

Peterson, Roger Tory. *All Things Reconsidered: My Birding Adventures*. Edited by Bill Thompson III. New York: Houghton Mifflin, 2006.

———. *Peterson Field Guide to Birds of Eastern and Central North America*. 6th ed. New York: Houghton Mifflin Harcourt, 2010.

Prather, Jonathan F., and Richard Mooney. "Neural Correlates of Learned Song in the Avian Forebrain: Simultaneous Representation of Self and Others." *Current Opinion in Neurobiology* 14 (2004): 496–502.

Reiner, Anton, et al. "The Avian Brain Nomenclature Forum: Terminology for a New Century in Comparative Neuroanatomy." *The Journal of Comparative Neurology* 473 (2004): E1–E6.

Rosner, Hillary. "Data on Wings." *Scientific American* 308, no. 2 (February 2013): 68–73.

Rotman, Brian. "Going Parallel." *SubStance: A Review of Theory and Literary Criticism* 29, no. 1 (2000): 56–79.

Savage, Candace. *Bird Brains: The Intelligence of Crows, Ravens, Magpies, and Jays*. San Francisco: Sierra Club Books, 1995.

Schaffner, Spencer. *Binocular Vision: The Politics of Representation in Bird-watching Field Guides*. Amherst: University of Massachusetts Press, 2011.

Sibley, David Allen. *The Sibley Field Guide to Birds of Eastern North America*. New York: Alfred A. Knopf, 2003.

———. *The Sibley Guide to Birds*. New York: Alfred A. Knopf, 2000.

———. *Sibley's Birding Basics*. New York: Alfred A. Knopf, 2003.

Stanger, Margaret A. *That Quail, Robert*. New York: J. B. Lippincott Company, 1966.

Stoll, John R. "Platte River Birding and the Spring Migration: Humans, Value, and Unique Ecological Resources." *Human Dimensions of Wildlife* 11 (2006): 241–54.

Sullivan, Brian L., Christopher L. Wood, Marshall J. Iliff, Rick E. Bonney, Daniel Fink, and Steve Kelling. "eBird: A Citizen-Based Bird Observation Network in the Biological Sciences." *Biological Conservation* 142, no. 10 (October 2009): 2282–92.

Sutton, Clay. "An Ecological Tragedy on Delaware Bay." *Living Bird* 22, no. 3 (Summer 2003): 30–37.

Tarvin, Keith, and Glen E. Woolfenden. "Blue Jay (*Cyanocitta cristata*)." In *The Birds of North America Online*, edited by A. Poole. Ithaca NY: Cornell Lab of Ornithology. http://bna.birds.cornell.edu/bna/species/469.

———. "Patterns of Dominance and Aggressive Behavior in Blue Jays at a Feeder." *The Condor* 99, no. 2 (April 1997): 434–45.

Taylor, H. R., and W. E. Harris. "An Emergent Science on the Brink of Irrelevance: A Review of the Past 8 Years of DNA Barcoding." *Molecular Ecology Resources* 12 (2012): 377–88.

Thoreau, Henry David. *Thoreau on Birds: Notes on New England Birds from the Journals of Henry David Thoreau*. Edited by Francis H. Allen. Boston: Beacon Press, 1993. First published 1910.

———. *Walden; Or, Life in the Woods*. New York: Dover, 1995. First published 1854.

United States Department of Agriculture (USDA). "2010 Managing Wildlife Damage Informational Notebook." Wildlife Services. https://www.aphis.usda.gov/wildlife_damage/content/wp_c_ws_2010_notebook.shtml.

———. "Estimating the Value of Resident Canada Goose Damage Management." National Wildlife Research Center. 2011. https://www.aphis.usda.gov/publications/wildlife_damage/2011/canada_goose_mgt.pdf.

———. "Fact Sheet—Controlling Starling Damage at Feedlots in West Virginia." Wildlife Services. January 2010. http://anr.ext.wvu.edu/r/download/56113.

———. "Factsheet: Management of Canada Goose Nesting." Wildlife Services. February 2011. https://www.aphis.usda.gov/publications/wildlife_damage/content/printable_version/fs_goosenst_WS_2pg.pdf.

United States Department of Agriculture, Animal and Plant Health Inspection Service (USDA)."Animals Taken by Component/Method Type and Fate by the Wildlife Services Program—FY 2008." 2009. https://www.aphis.usda.gov/wildlife_damage/prog_data/2008_pdr/content/wp_c_ws_PDR_G_Piechart_08.shtml.

———. "Animals Taken by Wildlife Services—FY 2010." 2011. http://www.aphis.usda.gov/wildlife_damage/prog_data/2010_prog_data/PDR_G/Basic_Tables_PDR_G/Table%20G_ShortReport.pdf.

———. "Animals Taken by Wildlife Services—FY 2011." 2012. https://www.aphis.usda.gov/wildlife_damage/prog_data/2011_prog_data/PDR_G/Basic_Tables_PDR_G/Table%20G_ShortReport.pdf.

———. "Partnerships and Progress." August 2009. https://www.aphis.usda.gov/wildlife_damage/downloads/partnerships%20in%20progress.pdf.

———. "Table G: Animals Taken by Wildlife Services—FY 2009." 2010. https://www.aphis.usda.gov/wildlife_damage/prog_data/2009_prog_data/PDR_G_FY09/Basic_Tables_PDR_G/Table_G_FY2009_Short.pdf.

———. "Wildlife Damage Management." 2012. https://www.aphis.usda.gov/wps/portal/aphis/ourfocus/wildlifedamage.

United States Department of the Interior (USDI). "Memorandum: Section 7 Consultation on the Proposed Regulation for Resident Canada Goose Management." October 11, 2005. https://www.fws.gov/migratorybirds/pdf/management/canada-geese/FEIS/Appendix17.pdf.

United States Fish and Wildlife Service (USFWS). "Endangered Species Act: Section Two." Endangered Species Program. http://www.fws.gov/endangered/laws-policies/section-2.html.

———. "Final Environmental Impact Statement: Resident Canada Goose Management." http://www.fws.gov/birds/management/managed-species/resident-canada-goose-management-final.php.

———. "Species Reports. Environmental Conservation Online System." http://ecos.fws.gov/tess_public/reports/ad-hoc-species-report?kingdom=V&status=E&status=T&status=EmE&status=EmT&status=SAE&status=SAT&mapstatus=1&fleadreg=on&fstatus=on&finvpop=on&header=Listed+Vertebrate+Animals.

Vantassel, Stephen M., Scott E. Hygnstrom, and Dennis M. Ferraro. "Urban Pest Birds: Controlling Damage." Lincoln: University of Nebraska–Lincoln, Institute of Agriculture and Natural Resources, Nebraska Extension, 2010. http://extensionpublications.unl.edu/assets/html/g2024/build/g2024.htm.

West, Meredith J., and Andrew P. King, "Mozart's Starling." *American Scientist* (March–April 1990): 105–14.

Whitman, Walt. *Specimen Days*. New York: Dover Press, 1995. First published 1883.

Wicks, Robert. "Literary Truth as Dreamlike Expression in Foucault's and Borges's 'Chinese Encyclopedia.'" *Philosophy and Literature* 27, no. 1 (2003): 80–97.

Wiggins, Andrea, and Kevin Crowston. "From Conservation to Crowdsourcing: A Typology of Citizen Science." *Proceedings of the 2011 44th Hawaii International Conference on System Sciences (HICSS)* (2011): 1–10.

Will, Kipling W., Brent D. Mishler, and Quentin D. Wheeler. "The Perils of DNA Barcoding and the Need for Integrative Taxonomy." *Systematic Biology* 54, no. 5 (October 2005): 844–51.

Wilson, Alexander. *American ornithology, or, The natural history of the birds of the United States: illustrated with plates engraved and colored from original drawings taken from nature*. Philadelphia: Bradford and Inskeep, 1814.

Wilson, E. O. "The Encyclopedia of Life." *Trends in Ecology and Evolution* 18, no. 2 (February 2003): 77–80.

———. *The Future of Life*. New York: Vintage, 2003.

Wolfe, Cary. *Animal Rites: American Culture, the Discourse of Species, and Posthumanist Theory*. Chicago: University of Chicago Press, 2003.

———. "Human, All Too Human: 'Animal Studies' and the Humanities." *PMLA: Publications of the Modern Language Association of America* 124, no. 2 (March 2009): 564–75.

Wood, Chris, Brian Sullivan, Marshall Iliff, Daniel Fink, and Steve Kelling. "eBird: Engaging Birders in Science and Conservation." *PLOS Biology* 9, no. 12 (December 2011): 1–5.

Yeates, David K., Ainsley Seago, Leigh Nelson, Stephen Cameron, Leo Joseph, and John Trueman. "Integrative Taxonomy, or Iterative Taxonomy?" *Systematic Entomology* 36, no. 2 (April 2011): 209–17.

Zinsser, William. "Watching the Birds." In *Peterson's Birds: The Art and Photography of Roger Tory Peterson*, edited by Roger Tory Peterson and Rudy Hogland, 1–21. New York: Universe Publishing, 2002.

# INDEX

*Page numbers in italic indicate illustrations.*

anthropomorphism: of blue jays, 3, 4,
8, 11–12, 15, 29; of Canada geese,
127–28; and conservation, 81–82;
pervasiveness of, 38–39, 62–65;
in species identification, 144–46;
of starlings, 47, 55, 60. *See also*
humans; orni-pomorphism
arctic habitats, xvii, xxi, 92, 164, 172
Armstrong, James W., 42, 61–62
*Arnie, the Darling Starling* (Corbo and
Barras), 39, 47–48, 57
art: for bird identification, 78; birds'
interiority in, 42, 61–63; blue jays
in, 2, 3, 7–10, 17, 30–33; and conservation, 92; and human-animal
relationships, 34–35, 61
Atlantic Ocean, 107. *See also* East Coast,
U.S.
Atlantic puffins, 31
Atlantic States Marine Fisheries Commission (ASMFC), 80
Audubon, John James: on bald eagles, 108;
on blue jays, xxii, 2, 3, 7–15, 9, 30–33,
35; and Canada geese, 130–31; killing
of birds, 161; perception of birds, 38–
39, 42–45, 53, 61–63, 81, 127–29
"The Avian Brain Nomenclature
Forum," 16–17
Avian Knowledge Network (AKN), 163
"Avian Nights" (Alexie), 40–41
Avise, John C., 140–41

Balakrishnan, Rohini, 143–44, 147–48
bald eagles, 38, 108–9, 116–17, 127
Baltimore orioles, 31
Barber, Theodore Xenophon, 175–76
Barras, Diane Marie, 39, 47–48
Barrow, Mark V., xviii
Beardsley, Sara, 154
Bekoff, Marc, 13, 17, 24–25, 27–28, 30,
33–34, 64–65
Berry, Wendell, 25, 34–35

"Beyond Birds" (Luke), 85–86
*Binocular Vision* (Schaffner), 77, 81, 108
biodiversity: in cities, 134; and classification, 143, 147–48, 152–55; data
on, 165–66; exchange value of, 174;
of geese, 108
biopolitical power: and classification,
152; and commodification of nature,
87, 96, 174; definition of, 117; and
interpellation, 53–54; management
of bird populations through, xix,
xxiii, 116–19, 122, 130, 135–37, 169–
70. *See also* government; politics
*Bioscience*, 90
bioterrorism, 121–22
bird banding, 101
bird biography: about blue jays, 3, 25–
29, 39; content of, 39–41, 48–55;
examples of, 42–48; interpellation
in, 41, 44–55, 59, 65; on visual
contact, 57. *See also* literature
*Bird Brains* (Savage), 3, 13
BirdCast, 163
*Birdcraft* (Wright), 81
birds: deaths of, xiv–xx, 79–86, 109,
120, 161; hope for, xiv–xvi, 171,
174–76; identification and classification of, xviii, xxi, xxiv, 73–74,
78, 82–87, 101, 144–66; instinctual
generalism of, 26–27; management
of populations, xix–xxii, 87–89,
92–94, 117–20, 126, 152, 169–
74; rescue of, 25–26, 39, 42–47;
responses to humans, 33, 44–45,
74–75; responses to predators, 21,
25, 61–63; similarity to humans,
33–34, 38–41, 70, 132–35; social
lives of, 59–61, 68–69; subjectivity
of, 41–50, 54–65. *See also specific*
*species*
birds, common, xvii–xviii, 36, 66, 172.
*See also* European starlings

Miquelon, xxi

Mississippi River, 107, 129

Missouri River, 129

mockingbirds, 9, 31

*Moonbird* (Hoose), 92

Mooney, Richard, 70

Mora, Camilo, 154

morality, 3, 6–17, 30–33, 81, 85, 108, 134. *See also* Christianity; ethics

Mozart, Wolfgang, 46, 48, 57, 59, 175

"Mozart's Starling" (West and King), 57, 59

Munson, Arthur M., 162

Myers, Kelley H., 88, 89

Nadesan, Majia, 117–19, 122, 135

naming: of Canada geese, 132; and interpellation, 40, 44, 47, 50, 53–55, 59; Jacques Derrida on, 48–50; and perception of animals, 64–65; of species, 153–54. *See also* birds, identification and classification of

"Naming Names" (Birke), 65–66

National Audubon Society, xvii–xviii, 87, 158–59, 166

National Environmental Policy Act, 121

National Oceanic and Atmospheric Administration, 172

National Park Service, 172

National Science Foundation, 166

Native Americans, 38, 40–41

natural selection, 141–42

nature: classification of, 144–58; and economy, 80–90, 93–97, 100, 174–75; human relationships with, 35, 38, 97, 98–99, 100–102, 133–34, 175–76. *See also* animals

Nealon, Jeff, 94–96, 117, 123, 124, 136

Nebraska, 88–89

Negri, Antonio, xxiii, 87, 94–96, 102, 174–75

Nel, Philip, 19, 20

Neves, Katja, 90

New Jersey, 73–74, 99–100, 113, 122. *See also* Delaware Bay

New Jersey Audubon Society, 80

New Jersey Department of Environmental Protection, 76

New York, 45–46, 66, 122

*New York Times*, 16–17

next-generation sequencing (NGS), 157

Nietzsche, Friedrich, 10–11, 94, 96, 144–46

*A Nietzschean Bestiary* (Acampora), 11

Niles, Lawrence, 80–81, 92, 97–101, 103, 170

Nixon, Richard, 172

nongovernmental agencies, xix, 90, 92, 117–18, 167, 173–74

North America: bird deaths in, xvi–xviii; bird species in, 83; blue jays in, 2; classification of birds in, 155–58; European starlings in, 45–46, 66; management of bird populations in, 110–11, 125, 126, 129, 170; study of birds in, xxi

North American Breeding Bird Survey (BBS), 166

North Dakota, 173

Oak Ridge National Laboratory, 166

Obama, Barack, 173

oil production. *See* resource extraction

"On Exactitude in Science" (Borges), 161–62

*On the Road* (Kerouac), xv

"On Truth and Lying in a Non-moral Sense" (Nietzsche), 10

*The Order of Things* (Foucault), 149

*Origin of Species* (Darwin), 10, 141–42

orni-pomorphism, 59–60. *See also* anthropomorphism

*Ornithological Biography* (Audubon), 7–8, 38, 42, 44

knot, 80, 91–99, 103; on seeing, 20, 25; of species identification, 141–43, 148, 153–56, 160–66; on starlings' behavior, 46. *See also* experimentation; genetics; ornithology
science, citizen, 81–83, 101–2, 158–67, 170–72. *See also* humans
*Scientific American*, 154
Seattle WA, 134
self, technologies of, 117
self-awareness, 38, 58–59, 63–65. *See also* cognitive ability
senses, 21–24, 55, 74, 86–87. *See also* sound; vision
sexing, 40, 44, 47, 54
Shakespeare, William, xxii
shorebirds, 73–76, 80, 88–92, 99, 110, 155. *See also* gulls; red knots
Sibley, David Allen, 2, 21, 78
*Sibley Field Guide to Birds of Eastern North America* (Sibley), 78
*The Sibley Guide to Birds* (Sibley), 2
*Sibley's Birding Basics* (Sibley), 78
*Silent Spring* (Carson), 120
singing. *See* communication
situated knowledge, 20–21
"60-Mile Tri-State Regional Canada Geese Populations Stabilization Project," 122
*Skylark Meets Meadowlark* (Gannon), 38
snow geese, 105
social marketing, 90–92, 99
Sonoma County CA, 51–54
sound, 55, 59–61, 68–70, 74. *See also* senses
South America, 92
South Jersey Bayshore Coalition, 80
Southwest, American, 172
sparrows, xix, 7, 18, 25, 37
spatiotemporal exploratory model (STEM), 162–63

species: concept of, 143–48; conservation of, 74–75, 78–79, 88–89, 116–18, 121; on Delaware Bay, 92; of geese, 107, 108, 112; identification and classification of bird, xviii, xxi, xxiv, 73–74, 78, 82–87, 101, 141–66; naming of, 153–54; relationships among, 38, 40–41, 51–55, 58–60, 63, 67, 68, 70, 104, 132–37; of titmice, 139–40; variations within, 132–33, 140–50, 155–59, 167–68
*Species of the Mind* (Allen and Bekoff), 34
"Split the Lark" (Dickinson), xvi, xix
Stanger, Margaret, 39, 44–45
State of the Birds 2009 report, 164–67
State of the Birds 2010 report, xvii
State of the Birds 2011 report, 163–67, 171–74
Steller's jays, 13, 27–28, 51–54. *See also* blue jays
St. Francis of Assisi, 174–75
Stoll, John R., 88–89
Stöwe, Mareike, 24
St. Pierre, xxi
Strom, Deborah, 173
*Sturnus vulgaris. See* European starlings
Sullivan, Brian L., 161, 162
swans, 105. *See also* waterfowl

Taft, William Howard, 173
Tarvin, Keith, 14, 27–28
taxonomy: of bird species, xviii, xxi, xxiv, 73–74, 78, 82–87, 101, 153–58; history of, 148–52, 167; iterative, 157; and species concept, 141–42, 144–47. *See also* birds, identification and classification of
TeraGrid, 166
Texas, 139–40, 145, 161
*That Quail, Robert* (Stanger), 39, 44–45

Wiggins, Andrea, 171
Wilbur, Richard, 56
wildlife rehabilitators, 46, 101
Wildwood NJ, 100
Wilkins, John, 149
Will, Kipling W., 156
willingness to pay (WTP), 88. *See also* value
Wilson, Alexander, 2
Wilson, E. O., 153, 154, 158

wind turbines, xvii, 163. *See also* energy development
Wolfe, Cary, 24, 48–49
woodpeckers, xiii, 37, 46
Woolfenden, Glen E., 14, 27–28
Wright, Mabel Osgood, 81

Yeates, David K., 157

Zink, Robert M., 140–41
Zinsser, William K., 30

www.ingramcontent.com/pod-product-compliance
Lightning Source LLC
Chambersburg PA
CBHW030931150426
42812CB00064B/2744/J